Digital Gender-Sexual Violations

This groundbreaking book argues that the fundamental issues around how victim-survivors of digital gender-sexual violations (DGSVs) are abused can be understood in terms of gender and sexual dynamics, constructions, positioning, and logics. The book builds upon Hall and Hearn's previous work, *Revenge Pornography*, but has been substantially reworked to examine other forms of DGSV such as upskirting and sexual deepfakes, as well as the latest research and debates in the field.

Facilitated by developments in Internet and mobile technologies, the non-consensual posting of real or fake sexually explicit images of others for revenge, entertainment, homosocial status, or political leverage has become a global phenomenon. Using discourse and thematic analytical approaches, this text examines digital, survey, and interview data on gendered sexual violences, abuses, and violations. The words of both the perpetrators and victim-survivors are presented, showing the impact on victim-survivors and the complex ways in which phallocentric power relations and existing hegemonic masculinities are reinforced and invoked by perpetrators to position girls and women as gendered and sexualised commodities to be traded, admired, violated, or abused for the needs of individual men or groups of men.

Hall, Hearn, and Lewis explore their research in a broader social and political context, evaluating and suggesting changes to existing legislative frameworks, education, victim support, and practical and policy interventions against DGSV, along with wider political considerations. This is a unique resource for students, academics, and researchers as well as professionals dealing with issues around digital gender-sexual violations.

Matthew Hall is Associate Professor at the British University in Egypt and Editor of the *Journal of Gender Studies*. As an interdisciplinary scholar, he has published in areas as diverse as health; new, mediated, and cyberspace identities; cognitive enhancement; body modification; disability; and image consciousness. Since 2017, his research has largely focused on digital gender-sexual violations.

Jeff Hearn is Professor of Sociology, University of Huddersfield, UK; Professor Emeritus, Hanken School of Economics, Finland; and Senior Professor, Human Geography, Örebro University, Sweden. He has worked on sexuality and violence for over 40 years, and on digitalisation since the late 1990s. He is co-managing editor of the *Routledge Advances in Feminist Studies and Intersectionality* book series.

Ruth Lewis is an Associate Professor in the Department of Social Sciences, Northumbria University, UK. Her research focuses on gender-based violence – particularly online and image-based abuse, GBV in universities, intimate partner violence, and lethal violence, as well as legal remedies – and feminist activism in response to these and other forms of misogyny.

Digital Gender-Sexual Violations

Violence, Technologies, Motivations

Matthew Hall
Jeff Hearn
Ruth Lewis

LONDON AND NEW YORK

Cover image: Getty

First published 2023
by Routledge
4 Park Square, Milton Park, Abingdon, Oxon OX14 4RN

and by Routledge
605 Third Avenue, New York, NY 10158

Routledge is an imprint of the Taylor & Francis Group, an informa business

British Library Cataloguing-in-Publication Data
A catalogue record for this book is available from the British Library

Library of Congress Cataloging-in-Publication Data
Names: Hall, Matthew, 1968- author. | Hearn, Jeff, 1947- author. |
Lewis, Ruth, 1966- author.
Title: Digital gender-sexual violations : violence, technologies,
motivations / Matthew Hall, Jeff Hearn, Ruth Lewis.
Description: Abingdon, Oxon ; New York, NY : Routledge, 2023. |
Includes bibliographical references and index. |
Identifiers: LCCN 2022017063 (print) | LCCN 2022017064
(ebook) | ISBN 9780367686116 (paperback) | ISBN 9780367686123
(hardback) | ISBN 9781003138273 (ebook)
Subjects: LCSH: Image-based sexual abuse. | Sex crimes. |
Computer crimes.
Classification: LCC HV6575 .H35 2023 (print) | LCC HV6575
(ebook) | DDC 362.8830285—dc23/eng/20220706
LC record available at https://lccn.loc.gov/2022017063
LC ebook record available at https://lccn.loc.gov/2022017064

ISBN: 978-0-367-68612-3 (hbk)
ISBN: 978-0-367-68611-6 (pbk)
ISBN: 978-1-003-13827-3 (ebk)

DOI: 10.4324/9781003138273

Typeset in Bembo
by codeMantra

Contents

Acknowledgements   vii
Disclaimer   ix
Abbreviations   xi

Introduction   1

PART 1
Framing and theorising digital gender-sexual violations   13

1 Words and concepts   15

2 Situating digital gender-sexual violations   27

3 Online interactions   46

4 Data and methods of analysis   57

PART 2
Empirical analyses of digital gender-sexual violations   71

5 Online textual abuse of feminists, *with*
   Michael Rowe and Clare Wiper   73

6 Upskirting, homosociality, and craft*man*ship   96

7 Revenge pornography   112

8 Some further forms of digital gender-sexual violations   129

PART 3
Wider implications and responses 143

9 Wider implications for workplaces, organisations, and
public spaces *with Charlotta Niemistö* 145

10 Socio-legal-technical considerations 161

11 Afterword: Key issues now and for the future 174

Index 183

Acknowledgements

While most of the material is published here for the first time, some has been updated from Hall and Hearn's 2017 book entitled *Revenge Pornography: Gender, Sexuality and Motivations*. Chapters 5 and 6 draw in part on previous texts, respectively:

Lewis, R., Rowe, M., & Wiper, C. (2016). Online abuse of feminists as an emerging form of violence against women and girls. *British Journal of Criminology*, *57*(6), 1462–1481.

Hall, M., Hearn, J., & Lewis, R. (2022). 'Upskirting', homosociality, and craftmanship: A thematic analysis of perpetrator and viewer interactions. *Violence Against Women*, *28*(2), 532–550.

We thank Michael Rowe and Clare Wiper at Northumbria University, UK, whose work contributes to Chapter 5, and Charlotta Niemistö at Hanken School of Economics, Finland, for her contributions to Chapter 9. We are grateful to editors and publishers for permission to reproduce this material here in revised form.

We would also like to thank Eleanor Taylor, Akshita Pattiyani, Alex Howard, and Tori Sharpe at Routledge who waited patiently for the manuscript and who saw it through to publication. We would also like to thank the anonymous reviewers for their constructive feedback.

It can be immensely challenging researching, analysing, and writing a book on what might be considered an emotionally demanding topic, in a seemingly continually changing terrain. Without the unstinting support of his co-authors, Jeff and Ruth, this book would have been almost impossible, and certainly onerous. Thus, Matthew's gratitude and thanks to them go beyond words. Matthew would also like to say a large thank you to his wife Tracy, who has suffered in silence being made aware of all the new forms of DGSVs that emerge. And, certainly not least, a big thanks to his family and friends for their continual support in what they might deem as a bizarre endeavour.

Jeff gives special thanks to Matthew and Ruth for being such congenial – and effective – co-writers and co-discussants, especially while we have worked on such unpleasant and violating material. Following our initial fortuitous meeting in Helsinki in October 2019, our only three-way meeting

IRL, it has been a pleasure to work together: working remotely does necessarily not mean social remoteness, but, in this case, close collegiality. Thanks also to Rukaya Al Zayani, Liisa Husu, Sofia Strid, Anne Laure Humbert, and Dag Balkmar.

Ruth would like to thank her co-authors, Matthew and Jeff, whom it has been a pleasure to work with, despite the distinctly unpleasurable topic of this book. Thanks also to collaborators, Sundari Anitha, Mike Rowe, and Clare Wiper. I have been lucky to work with you all on this topic and your insights, support, and analysis have made me a better scholar.

Disclaimer

Digital gender-sexual violations are heinous acts that can, and do, devastate the lives of victim-survivors and those around them. This is so much so that, as a result, victim-survivors have been known to take their own lives. These are phenomena to be opposed and stopped.

In order to be able to examine perpetrator motivations and interactions and see the ways in which victim-survivor materials are used and disseminated, on what platforms, we have had to access some very unsavoury Internet websites and platforms. The Internet data analysed in this book is drawn primarily from two Internet platforms – the now closed dedicated revenge pornography website MyEx.com, and The Candid Zone, which hosts upskirting materials and posts amongst a plethora of other sexualised materials of women and possibly, also girls. We have also examined the following pornographic deepfake dedicated websites: MrDeepFakes, AdultDeepFakes.com, Deepfakeporn.net, FamousBoard.com, SexCelebrity.net, MrDeepFakes.com, CelbJihad.com. CFake.com, as well as the spycam website SpyArchive.com, and more general pornography websites such as PornHub, Xvideos, Heavy-R, and the related search engine, The Porn Dude. None of these required membership; they are freely available on the Internet. While we sought permission to reproduce material for analysis from MyEx.com and The Candid Zone on several occasions, no response was received. For analytical purposes, we reproduce perpetrators' written electronic data in full. The reader should therefore be aware that the electronic text in this book is reproduced verbatim and as such some readers might find its content disturbing.

Pornography that involves the sexual abuse of children is illegal in the United Kingdom under the Protection of Children Act 1978 (PCA 1978) and section 160 of the Criminal Justice Act 1988 (CJA 1988) (Crown Prosecution Service, 2020). Given a significant amount of sexting involves minors and some sexting is reported to end up on revenge porn websites, we have made every effort to confine the research to text and accompanying images where it was claimed that the victim was over 18 years of age and also where the victim appeared so. Where we thought minors might have been involved such as on The Candid Zone with threads that referred to 'teens', or 'highschool', for example, we reported these to the Internet Watch Foundation.

This book is also designed to provide information to readers only. It is sold with the understanding that the publisher is not engaged to render any type of psychological, legal, or any other kind of professional advice. The content of each chapter is the sole expression and opinion of the authors, and not that of the publisher. Neither the publisher nor the author shall be liable for any physical, psychological, emotional, financial, or commercial damages, including, but not limited to, special, incidental, consequential, or other damages.

Abbreviations

AI	Artificial intelligence
AGI	Artificial generalised intelligence
DA	Discourse analysis
DGSV	Digital gender-sexual violation
DIPV	Digital intimate partner violence
DV	Domestic violence
EU	European Union
FRA	Fundamental Rights Agency
GBV	Gender-based violence
IBSA	Image-based sexual abuse
ICTs	Information and communication technologies
Incels	Involuntary celibates
IPV	Intimate partner violence
MGTOW	Men Going Their Own Way
NCII	Non-consensual intimate images/imagery
TA	Thematic analysis
UN	United Nations
VAW	Violence against women
VAWG	Violence against women and girls

Introduction

Introduction

The Internet never forgets.[1] And that permanent digital record, a blessing when it summons a moment we want to recall with the click of a
mouse, can be a weapon in more sinister hands when it preserves ones
we would like to forget. Controlling the distribution of the acts we want
back, from mere silly poses for a camera to the most intimate deeds, has
become a fact of life in the digital age, taking us into uncharted legal and
ethical territory. And few expressions of this exploitative power are as
disturbing as what is known as revenge porn, the posting online of sexually explicit photos or videos by a former partner seeking retribution.

(Penney, 2013, p. 1)

Although Jonathon Penney's (2013) warning about the misuse of the Internet relates specifically to what has become known colloquially as 'revenge
pornography'[2] and is demonstrable by high profile examples of online digital
gender-sexual violation (DGSV), such as *The Fappening*[3] (Moloney & Love,
2017), it is highly applicable to many other forms of DGSV. The taking and
sharing of intimate images of people (e.g., upskirting[4]), or the making and
sharing of fake intimate images (e.g., pornographic deepfakes[5]), are some
of the other forms of DGSV the Internet is now used for, and a reason we

---

1 Although some materials disappear or end up in silos in what is termed 'URL rot' or 'link
  rot' (Sampath Kumar & Vinay Kumar, 2013), intimate sexualised materials seldom expire.
2 The term, typically used in the media and colloquially, is better understood as the
  non-consensual distribution of explicit images by (ex-)partners to seek revenge, as we
  discuss in Chapters 1 and 7.
3 The term refers to the August 2014 non-consensual disclosure of explicit images of around
  100 female celebrity A-listers (Radhika, 2014).
4 Upskirting refers to the non-consensual act of taking photographs or recordings from
  underneath someone's skirt or dress. We discuss this form of violation in more detail in
  Chapter 7.
5 Pornographic deepfakes are a form of synthetic media in which one person's image is
  swapped for another person's who is involved in some form of explicit image or act. We
  discuss deepfakes and other forms of DGSV in Chapter 8.

DOI: 10.4324/9781003138273-1

decided to broaden the scope of this book, rather than simply update our previous book entitled *Revenge pornography: Gender, sexuality and motivations* (Hall & Hearn, 2017).

Making public sexually explicit (non)consensual images of others with new technology is nothing new. Communication technologies, whether labelled as 'new' or not, have repeatedly been taken up by those wishing to create or represent sex and sexuality, and pornographers, in particular, have done so in a more or less organised way. Rosen's (2010) *Beaver Street: A history of modern pornography* highlights the historical and symbiotic relationship between pornography and technology. Increasingly complex modern technologies, such as artificial intelligence[6] and augmented reality,[7] have developed from the peep show, photography and film, and associated histories of 'the real', the glossy image, the pin-up, the film star, and the film icon. Early filmmakers were not slow to exploit sexual display on the screen, with sexual themes figuring in clear, conscious, and sometimes less conscious ways. Telephones brought 'call girls'; specialist telephone sexual services, sex lines, and telephone sex followed.

Video and television technologies have led to sex videos, sex channels, and sex pay TV. Johnson (1996) points out the pornography industry always accelerated the growth of new technologies such as video recorders and cameras and more recently the Internet, smartphone, and other portable devices because they appealed to creators and consumers of pornography. Their appeal centred on being able to produce explicit images in the privacy of one's home without having to go to the store to get a film developed. "Videotape first emerged as a cheap and efficient alternative to film (later kinescope) for TV production. Its development for home use owes its birth to Sony and Betamax but its maturity to porn" (Johnson, 1996, p. 222). Conversely, new technologies such as the Internet allow the consumption of explicit material at home, and as such, the porn industry has gained a new audience of people willing to watch their films; "(i)nstead of travelling to a disreputable store, viewers could watch films at their convenience at home" (Johnson, 1996, p. 222).

Information and computer technologies (ICTs), and specifically the Internet, have raised possibilities of techno-sex, high-tech sex, non-connection sex, mobile phone sex, and virtual sex. New forms of sex, sexual storytelling, sexual genres, sex talk shows, and digital sexual media have mushroomed. Indeed, ICTs are themselves part of the broader histories of the publicisation (Brown, 1981) of sexuality and technologies of the senses. There are daily reports of how ICTs are changing how sexuality is done and experienced

---

6 Artificial intelligence (AI) refers to the ability of a machine to perform activities typically considered as requiring intelligence such as navigating, large-scale data processing, and machine learning (see Yao et al., 2019). AI is a broad term including narrow (or weak) AI and general AI (AGI) or strong AI, as well as several other sub-types.

7 Augmented reality refers to the merging of a view of the 'real-world' upon a digital image in 'real time' (Steffen et al., 2019). We discuss the current and potential future implications of this development for DGSVs in more detail in Chapter 8.

in chat lines, Internet dating, email sex, cybersex, cyberaffairs, and falling in love on the Net, hence providing new channels for sexuality, sexual communication, sexual citizenships, and sexualised violence (Hearn, 2006). Speed and ease of ICTs create many possibilities for new forms of cybersexual experimentation, such as mixed or multi-media sex, interactive sex, and interactive pornography.

There are many further ways in which people use ICTs and the Internet for sexual purposes. These may draw on the increasing range of online information and discussion forums on all manner of sexual aspects that are to be found on the Internet. In addition, there are increasing moves from more passive use of the Internet information to more active engagement and creation on interactive sites by those who might be described as competent online sexual agents (Döring, 2009). Above all, the Internet has brought all this and more into one "single medium to which a still increasing number of people have access due to technological advances and decreasing prices" (Daneback & Ross, 2011, p. 3).

Online uses of ICTs for sexual purposes are now normalised in many parts of the world, and especially so, but not only, for younger people. For example, Wright, Bryant, and Herbenick's (2021) recent analysis of the US National Survey of Porn Use, Relationships, and Sexual Socialization (NSPRSS) found that 84.4% of 14- to 18-year-old males and 57% of 14- to 18-year-old females have viewed pornography. A survey (Regnerus, Gordon & Price, 2016) comparing pornography consumption of 18- to 40-year-olds found that as many as 70% of men and 40% of women had reported viewing pornography. But whilst statistics are contestable, it would seem accessing sexual content is popular. Indeed, with regard to the 'premier' dedicated pornographic website, Pornhub (2019: https://www.pornhub.com/insights/2019-year-in-review), the popularity of consumption showed no signs of decreasing.

Other digital sexual behaviours are now common. For example, a recent meta-analysis of 39 studies on adolescent sexting[8] found 14.8% had sent a 'sext', and 27.4% had received one, and these figures tend to rise with age (Madigan et al., 2018), and a meta-analysis (Mori et al., 2020) of emerging adult (18–29 years of age) sexting found that 38.3% had sent a 'sext', 47.7% had received one, and 15% had forwarded a sext without consent. However, a ten-country study (Morelli et al., 2020) shows non-consensual and pressured sexting to be higher.

However, such statistics neglect Internet use for some other kinds of sexual purposes such as educational purposes, ambiguities in what is meant by "sexual content", and whether use implies any relation to sexual arousal. They also do not take account of likely under-reporting by some people, particularly some women, who claim *not* to use the Internet for sexual purposes, but still

---

8 Sexting refers to the sending, receiving, or forwarding of a sexually explicit image between portable devices.

report that they engage in online sexual activities (Daneback & Ross, 2011). Under-reporting may be for a variety of further reasons, including gendered and sexual taboos, cultural notions of sexual respectability, and normalisation of everyday ICT use, whether sexual or not. Also, such generalised figures can obscure some broad demographic tendencies, for example, in some surveys, women's lesser and men's greater use, younger people's greater and older people's lesser use, and bisexuals' greater use than heterosexuals and homosexuals.

Of particular relevance for our current concerns is the normalisation of access to, and use of, pornography. Men tend to access and use pornography, online or not, more than women, with less gender difference for younger people, and declining use with age. According to a recent UK study (Puccio & Havey, 2016), the average age for first exposure to online pornography is 11, and, of 3,000 13- to 18-year-old boys surveyed, 81% said they had looked at online pornography.

Such broad tendencies have multiple effects, especially on younger people. For example, Massey and colleagues' (2021) systematic review of the literature on young people's pornography consumption and sexual relationships found several links to sexual risk-taking for young women and young men (condom use, group sex, alcohol/drug sex). Young males also had tendencies to: be less concerned about sex acts hurting their partner; not ask for permission to do sex acts and claim they 'slipped' from vaginal to anal sex; engage in coercive and dominant behaviours, such as slapping and hair pulling; and be more concerned with their own sexual pleasure than their partner's. However, the authors did point out that whilst correlations exist, that does not mean causality, as enjoying watching violent pornography does not *necessarily* mean it informs sexual practices. It is now clear that pornography – that is, online pornography – is part and parcel of many children's, young people's, and indeed adults' lives.

At the same time, the Web and ICTs more generally have facilitated, in many ways, new forms of relatively easy and virtual violation and abuse, by Twitter, social networking sites (SNSs), or other means. The European Union's Fundamental Rights Agency (FRA, 2014) interview survey of 42,000 women in all 28 EU countries on experiences of violence against women addressed three types of acts that could be considered cyberstalking – that is, which involve the use of the Internet, email, or mobile phones:

- Sending emails, text messages (SMS), or instant messages that are offensive or threatening;
- Posting offensive comments about the respondent on the Internet; and
- Sharing intimate photos or videos of the respondent, on the Internet or by mobile phone.

They add that to be considered as stalking, these and all the other acts described in the survey must take place repeatedly and be perpetrated by the same person. Based on these definitions, the FRA survey authors estimate that 5% of women in the European Union have experienced one or more forms of cyberstalking since the age of 15, and 2% have experienced it in the 12 months preceding the survey. Taking the victim-survivor's[9] age into consideration, the 12-month rates vary from 4% among 18- to 29-year-olds to 0.3% among women 60 years old or older. Not surprisingly, there appear again to be important variations across age and generation.

Having said that, reliable information about who exactly perpetrates and experiences DGSV, across different contexts and social divisions, is still limited. However, research on image-based sexual abuse shows men aged 1639 years are perpetrators more often than women of that age, with ratios of one in five and one in eight, respectively, with LGBTIQA+ people reporting relatively higher victimisation (Powell et al., 2020). Dedicated 'revenge porn' sites have 90 or more percent men users (Hall & Hearn, 2017), and one recent estimate reported women as 27 times more likely to be harassed online than men.[10] While digital intimate partner violence affects all ages, Marganski and Melander (2018) note that young adults have the highest rates of technology use and are at highest risk of intimate partner violence (see Powell et al., 2020).

There would appear to be both significant differences and significant continuities between the ubiquity of what might be called stranger pornography online, and its widespread negative pressures and effects, especially on young women, but also young people more generally, and the more personally directed and repeated online violations, including revenge pornography, from known others. An important caveat here is that what has been hitherto a basic distinction between knowing and not knowing someone is becoming blurred, especially for younger generations. Similarly, notions of privacy, anonymity, and confidentiality are not so absolute for some people. At the risk of over-generalisation, Daneback and Ross (2011, p. 7) state:

> It has ... been suggested that younger and older people (in relative terms) have different concepts of anonymity with regard to sexually related activities on the Internet. It seems that by anonymity, young people mean not having to express sexually related details face to face (but they have no problems displaying a picture of themselves while doing it), whereas older people equate anonymity with not being seen or known.

Pornography, online pornography, and online violation can indeed be intertwined in complex ways, both societally and individually. It should be

---

9 'Victim' and 'survivor' are at times used interchangeably by some of the sources we draw upon. We recognise that the correct term should be determined by context, and that 'survivor' or 'victim-survivor' is more appropriate than 'victim' in many instances.

10 Written evidence (OSB0097) from Glitch, the UK charity to end online abuse, to the UK Parliamentary report on Draft Online Safety Bill (2021, p. 13).

added that, for some people, these developing and unstable connections can be intensified in and through what have become known, in psychological parlance, as 'Internet addiction' (Young, 1996), 'virtual addiction', 'cyber addiction', or indeed 'pornography addiction'. Some studies report young men's greater propensity for 'compulsive use of the Internet', and also how this may, in turn, link with psychological tendencies towards, for example, depression, loneliness, low self-esteem, experience of low parental involvement or conflict (for example, Ayas & Horzum, 2013; Aydin & Sari, 2011; Wiederhold, 2016), and co-addictions, and at times also psycho-sexual problems (Sussman, Lisha & Griffiths, 2011).

Furthermore, various forms of online abuse have a socio-spatial and geopolitical aspect that can be both local and global. Once on the Web, they can be accessed from anywhere in the world, the global digital public space. Incipient 'globalisation' of sexuality and abuse through ICTs can be produced through local and globalised social practices. ICTs have multiple impacts on sexuality, with changing forms locally and globally. Although this relationship has, in strictly quantitative and commercial terms, been mutually beneficial for the porn industry, some sectors of the porn industry have, as a consequence, stagnated or declined. For example, the speed and relative anonymity of the Internet, and especially in the Dark Net, has meant that the distribution and viewing of recordings of child sexual abuse have been extended. One of the more recent consequences of the relationship between pornography and the development of Internet and smartphone technologies has been the number of people reporting harassment, humiliation, invasion of privacy, and loss of reputation as a result of various forms of DGSV (Powell et al., 2020).

In Chapter 1 *Words and concepts*, we explore the various commonplace and more specialist terminologies for DGSVs, as used by policy organisations, legislators, ICT companies, academics, activists, media outlets, as well as by those individuals, groups, and organisations that perpetrate violations or who experience their effects most directly. We consider this matter in terms of naming, that is, the naming of the key elements that make up the field, and some of the connections between them. We argue that it is important to bear in mind that gender and sexuality are not fixed terms, but are influenced by environmental, societal, and socio-technological changes, and that the gender-sexualing or sexual-gendering of technologies needs to be borne in mind as a backcloth to the analysis of digital gender-sexual violations. Digitalisation, gender and sexuality, and violence and violation all come together in the concept of DGSV.

Chapter 2 *Situating digital gender-sexual violations* shows how DGSVs can be situated and understood from different traditions and perspectives. The first perspective we discuss is to see DGSV in terms of gender-based violence and kindred framings. The broadening of understandings of what is meant by violence by feminist theory and practice means DGSV can be located within the continuum or continua of GBV, sexual violence, and men's violence against women and children more broadly, both individually and structurally (Yadav & Horn, 2021). Following this logic further, DGSV can be seen as gender, gendered, sexual, gender-sexual (violent) practices. These practices may be interpreted as structured action, resulting from the gender-sexual social order and social structures, sometimes called patriarchy, and/or as a way of doing gender, doing sexuality, or doing gender/sexuality performatively. Third, DGSVs can be understood as practices done by, through, and with technologies. As such, they can be viewed as another part of the technologisation of social life, sexualities, and violences, in their multifarious possibilities that harm another, often intentionally, and often repeatedly. The fourth perspective focuses on how technology is not only gendered, but gender is technologised across the human/machine, human/non-human boundaries (Haraway, 1991). Fifth, DGSV can be seen, in part, as allied to societal trends towards pornographisation, that is, a relatively new form or genre of pornography where the private is made public (Empel, 2011). Sixth, DGSV can be characterised as digital hate, misogyny, and part of the manosphere – the collection of Internet platforms and websites that promote more dominant and misogynistic masculinities (Ging, 2019). Seventh, DGSVs can also be framed as borderlessness, difficult-to-control, and transnational – in their production, consumption, interventions to counter them, and very existence as a new online-offline configuration (Hearn & Hall, 2021). Finally, DGSV is presented as part of publicisations and online narratives whereby public interest and concern for some mass media and governmental actors has led to demands for more legal or regulatory controls.

Since DGSV are largely facilitated by Internet websites and platforms, Chapter 3 *Online interactions* explores how people interact and communicate in these spaces. We show that people interact on multiple levels such as narrative, interactive, communicative, adaptive and productive, as well as through a variety of media such as email, social media, forums, and chat rooms. The vast array of ways people can engage with online sources and each other can influence how people present themselves when surfing the web (Tyler & Feldman, 2005). We argue this has important implications for the study of DGSV since it allows us to see what motivates people to undertake such activities and how they account for their actions. We explore how people present themselves, which includes discussions around online deception and 'real' identities that mirror offline identities. This chapter concludes with us outlining our position in which we see identities as co-constructed in interactions regardless of the online or offline medium, along with the important and topical question of online privacy.

The final chapter of Part One, Chapter 4 *Data and methods of analysis,* sets out our data selection, collection, and the two analytical approaches we deployed – Thematic Analysis (Braun & Clarke, 2012) and Analysis (Potter, 1996) – to our different on- and off-line datasets from a survey, interviews, and electronic communications. Different datasets often require similar, or markedly different, forms of analysis in order to highlight different features, such as motivations, impacts, social norms, power structures, and relationships between people. This chapter highlights our analytical approaches and processes deployed in the analytical chapters indicating the benefits of a multimodal approach to data analysis across, and within, different studies that have an overarching focus – digital gender-sexual violations. This chapter concludes by highlighting the difficulties of working with topics such as sexual violence, abuse, and violations, some of the key ethical considerations involved, and the impacts that work may have on researchers.

Chapter 5 *Online textual abuse of feminists* begins Part Two, where we explore *Empirical Analyses of DGSVs*. Although feminists are not the only people who are targeted for online abuse, they do tend to be routinely targeted for DGSV, and this tells us something important about contemporary gender relations. In this chapter, we discuss the *types* of online abuse to which they are subjected as well as the *function* of that abuse. We consider what purpose it serves in contemporary society, its links with the anti-feminist manosphere and with violence (sometimes fatal) that occurs offline. We also draw on data from the first study of online abuse directed at feminists (Lewis, Rowe & Wiper, 2017), to consider online abuse as a political strategy to subdue or silence women's and feminists' engagement in political campaigns, discourse, and debate.

In Chapter 6 *Upskirting, homosociality, and craftmanship* we explore this form of DGSV as men's homosocial interaction created through creating in-group identity on The Candid Zone, a website dedicated to surreptitiously taken photos of women's bodies, which is bolstered by positioning the activity as risky and requiring courage, and the demonstration of craftmanship through their photographic skills. But unlike other forms of DGSV such as 'revenge porn', our analysis highlights how the intrusion into the woman's personal and body space seems to be part of the attraction, in both senses, for many of the men. Homosocial misogyny is reproduced through women as currency, initially close up, then at a relative distance, in a dispersed way amongst an online community of men. However, in contrast to more obviously gross forms of misogyny, we have termed this 'polite misogyny' because of the politeness of much of the homosocial discourse, and as it seems to have some commonality with what some see as notions of supposedly chivalrous behaviour, whereby the male gaze appraises and 'appreciates' the female body, as (if it were) an object, an antique vase or a fine wine (Appelbaum, 2017), or even a hunting trophy.

In our previous book *Revenge pornography: Gender, sexuality and motivations* (Hall & Hearn, 2017), we drew upon data from the, then, dedicated revenge porn website MyEx.com, which has since been closed by the US Federal Trade Commission and the State of Nevada in 2018 because of changes in legislation and the impact it has on victim-survivors. But, whilst there remains a number of other revenge porn dedicated websites, our analytical findings (e.g., how gender and sexuality are invoked in accounting for DGSV and perpetrators motivations) still remain useful and valid. However, that analysis spanned four distinct chapters on different poster-postee permutations: male-to-female, female-to-male, male-to-male, female-to-female. In broadening the scope of this book, we have combined these four chapters into one: Chapter 7 *Revenge pornography*. However, in order to broaden the scope of this book, we have chosen exemplars to highlight the key points for the reader.

Chapter 8, *Some further forms of DGSV*, concludes this section by briefly covering four of these forms – deepfake pornography, spycamming, cyberflashing, and sexual happy slapping, and some of the related issues arising. For example, we discuss the issue of (non)consent and coercion with taking, making, disseminating, or receiving explicit images and how these vary between forms of DGSV (e.g., consent to take an image but not to disseminate, as is often the case in revenge porn, or consent to take but not to receive, as with cyberflashing). We explore also perpetrator motivations (e.g., profit, homosocial status), their implications for victim-survivors (e.g., accountability), and associated difficulties for legal systems, for example, the prosecution of perpetrators (e.g., ownership and use of images), and the development of legislation (e.g., on intent to harm). Such issues become even more blurred in different contexts, such as taking explicit images in public spaces (e.g., on a beach), or in various cultural contexts (e.g. a person in a state of religious undress).

Part 3, *Wider implications and responses* begins with Chapter 9, *Wider implications for workplaces, organisations, and public spaces*. We highlight how DGSVs have many wider implications beyond the immediate harm and personal lives of victim-survivors. These include impacts on family, and wider communities, education, social life, politics, leisure, and the worlds of work. In this chapter, we elaborate on some of these impacts, with a focus on work and workplaces, and also other institutional, organisational, and 'non-work' times and places, such as associations, schools, colleges and universities, community facilities, political and social movement organising, religious organisations, and sports clubs – all of which clearly have their own online presence.

Chapter 10 *Socio-legal-technical considerations* begins by exploring the legal and governmental responses to DGSVs. We explore some of the transnational issues related to DGSV and how the absence of international laws impinges the prosecution of DGSVs. While people are now being convicted of this crime through changes in the laws in some countries, we show that it is still difficult for victim-survivors to bring lawsuits or take action against the perpetrators and the host websites. Building on previous chapters, we look at the issue of consent and responses to this, including difficulties in prosecution due to questions of the copyright of images. These difficulties might be addressed via the European Union General Data Protection Regulation (GDPR). We continue the chapter with two sections that focus on victim-survivor support and empowerment services, such as 'Stop-Non-Consensual Intimate Image Abuse' (StopNCII.org), which generates a hashtag for a victim-survivor's intimate images so that it may be removed swiftly. The final section explores education, awareness-raising, campaigns, and interventions such as teaching about non-violent conflict resolution, communication skills, help-seeking, unequal gender norms, power and control in relationships, and the normalisation of digital gender-sexual violations.

Our final chapter *Afterword: Key issues now and for the future* offers further considerations on several ongoing themes. First, we address the question of what we mean by sex, gender, and sexuality, and the continuing set of societal debates, that are especially variable when viewed internationally, on the possible usages of 'sex' and 'gender', and their connections. Given men tend to be the main perpetrators of DGSV, we explore how they talk and write about these and how they account for them. Consideration is also given to binary gender and sexuality positions in doing violence. The display of gender and sexual positions is through antagonism, violation, power, and control, towards those who are, or have been, the object of desire, thus raising questions related to gender-sexual dynamics, with their frequently binary 'logic', and how these are complicated further by the technological affordances. We explore the power practices of micro-techno-masculinities in DGSV, and some men's gendered power practices in their engagement with technological patriarchies. DGSV throws up questions about experiences of both space and time and in particular how patriarchy and misogyny co-exist, are reinforced, and practiced, through and by off-/on-line spaces. The future of DGSV and the various forms are considered, and we suggest that although some policymakers and technology developers have responded to some concerns of the misuse of smartphones (such as, for upskirting, banning the silent smartphone camera apps), additional considerations and actions on current, new, and emerging technologies (e.g., augmented reality) will be needed in the future by researchers, policymakers, activists, and technology developers. We conclude this chapter, and the book, by highlighting that despite the misuse of technologies and on-/offline spaces in order to do harm, they also provide activists with resources to address these through campaigns and awareness raising so that in the future technological affordances and on-/offline spaces will become much safer spaces.

References

Appelbaum, R. (2017). *The aesthetics of violence.* London: Rowman & Littlefield.

Ayas, T., & Horzum, M. B. (2013). Relation between depression, loneliness, self-esteem and internet addiction. *Education, 133*(3), 283–290.

Aydin, B., & Sari, S. V. (2011). Internet addiction among adolescents: The role of self-esteem. *Procedia Social & Behavioral Sciences, 15*(1), 3500–3505.

Braun, V., & Clarke, V. (2012). Thematic analysis. In H. Cooper, P. M. Camic, D. L. Long, A. T. Panter, D. Rindskopf & K. J. Sher (Eds.), *APA handbook of research methods in psychology, Vol. 2. Research designs: Quantitative, qualitative, neuropsychological, and biological* (pp. 57–71). Washington, DC: American Psychological Association.

Brown, C. (1981). Mothers, fathers, and children: From private to public patriarchy. In L. Sargent (Ed.), *Women and revolution: The unhappy marriage of marxism and feminism* (pp. 239–267). New York/London: Maple/Pluto.

Daneback, K., & Ross, W. M. (2011). The complexity of internet sexuality. In R. Balon (Ed.), Sexual dysfunction II: Beyond the brain-body connection. *Advances in Psychosomatic Medicine, 31*, 1–14.

Döring, N. (2009). The Internet's impact on sexuality: A critical review of 15 years of research. *Computers & Human Behavior, 25*(5), 1089–1101.

Draft Online Safety Bill. (2021). *London: House of Commons and House of Lords.* 10 December. Retrieved from: https://committees.parliament.uk/publications/8206/documents/84092/default/

Empel, E. (2011). (XXX) Potential impact: The future of the commercial sex industry in 2030. *Manoa: Journal for Fried and Half Fried Ideas (About the Future).* December. Retrieved from: www.friedjournal.com/xxxpotential-impact-the-future-of-the-commercial-sex-industry-in-2030

FRA (Fundamental Rights Agency). (2014). *Violence against women: An EU-wide Survey.* Vienna: FRA. Retrieved from: https://fra.europa.eu/en/publication/2014/violence-against-women-eu-wide-survey-main-results-report

Ging, D. (2019). Alphas, betas, and incels: Theorizing the masculinities of the manosphere. *Men and Masculinities, 22*(4), 638–657.

Hall, M., & Hearn, J. (2017). *Revenge pornography: Gender, sexualities and motivations.* Abingdon: Routledge.

Haraway, D. J. (1991). *Simians, cyborgs and women: The reinvention of nature.* New York: Routledge.

Hearn, J. (2006). The implications of information and communication technologies for sexualities and sexualized violences: Contradictions of sexual citizenships. *Political Geography, 25*(8), 944–963.

Hearn, J., & Hall, M. (2021). The transnationalization of online sexual violation: The case of 'revenge pornography' as a theoretical and political problematic. In Y. R. Zhou, C. Sinding & D. Goellnicht (Eds.), *Sexualities, transnationalism, and globalization: New perspectives* (pp. 92–106). New York: Routledge.

Johnson, P. (1996). Pornography drives technology: Why not to censor the Internet. *Federal Communications Law Journal, 49*(1), 217–227.

Lewis, R., Rowe, M., & Wiper, C. (2017). Online abuse of feminists as an emerging form of violence against women and girls. *British Journal of Criminology, 57*(6), 1462–1481.

Madigan, S., Ly, A., Rash, C. L., Van Ouytsel, J., & Temple, J. R. (2018). Prevalence of multiple forms of sexting behavior among youth: A systematic review and meta-analysis. *JAMA Pediatrics, 172*(4), 327–335.

Marganski, A., & Melander, L., (2018). Intimate partner violence victimization in the cyber and real world: Examining the extent of cyber aggression experiences and its association with in-person dating violence. *Journal of Interpersonal Violence, 33*(7), 1071–1095.

Massey, K., Burns, J., & Franz, A. (2021). Young people, sexuality and the age of pornography. *Sexuality & Culture, 25*(1), 318–336.

Moloney, M. E., & Love, T. P. (2017). # The fappening: Virtual manhood acts in (homo) social media. *Men and Masculinities.* doi: 1097184X17696170.

Morelli, M., Chirumbolo, A., Bianchi, D., Baiocco, R., Cattelino, E., Laghi, F., & Drouin, M. (2020). The role of HEXACO personality traits in different kinds of sexting: A cross-cultural study in 10 countries. *Computers in Human Behavior, 113*, 106502. doi: 10.1016/j.chb.2020.106502.

Mori, C., Cooke, J. E., Temple, J. R., Ly, A., Lu, Y., Anderson, N., Rash, C., & Madigan, S. (2020). The prevalence of sexting behaviors among emerging adults: A meta-analysis. *Archives of Sexual Behavior, 49*(4), 1103–1119.

Penney, J. (2013). Deleting revenge porn. *Policy Options Politiques*. November. Retrieved from: http://policyoptions.irpp.org/fr/issues/vive-montreal-libre/penney

Pornhub. (2019). The 2019 Year in Review. 11 December. Retrieved from: https://www.pornhub.com/insights/2019-year-in-review

Potter, J. (1996). *Representing reality: Discourse, rhetoric and social construction*. London: Sage.

Powell, A., Scott, A. J., Flynn, A., & Henry, N. (2020). Image-based sexual abuse: An international study of victims and perpetrators. Technical Report. February. RMIT University, Melbourne. doi: 10.13140/RG.2.2.35166.59209.

Puccio, D., & Havey, A. (2016). *Sex, likes and social media: Talking to our teens in the digital age*. London: Vermilion.

Radhika, S. (2014). Jennifer Lawrence photo leak: Let's stop calling this hacking 'The Fappening'. *The Telegraph*. 2 September. Retrieved from: www.telegraph.co.uk/women/womens/life/11069829/Jennifer-Lawrence-photo-leak-Lets-stop-calling-this-hacking-The-Fappening.html

Regnerus, M., Gordon, D., & Price, J. (2016). Documenting pornography use in America: A comparative analysis of methodological approaches. *The Journal of Sex Research, 53*(7), 873–881.

Rosen, R. (2010). *Beaver street: A history of modern pornography: From the birth of phone sex to the skin mag in cyberspace: An investigative memoir*. London: Headpress.

Sampath Kumar, B. T., & Vinay Kumar, D. (2013). HTTP 404-page (not) found: Recovery of decayed URL citations. *Journal of Informetrics, 7*(1), 145–157.

Steffen, J. H., Gaskin, J. E., Meservy, T. O., Jenkins, J. L., & Wolman, I. (2019) Framework of affordances for virtual reality and augmented reality. *Journal of Management Information Systems, 36*(3), 683–792.

Sussman, S., Lisha, N., & Griffiths, M. (2011). Prevalence of the addictions: A problem of the majority or the minority? *Evaluation and the Health Professions, 34*(1), 3–56.

Tyler, J. M., & Feldman, R. S. (2005). Deflecting threat to one's image: Dissembling personal information as a self-presentation strategy. *Basic & Applied Social Psychology, 27*(4), 371–378.

Wiederhold, B. K. (2016). Low self-esteem and teens' internet addiction: What have we learned in the last 20 years? *Cyberpsychology, Behavior, and Social Networking, 19*(6), 359.

Wright, P. J., Bryant, P., & Herbenick, D. (2021). Preliminary insights from a U.S. probability sample on adolescents' pornography exposure, media psychology, and sexual aggression. *Journal of Health Communication: International Perspectives, 26*(1), 39–46.

Yadav, P., & Horn, D. (2021). Continuums of violence: Feminist peace research and gender-based violence. In T. Väyrynen, S. Parashar, É. Feron, & C. C. Confortini (Eds.), *Routledge handbook of feminist peace research* (pp. 105–114). London: Routledge.

Yao, M., Sohul, M., Marojevic, V., & Reed, J. H. (2019). Artificial intelligence defined 5G radio access networks. *IEEE Communications Magazine, 57*(3), 14–20.

Young, K. S. (1996). Internet addiction: The emergence of a new clinical disorder. *CyberPsychology & Behavior, 1*(3), 237–244.

Part 1

Framing and theorising digital gender-sexual violations

1 Words and concepts

Introduction

New, advanced ICTs (information and communication technologies) appear to be a mixed blessing. They transform social, human, posthuman, and environmental possibilities in what seem to be many positive ways, at the same time summoning up new negativities, violences, and abuses – as with gender and sexual violations. So, what are digital gender and sexual violations, or rather digital gender-sexual violations (DGSV hereafter)? And how are we to map the terrain of DGSV? This book explores the parameters of various digital violences, including 'revenge pornography', upskirting, sexual 'happy slapping', spycamming, cyberstalking, sexual deepfakes, and deepnudes, and much more.

In this opening chapter, we begin by discussing the various terms used to address such digital gender-sexual violence, abuse, and violation. These very terms cover a very wide range of practices and are named in a wide range of ways. They are in both common and more specialist, usage, by policy organisations (e.g., UK Safer Internet Centre), legislators, ICT companies, academics, activists, media outlets, as well as those individuals, groups, and organisations that perpetrate violations or those who experience their effects most directly. We consider this matter in terms of naming, the key elements that make up the field, and some of the connections between them.

Naming

The arena of digital sexual violence, abuse, and violation goes under a number of overall names. This process of naming itself can be far from innocent, with different terminologies suggesting different emphases, framings, and even socio-political orientations. One first way of representing the whole diverse field of activity is by couplets, combining the technological and the abusive, with the technological preceding the abusive. Thus, relatively early used terms include electronic victimisation (Bennett et al., 2011), online abuse, Internet abuse, cyberabuse, cyber violence (Al-Alosi, 2017; Petersen & Densley, 2017), or perhaps commonly online misogyny (Lewis, Rowe & Wiper, 2018; also,

DOI: 10.4324/9781003138273-3

Jane, 2016). More recently, the term, tech abuse, has come into use, as, for example, by the London-based domestic violence charity, Refuge. Such couplets as online abuse, cyberabuse, and tech abuse bring together the two elements, sometimes even-handedly, often with the abuse as the dominant element, as an overarching frame, without further explicit gendered reference.

Some of the most well-used terms that are now in circulation place technology, as a more general term, at the forefront, as in: technology-facilitated sexual violence (TFSV) (Henry, Flynn & Powell, 2020; Henry & Powell, 2016, 2018); technology-facilitated sexual abuse (TFSA); technology-facilitated abuse (eSafetyCommissioner, n.d.; VAWnet, n.d.); technology-facilitated coercive control (TFCC) (Dragiewicz et al., 2018); technology-facilitated violence and abuse (Bailey, Flynn & Henry, 2021); gender-based violence facilitated by technology (Jatmiko, Syukron & Mekarsar, 2020); and digital technologies and gender-based violence (Barter & Koulu, 2021) – even abuse of technology (Woodlock, 2017). We argue that to focus this genre of terms on technology, and often also its affordances, as the facilitator of violence obscures the social context, formation, and perpetration of violence itself, so that the violence is seen as a technological (in the narrower sense) matter (see Vera-Gray, 2017).[1]

A slightly different naming – and thus focus – is with image-based sexual abuse (IBSA) (DeKeseredy & Schwartz, 2016; Henry & Flynn, 2019; McGlynn & Rackley, 2017; Powell et al., 2019). This term names, or appears to name, the image and the visual as primary, as basic, and in that sense may play down other aspects of abuse, such as verbal, written, sonic abuse, as well as further possible contextual aspects. Also, interestingly, in some legal discussions, for example, in the UK Law Commission, the term, intimate image abuse, has been used, not with reference the intimacy of the relationship, as in intimate partner violence, but in terms of the invasion of intimate privacy and the violation of personal bodily integrity, as in taking, sharing, and distribution of photographs or videos of intimate parts of the body without consent.

The emphasis on lack of consent in sharing and distribution is highlighted in the terms, non-consensual distribution of sexually explicit media, non-consensual distribution of private sexual material, and non-consensual sharing or distribution of intimate images or imagery (NCII) (e.g., Walker et al., 2021). Such terms, referring to the distribution of sexually explicit images or videos that were initially shared with the expectation that they would remain private, are well used in both academic and activist circles, for example, the UK-based StopNCII.org, and the US-based Cyber Civil Rights Initiative. Responsibility around consent is not only framed as concerning the immediate party or parties involved, but also is increasingly extended to the intermediaries, such as technology companies and their platforms (see, for example, Suzor, Seignior & Singleton, 2017; Suzor et al., 2019).

---

1 Jeff Hearn thanks Rukaya Al Zayani (2020) for fruitful discussions on this particular and many other issues.

These alternative terms are sometimes also applied in more limited or more precise ways, and thus with slightly different nuances, for example, technology-facilitated domestic violence, technology-facilitated domestic and family violence (Douglas, Harris & Dragiewicz, 2019), technology-facilitated sexual assault (Powell & Henry, 2017), technology-facilitated stalking and unwanted sexual messages/images (DeKeseredy et al., 2019), digital-coercive control (DCC) (Harris and Woodlock, 2019), and cyber psychological abuse (Leisring & Giumetti, 2014).

Another way of framing these abuses is in terms of the **form of relationship**, currently or previously, between the perpetrator(s) and those targeted, or indeed the absence of any previous relationship in-real-life (IRL) or online. In particular, reference is sometimes specifically made to, for example, partner cyber abuse (Taylor & Xia, 2018), digital intimate partner violence (Hearn et al., 2021), digital dating abuse (DDA) (Bennett et al., 2011; Brown & Hegarty, 2018), or partner abuse, control, and violence through Internet and smartphones (Gámez-Guadix, Borrajo & Calvete, 2018).[2]

Placing online abuse in the context of, for example, intimate partner violence, raises several issues, perhaps most obviously the relation of such online abuse to the huge existing body of theory, research, policy, intervention, and practice in that area. More specifically, it is clear that among those experiencing intimate partner violence many also experience various online abuses. For example, Refuge (2020), the UK domestic violence charity, found in 2019 that 72% of their service users had experienced abuse through technology, and 85% of respondents surveyed by Women's Aid (2020) in 2015 reported that the abuse they received online from a (ex-)partner was part of a pattern of abuse experienced offline (Hadley, 2017). On the other hand, some terminologies, such as upskirting or downblousing, and, in some contexts, cyberstalking or trolling, may suggest the lack of a previous or known relationship.

Sometimes, slightly confusingly, more **specific forms of abuse**, such as cyberstalking, 'revenge pornography', or 'stolen' or 'leaked' sex tapes, are sometimes used loosely as a catch-all for a broader collection of online abusive acts and activities. Specific terms for the many specific terms and types of abuse can be often framed around or focused on more particular forms of acts or actions, frequently but not always interpersonally orientated. Further examples include: intimate partner violence (IPV), online surveillance by partners, GPS stalking, tracking, Internet- and image-based abuse, reputation abuse, abuse via banking technology and transfers (including abusive messages on bank statements via tiny transfers of money), hacking, electronic sabotage, spycamming, deepfakes, impersonation, unwanted contact via social media, posting embarrassing information about the partner or ex-partner, cyberstalking, monitoring partner's or ex-partner's online communication,

---

2 For an invaluable resource on research papers on technology used in intimate partner violence, see IPVTechBib (2021).

non-consensual sexting and nudes, spyware recording key-loggings and key-strokes, trolling, doxing, and use of the Internet of Things (IoT) (see, for example, Al-Alosi, 2017; Dragiewicz et al., 2018; Duerksen & Woodin, 2019; Powell & Henry, 2018; Woodlock et al., 2020;).

Finally, sometimes, the explicit recognitions of technology, **gender, and sexuality are omitted**, so that the framing and naming of these activities are made without gendering and within a somewhat different field of activity, for example, hate speech, within or into which gender and sexual violations are incorporated. In contrast, in this book we use the overarching concept of DGSV.

Elements

Let us now look at the three major aspects and elements that make up the field of digital sexual violence in a little more detail: **the 'digi', the 'sexual', and the 'violent'**. First, what is meant by the technological or the digital? Second, what is meant by gender and sexuality? Third, what is meant by violence, abuse, and violation? And then there is the key question, how do these three elements interconnect, and how are they understood to interconnect, as with, for example, 'digital gender-sexual violations', in their various forms and guises? (see Figure 1.1).

The first of these goes by several labels: digital or just digi, cyber, online, Internet, or simply technology or technological. These clearly overlap, but they are not necessarily coterminous. The digital refers to the production and circulation of data expressed as a series of the digits, 0 and 1. The digital or the cyber are not necessarily online or on the Internet, at least in the everyday sense of those terms, even if much human-to-human digital communication is conducted that way. The IoT shows how there can be machine-to-machine communication, without passing via the Internet or being accessible online. Somewhat similarly, the contents of the Deep Web are not indexed by standard web search-engines, and so are less accessible to most people. The digital has many features and characteristics, such as the possibility of real-time automation and contextual interactivity, and what is usually called artificial intelligence (AI).

Figure 1.1 The potential complex interconnectivities between the three elements.

It is perhaps worth mentioning that the alternative term, cyber, can also be used: indicating the relating to or characteristic of the culture of computers, information technology, and virtual reality, and concerning all aspects of computing, including storing data, protecting data, accessing data, processing data, transmitting data, and linking data. However, the prefix, cyber, is less preferred to the digital, as the former has become somewhat devalued (Coe, 2015). The notion of cyber might be considered over-used in cultural discourse, for example, in relation to style and some less than clear immateriality in numerous diverse and contradictory ways, as with, say, cyberpunk. Furthermore, the usage of cyber in some overly optimistic variants of cyberfeminism (see Bray, 2007) and even with generic interpretations of cybernetics as the broad science of communications add to the potentially confusing mix.

Importantly, the concern with the digital or the cyber is clearly not the same as **the virtual, the visual, the symbolic, or the representational**, when applied to violence and abuse, as in image-based abuse. The virtual, the visual, the symbolic, or the representational are all far from new, and indeed all are ancient (Shields, 2002). Rather, certain technologies have made their transfer of the visual, the symbolic or the representational swifter and easier – so that the virtual is more present, more complex, and probably more ambiguous than in previous historical periods.

Then, there is the question of how technologies, in, say, the digital or visual sense, are specifically invoked and connected to violence and abuse. As noted, technology-facilitated has become a popular phrasing. So, in that terminology, it is the technology that *facilitates* – makes easy or at least easier – the abuse. Technology is given (some form of) agency. We are critical of this way of thinking about digital abuse, criticism made all the more urgent with the growth of various forms of AI, especially those forms designed to commit digital abuses. The use of 'facilitated' is distinct from the use of the term 'based', as in 'image-based abuse'. Other possible, less determined or determining terms, might be, for example, 'technology-located' or 'technology-related' or 'through the medium of technology'.

The second set of elements concerns **gender** (as in 'gender-based violence'), **sex,** the **sexual, and sexuality**. Again, these are clearly not equivalents, with the explicit named emphasis usually either on gender or the sexual, with its ambiguities, in English, of sex and sexuality. All these terms can have different meanings and connotations, for example, ranging from using sex as biologically essentialist to sex as gendered, or from using gendered as a cultural construction of given sex to gender as a wide-ranging social construction of social reality, including the social construction of sex. Moreover, terms that are similar to 'sex' and 'gender' can have quite different connotations and nuances in languages other than English. Understandings of the relations between sex and gender, with their own different meanings, have become more complex in recent years, for several reasons. There has been dissatisfaction in some feminist theorising with the strict separation of sex and gender, and even with the very concepts themselves, even whilst some wish to retain a strict separation of sex and gender. Much greater public and academic debate and explicit politics on queer and transgender, in their various forms, have prompted questioning of what is meant by sex and gender.

Furthermore, in terms of our own focus, assumptions regarding sex and/ or gender can be complicated in the virtual world, with multiple possibilities for diverse digital (re)presentations, visualisations, and violations that are not easily categorisable or recognisable as only and specifically sexed, sexual, or gendered. Rather, they may seem to convey some combination of sex, sexuality, and gendering. With digitalisation and augmented reality/ies, including with the use of faking technology of 'bodies', the relation of what is to be called sex, or sexuality, or gender may be(come) more obscured. Accordingly, it may be difficult or impossible to say if digital violations are best framed as sexed violation, sexual violation, or gender violation. For example, a deepfake may be simultaneously sexed, gendered, and sexual. At times, the confusion between sex and gender, not least through the embedding in the virtual, points to the need for a metacategory – such as gex – that acts as an umbrella term, not making assumptions of any equivalence or prioritising of sex or gender (Hearn, 2012).

Sometimes, a more specific focus is placed on women as violated, as in, for example, digital, online, or cyber violence against women, as emphasised in, for example, the work of the European Institute for Gender Equality (n.d.) and UN Women (2020).

The third element concerns the invocation of **violence, abuse, and violation**, sometimes also named as aggression(s), with its more psychological connotations, or coercion or coercive control, with its established connotations, in particular, from understandings of intimate partner violence (Stark, 2007).

Connections

These elements noted interconnect in various ways. There are links between, first, technology, second, gender and sexuality, and, third, violence. The question is how to speak – and write – about these connections (see Figure 1.2). First, in the field of activities we are discussing, technology of some sort is involved in the violences and violations – but which technologies are involved and above all how are they involved?

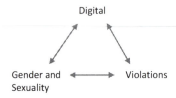

Figure 1.2 Interconnectivity between the digital, gender and sexuality, and violations.

In direct physical violence, the body is used as technology, with arms, hand, feet, head, and so on used as technologies of the body to do violence. Similarly, there are multitude forms of violence with weapons, either purpose-built, like daggers, or adapted, like baseball bats, or improvised, like saucepans. Involving personal body parts even less directly and thereby creating some distance between the perpetration and experience of violence are the technologies of wider or even mass violence, within or outside war – guns, bombs, and the rest.

Violence is always with-something, if not by-something. There is always some kind of assembling, though not in the usual sense of assemblage. The technologies that we are concerned with in this book are complex, 'machinic', and concerned with not just mechanical or analogue machines, but complex, 'new(er)', advanced, digital technologies. To label the kind of violences and violations, we are concerned with as *simply* 'technological', or tech, is limiting and may potentially obscure human agency, inventiveness, and interaction in relation to technologies.

So, to summarise so far, violences and violations involve technologies, in the widest sense – of the self, of the gendered-sexual body, of weapons, of things, of machines, of complex machines, and so on. There are non-machinic technologies of violence and machinic technologies of violence, which can be more or less complex, and more or less interpersonally directed. As already noted, these complex machinic technologies of violence go by various names: cyber, Internet, online, 'new', advanced, virtual, information (as in IT or ICT), connective, or as we prefer digital. Not all digital technologies, and associated violences, are online or on the Internet.

So, these violences are in part prosthetic, beyond the immediate body, as are the violations. They are violations and violences in their intention to harm and in their harm caused and experienced, even if the agency and the effect are mediated through (semi-)autonomous systems, for example, in-stalling overt or covert video surveillance in all domestic rooms, with their potential use for violation and coercive control. They are likely to also entail intention to harm, but this is not necessarily so, at least in a clear and con-scious way (see pp. 30–33, 179–180). Moreover, with the abusive use of the IoT, the violence and violation concerned can be systemic and long-term, as in continuous surveillance and monitoring, rather than reducible to a specific act, time, and place.

The next set of questions is: how are these connections of the digital and the (new) technological, and violence and violations, gendered and/or sexual? Are we talking about gendered or sexual violence that operates through the digital or digital violence that is gendered or sexual violence that is digital in its medium? Should we talk of digital sexual violation or perhaps more accurately sexual digital violation? Is it "sexual violation" of the digital type or digital violation of the sexual type? In several senses both are accurate, but what seems to have happened in the naming and conceptualising of this range of activity is that the *established* field of sexual violence has had the digital (or cyber and so on) *added on*. This adding on needs, at the very least, to be interrogated and questioned. Would it perhaps be more accurate to speak of DGSV?

The order of adjectives – for example, in this case digital and sexual – may seem innocent, but matters. Following the usual conventions, adjectives describing material precede those describing type. So, which is the more material – the digital or the sexual? Which is the type? Which is qualifying which? And why not reverse the whole combination and speak of, say, violent sexual digitality or violent technological sexuality? These are some of the questions that inform our approach to the discussions in the book. It can be all too easy to ascribe self-evident materiality and material causation to technology, operating in a machinic, deterministic way, that then refashions gender-sexual power relations, perhaps assumed to be more malleable, whilst in fact being no less material.

Meanwhile what is meant and what is happening in terms of how gender, sex, and sexuality are themselves being constructed and reconstructed through the digital, ICTs and the rest? The sexual and the gendered are also mediated by the digital. There is a multitude of ways in which gender and sexuality are being affected by and through ICTs, from online affairs to the multiplication of gender and sexual identities. Although such issues are not the prime focus of this book, it is important to bear in mind that gender and sexuality are not fixed and immune from all manner of changing environmental, societal, and socio-technological influences (see pp. 174–175).

And finally, in this section is the question of how the technology and the technological, specifically the digital and digital technologies, themselves intersect with gender and sexuality, and may be gendered and sexualed,[3] and even violent (Salter, 2018; Shelby, 2020). Certain technologies and their affordances, or socio-technologies and their social affordances, can in themselves be potentially gender-sexual-violating. For example, the social affordances of different technologies – enabling technical control engendering trust, creating conditional communality, and so on – make possible the easy shift from trust to violation (Hearn, 2014). In discussing the relations of technology and the dynamics of sexual assault, the US National Network to End Domestic Violence, Safety Net Project (2017) points out:

> Sex offenders manipulate positions of trust to gain access to victims, or to avoid being held accountable for their actions. These positions of trust include those within social groups, faith communities, schools, workplaces, health care settings (including in-home care), and legal settings (jails, prisons, immigration facilities or juvenile detention).

---

3 'Sexualed' is used to indicate having sexual meaning, rather than the more explicit notions of sexualised and sexualisation (Hearn & Parkin, 1987)

It has become a widely employed, almost a fixed, axiom to see the gendering of technology as a matter of social construction. However, a more open-ended appreciation of the gendering of technology, for example, as seen through the lens of sexual difference theory (Obreja, 2012), might yield more diverse and embodied interpretations. Both the speed and the manufactured 'instant gratification' of much new technology impacts on gendered-sexual time and gender-sexual-bodily rhythms and experiences, in ways that may be difficult to reduce to social construction. For example, a digital violating communication may be sent from the other side of the world and then be received almost instantly when the recipient is about to go to sleep, or the arrival of a deeply offensive deepfake may bring a profound reaction and revulsion in the bodily, visceral, affective, sexual-gendered experience. Such events emphasise the material reality of sexed-gendered bodies in ways that might challenge some notions of disembodied gendering.

To say all this is not to reify technologies, less still to remove agency and intention in doing violation, but rather to recognise the deep structure of some technological change. Again, these issues are not the prime focus of the book, but the gender-sexualing or sexual-gendering of technologies needs to be borne in mind as a backcloth to the analysis of digital sexual violations. Digitalisation, gender and sexuality, and violence and violation all come together in the concept of DGSV and the discussions that we continue in this book.

References

Al-Alosi, H. (2017). Cyber-violence: Digital abuse in the context of domestic violence. *University of New South Wales Law Journal, 40*(4), 1573–1603.

Al Zayani, R. (2020). *A systematic review of technology-facilitated violence.* unpub. ms. Örebro: Örebro University.

Bailey, J., Flynn, A., & Henry, N. (Eds.). (2021). *The Emerald international handbook of technology-facilitated violence and abuse.* Bingley: Emerald.

Barter, C., & Koulu, S. (2021). Special issue: digital technologies and gender-based violence – mechanisms for oppression, activism and recovery. *Journal of Gender-Based Violence, 5*(3), 367–375.

Bennett, D. C., Guran, E. L., Ramos, M. C., & Margolin, G. (2011). College students' electronic victimization in friendships and dating relationships: Anticipated distress and associations with risky behaviors. *Violence and Victims, 26*(4), 410–429.

Bray, F. (2007). Gender and technology. *The Annual Review of Anthropology, 36,* 37–53.

Brown, C., & Hegarty, K. (2018). Digital dating abuse measures: A critical review. *Aggression and Violent Behavior, 40,* 44–59.

Coe, T. (2015). *Where does the word cyber come from?* 28 March. Retrieved from: https://blog.oup.com/2015/03/cyber-word-origins/

DeKeseredy, W. S., & Schwartz, M. D. (2016). Thinking sociologically about image-based sexual abuse: The contribution of male peer support theory. *Sexualization, Media & Society, 2*(4). doi: 10.1177/2374623816684692.

DeKeseredy, W., Schwartz, M., Harris, B., Woodlock, D., Nolan, J., & Hall-Sanchez, A. (2019). Technology-facilitated stalking and unwanted sexual messages/images in a college campus community: The role of negative peer support. *SAGE Open*, *9*(1), 1–12. https://doi.org/10.1177/2158244019828231

Douglas, H., Harris, B. A., & Dragiewicz, M. (2019). Technology-facilitated domestic and family violence: Women's experiences. *The British Journal of Criminology*, *59*(3), 551–570.

Dragiewicz, M., Burgess, J., Matamoros-Fernández, A., Salter, M., Suzor, N. P., Woodlock, D., & Harris, B. (2018). Technology facilitated coercive control: Domestic violence and the competing roles of digital media platforms. *Feminist Media Studies*, *18*(4), 609–625.

Duerksen, K. N., & Woodin, E. M. (2019). Technological intimate partner violence : Exploring technology-related perpetration factors and overlap with in-person intimate partner violence. *Computers in Human Behavior*, *98*, 223–231.

EIGE (n.d.). *Cyber violence against women*. Retrieved from: https://eige.europa.eu/gender-based-violence/cyber-violence-against-women

eSafetyCommissioner (Australian Government). (n.d.). *What is technology-facilitated abuse?* Retrieved from: https://www.esafety.gov.au/key-issues/domestic-family-violence/technology-facilitated-abuse

Gámez--Guadix, M., Borrajo, E., & Calvete, E. (2018). Partner abuse, control and violence through internet and smartphones: Characteristics, evaluation and prevention. *Papeles del Psicólogo*, *39*(3), 218–227.

Hadley, L. (2017). *Tackling domestic abuse in a digital age*. A Recommendations Report on Online Abuse by the All-Party Parliamentary Group on Domestic Violence. Bristol: Women's Aid Federation of England.

Harris, B. A., & Woodlock, D. (2019). Digital coercive control: Insights from two landmark domestic violence studies. *The British Journal of Criminology*, *59*(3), 530–550.

Hearn, J. (2012). Male bodies, masculine bodies, men's bodies: The need for a concept of gex. In B. S. Turner (Ed.), *Routledge handbook of body studies* (pp. 307–320). London: Routledge.

Hearn, J. (2014). Sexualities, organizations and organization sexualities: Future scenarios and the impact of socio-technologies (A transnational perspective from the global "North"). *Organization: The Critical Journal of Organization, Theory and Society, 21*(3), 400–420.

Hearn, J. Hall, M., Lewis, R., & Niemistö, C. (2021). *The spread of digital intimate partner violence*. Unpublished manuscript.

Hearn, J., & Parkin, W. (1987). *'Sex' at 'work': The power and paradox of organisation sexuality*. New York: St Martin's Press.

Henry, N., & Flynn, A. (2019). Image-based sexual abuse: Online distribution channels and illicit communities of support. *Violence Against Women*, *25*(16), 1932–1955.

Henry, N., Flynn, A., & Powell, A. (2020). Technology-facilitated domestic and sexual violence: A review. *Violence Against Women*, *26*(15–16), 1828–1854.

Henry, N., & Powell, A. (2016) Sexual violence in the digital age: The scope and limits of criminal law. *Social & Legal Studies*, *25*(4), 397–418.

Henry, N., & Powell, A. (2018). Technology-facilitated sexual violence: A literature review of empirical research. *Trauma, Violence, & Abuse*, *19*(2), 195–208.

IPVTechBib. (2021). *Selected Research Papers on Technology used in Intimate Partner Violence*. Retrieved from: https://ipvtechbib.randhome.io/year.html

Jane, E. (2016). *Misogyny online: A short (and brutish) history.* London: Sage.

Jatmiko, M. I., Syukron, M., & Mekarsar, Y. (2020). Covid-19, harassment and social media: A study of gender-based violence facilitated by technology during the pandemic. *The Journal of Society & Media, 4*(2), 319–347.

Leisring, P. A., & Giumetti, G. W. (2014). Sticks and stones may break my bones, but abusive text messages also hurt: Development and validation of the Cyber Psychological Abuse scale. *Partner Abuse, 5*(3), 323–341.

Lewis, R., Rowe, M., & Wiper, C. (2018). Misogyny online: Extending the boundaries of hate crime. *Journal of Gender Based Violence, 2*(3), 519–536.

McGlynn, C., & Rackley, E. (2017). Image-based sexual abuse. *Oxford Journal of Legal Studies, 37*(3), 534–561.

National Network to End Domestic Violence, Safety Net Project. (2017). *Technology safety.* Retrieved from: https://www.techsafety.org/technology-and-sa

Obreja, M. (2012). *Technology and Sexual Difference,* PhD diss. Linköping: Linköping University Electronic Press.

Petersen, J., & Densley, J. (2017). Cyber violence: What do we know and where do we go from here? *Aggression and Violent Behavior, 34,* 193–200.

Powell, A., & Henry, N. (2017). *Sexual violence in a digital age.* Houndmills: Palgrave Macmillan.

Powell, A., & Henry, N. (2018). Policing technology-facilitated sexual violence against adult victims: Police and service sector perspectives. *Policing and Society, 28*(3), 291–307.

Powell, A., Henry, N., Flynn, A., & Scott, A. J. (2019). Image-based sexual abuse: The extent, nature, and predictors of perpetration in a community sample of Australian residents. *Computers in Human Behavior, 92,* 393–402.

Refuge. (2020). *72% of Refuge service users identify experiencing tech abuse.* Retrieved from: http://www.refuge.org.uk/72-of-refuge-service-users-identify-experiencing-tech-abuse/

Salter, M. (2018). From geek masculinity to Gamergate: The technological rationality of online abuse. *Crime, Media, Culture, 14*(2), 247–264.

Shelby, R. M. (2020). Techno-physical feminism: Anti-rape technology, gender, and corporeal surveillance. *Feminist Media Studies, 20*(8), 1088–1109.

Shields, R. (2002). *The Virtual.* London: Routledge.

Stark, E (2007). *Coercive control: How men entrap women in personal life.* Oxford: Oxford University Press.

Suzor, N., Seignior, B., & Singleton, J. (2017). Non-consensual porn and the responsibilities of online intermediaries. *Melbourne University Law Review, 40*(3), 1057–1097.

Suzor, N., Dragiewicz, M., Harris, B., Gillett, R., Burgess, J., & Van Geelen, T. (2019). Human rights by design: The responsibilities of social media platforms to address gender-based violence online. *Policy & Internet, 11*(1), 84–103.

Taylor, S., & Xia, Y. (2018). Cyber partner abuse: A systematic review. *Violence and Victims, 33*(6), 983–1011.

UN Women. (2020). *Take five: Why we should take online violence against women and girls seriously during and beyond COVID-19.* 21 July. Retrieved from: https://www.unwomen.org/en/news/stories/2020/7/take-five-cecilia-mwende-maundu-online-violence

VAWnet (n.d.) *Technology-Facilitated Abuse.* https://vawnet.org/sc/technology-assisted-abuse

Vera-Gray, F. (2017). "Talk about a cunt with too much idle time": Trolling feminist research. *Feminist Review, 115,* 61–78.

Walker, K., Sleath, E., Hatcher, R. M., Hine, B., & Crookes, R. L. (2021). Nonconsensual sharing of private sexually explicit media among university students. *Journal of Interpersonal Violence, 36*(17–18), NP9078-NP9108.

Women's Aid. (2020). Online and digital abuse. Retrieved from: https://www.womensaid.org.uk/information-support/what-is-domestic-abuse/onlinesafety/

Woodlock, D. (2017). The abuse of technology in domestic violence and stalking. *Violence Against Women, 23*(5), 584–602.

Woodlock, D., McKenzie, M., Western, D., & Harris, B. (2020). Technology as a weapon in domestic violence: Responding to digital coercive control. *Australian Social Work, 73*(3), 368–380.

2 Situating digital gender-sexual violations

Introduction

Digital gender-sexual violations (DGSVs), in their many and various forms – cyberbullying, online aggression, 'flaming', stalking, trolling, and much more – can be understood from several different traditions and perspectives. Our own work, both separately and together, across this broad field of activity has developed from a wide range of earlier studies, research projects, and interventions. These include those focused on: violence against women, intimate partner violence, image-based sexual abuse (IBSA), non-consensual intimate images (NCII) and 'revenge pornography', online abuse against feminists, violence in and around organisations, organisational policies on well-being, ICTs and sexuality, online communities and discourses, and strategies of resistance to violence. All these areas of work, and their associated theoretical and political traditions, have influenced our work in multiple ways. They also suggest different ways of situating DGSVs.

Accordingly, this chapter considers these violations through a number of overlapping perspectives. We begin with the framing of gender-based violence and abuse, and then their concomitant gender-sexual practices, before turning to technologisation, with specific focus on information and computer technologies, their affordances and various blurrings, and then the construction of gender-technologisation, seen through technofeminist scholarship. The chapter continues with a focus on pornographisation and visuality. Finally, we consider three broader ways of situating DGSVs, namely, as part of what we call digital hate, misogyny, and the manosphere; as transnationalisation, through the spread of transnational processes; and as publicisations and online narratives.

Gender-based violence

First, digital gender-sexual violations can be clearly understood as forms of and part of the broad range and continua of *gender-based violence and abuse* (GBV), and kindred framings, notably *men's violence against women and girls* (VAWG), *violence against women and children*, and *sexual violence*, including of

DOI: 10.4324/9781003138273-4

(former) intimate partners (see Boyle, 2019; Graaff, 2021). Feminist theory and practice has broadened understandings of what is meant by violence, well beyond what might be included within criminal codes, has highlighted its gender and sexual dimensions, and has demonstrated the pervasiveness of such violence (for example, Hagemann-White et al., 2008; Hanmer & Itzin, 2000; Stark, 2007). Recent figures from the World Health Organisation (WHO, 2021) show an estimated 30% of women worldwide have experienced some form of physical and/or sexual violence. Twenty-seven percent of women worldwide reported experiencing sexual abuse by their partners, and as many as 38% of murders of women worldwide are committed by an intimate partner. DGSV can be seen as part of the huge range of gender-based and sexual violence, and men's violence against women.

In contrast to narrower, often gender-neutral, definitions of violence, there are now vast bodies of literature, both feminist and non-feminist, that discuss the meanings of violence, abuse and violation, and the experiences thereof, in broader and more inclusive ways.[1] Violence and abuse may thus include physical (hitting, shoving, kicking, biting, or throwing things), psychological and emotional (yelling, controlling actions, humiliating, demeaning, making threats), sexual (rape, sexual assault, non-consensual sexual acts, applying pressure to consent to do something sexual), and economic violence, violence to property and pets, control of access to family and friends, health services and reproductive rights, coercive control, abuse of bodily integrity, and representational violence. The concept of the continuum of (sexual) violence has been well used to grasp this range (Kelly, 1988). Violence has also been theorised as a gendered structural phenomena in state formation (Tilly, 1990), and in feminist political economy across multiple levels and spheres of social reproduction (for example, Gentry, Shepherd & Sjoberg, 2018; Meger, 2016; True, 2012). Seen thus, violence ranges from war, genocide, and homicide to assaults and coercive controls, as well as symbolic violence (Bourdieu, 1998), systemic violence (Žižek, 2008), colonial violence, and slow violence (Nixon, 2011).

DGSV can be located within the continuum or continua of GBV, sexual violence, and men's violence against women and children, stretching across war and 'peace', interpersonal and structural violence, and other violent processes (Blumenstein & Jasinski, 2015; Cockburn, 2004, 2014; Yadav & Horn, 2021). Seen thus, it is not surprising that the idea of a single continuum of (sexual) violence has been extended in feminist theorising and policy contexts (Boyle, 2019; Buiten & Naidoo, 2020; Graaff, 2021; Lewis, Rowe & Wiper, 2017;).

---

1 Despite this broadening, some feminists have argued for limiting the concept of 'violence' to physical violence and illegal violence, that is criminal, violence: "For the purposes of a theory of change – in order to potentially make visible the relationship between violence and other forms of power and to identify the levers of transformation – it is better to restrict the concept of 'violence' to a specific and precise definition connected to *intended physical acts that cause harm*" (Walby et al., 2017, p. 4; our emphases).

This includes attending to the differential ways violence operates both materially and representationally, as in online 'image-base abuse' (McGlynn, Rackley & Houghton, 2017) and pornography, with the dual realities of material practices (real fleshly bodies doing real things) and forms of representation (staged, photographed, filmed, and so on) (Boyle, 2014). DGSVs can also be encompassed within the deadly, damaging, dispersed, and diffuse regimes of violence (Hearn et al., 2020, 2022) that are not immediately or directly physical on the fleshy body, even though they have harmful physical bodily effects on the violated and the abused.[2]

In situating DGSV as GBV, emphasis is placed clearly on gendered power, control, and the intention to harm that are exerted and reproduced, structurally and interpersonally. The crux of DGSV as GBV is then the enactment and imbalance of gender-sexual power, often, facilitated by the perpetrator's ability to remain anonymous and (superficially) distant. Seen as GBV, many DGSVs share features of forms of intentional harming, for example: reputation damage by spreading malicious gossip, rumours or photos, that may be manipulated, as in IBSA; intent to threaten or induce fear in the targeted person by circulating or sending repeated messages and photos, as in cyberstalking; sharing of or tricking someone into revealing aspects of their private life, with intent to embarrass them, as in doxxing; repeatedly sending offensive, rude, and insulting messages or photos to the victim-survivor or people they know, as in harassment; videoing someone being swarmed by a group, then posting it online to platforms such as YouTube (Lacey, 2007).

In many ways, seeing DGSV as GBV acts as an umbrella framing of the subsequent approaches to situating DGSV including as exemplars of forms of violences that are novel, continuing to change, and, in that sense, unfinished.

Gender-sexual practices

Following this logic further, DGSV can be seen as gender, gendered, sexual, *gender-sexual* (violent) *practices*. These practices may be interpreted as structured action, resulting from the gender-sexual social order and social structures, sometimes called patriarchy, and/or as a way of doing gender, doing sexuality, or doing gender/sexuality performatively. Either or both ways, it is part of the gender-sexual matrix, dominantly heterosexual, that (re)produces gender categorisations and places them into effect. The possible

---

2 Landrine and Klonoff (1997) suggest that it is the presence and exposure to oppressive (in their case, sexist) acts rather than the victim-survivor's subjective appraisals of such acts that better predict negative symptoms. Krieger and Sidney (1996) from a US survey of 4,000 black and white young adults report that blood pressure was highest for working-class black adults who accepted discrimination as 'a fact of life' or who denied they experienced discrimination, and lower for those who challenged unfair treatment. 'Accumulations of microaggressions' can affect self-confidence and self-respect of those targeted (Benokraitis, 1998, pp. 8–10).

overlapping, and non-prioritisation, of gender over sexuality, and indeed *vice versa*, noted here is part of the actual and potential instability of both of the two categories. This is made explicit in some versions of queer theory or queerfeminism, as theoretically inspired by Foucault or Butler or driven by direct subversive political action.

Having said that, as gendered, or intersectionally gendered, or gender-sexual practices, DGSV appear to be most often and mainly a matter of the *practices of men and masculinities* (Connell, 1995) or similar concepts, such as *manhood acts* (Schwalbe, 2013) that happen to take place with the use of or via ICTs. They thus can be instances of patriarchal, sexist, hegemonic and dominant forms of masculinities and manhood, and complicit, subordinated, marginalised, ambivalent, resistant, and counter-patriarchal forms. This is certainly not to stereotype such practices, but to see men's digital violent practices, and the discourses employed within and around them, as part of the diverse repertoires of men and masculinities, and in this sense perhaps less novel, less original, than they may appear to some or in some debates. In this view, DGSV may be understood as more about gendered-sexual positions, positionings, practices, within current, and changing, gender-sexual orders, and less about the specific and rapidly changing affordances of ICTs – to which we now turn.

Technologisation

Digital gender-sexual violations are done *by, through and with technologies, in this context, information and communication technologies (ICTs)*, whether through the sharing of explicit images and abusive written text via, say, cell phones within a specific locality or community, or accessing tailor-made online platforms, or the Internet of Things (IoT). Seen thus, DGSVs are part of the technologisation of socialities, sexualities, and violences, in their multifarious possibilities – that is, online and other technologically linked activity and activity that harms another, often intentionally so, and often repeatedly, where the victim-survivor is typically unable to defend themselves (Slonje, Smith & Frisén, 2013).

Importantly, ICTs have a number of distinctive features: time/space compression of distance and physical separation, instantaneousness in real time, asynchronicity, reproducibility of images, creation of virtual bodies, blurring of the 'real' and the 'representational'. More specifically, the affordances of computerised communication networks include broader bandwidth; wireless portability; globalised connectivity; personalisation (Wellman, 2001); and blurrings, even the abolition, of the strict boundary between online and offline, and between 'codex' (print) and 'net' (non-print) (Gilbert, 2013).

Digital gender-sexual violations exploit those characteristics and affordances, elaborate them in all sorts of ways, with open-ended and undefined possibilities and effects. Scholars such as Attwood (2009), Empel (2011), Dines (2010), Durham (2009), Levin and Kilbourne (2009), and Paasanen,

Nikunen and Saarenmaa (2007) point out that the boundary between public and private is shifting from one of censorship to an 'informed' consumer culture. That is, the relationship between the two spheres is becoming more fluid and porous with sex often taking centre stage, as it is between online and offline. DGSV can thus be seen in terms of the processual nature of the interactive web, in which 'produsers', 'prosumers', and other hybrids create the web interactively (see Whisnant, 2010, discussed below in relation to the production and consumption of pornography), as evidenced in do-it-yourself pornography, selfies, celebrity selfies, naked selfies, reality media, online lives, neknominate (drinking) challenges, and the rest.

This raises more and more complex issues of blurred and blurring boundaries, for example, how DGSVs can be simultaneously embodied and virtual. For example, a particular IBSA posting may reference, implicitly or explicitly, another earlier topic or social occasion offline and offscreen, positive or negative, for one, both, or more parties, which would not be decipherable by an uninvolved party or viewer. Such phenomena are irreducible to one form or possibility, may be multi-medial, multi-modal, multi-vectoral, and may only be understandable in the context of the range of further social practices beyond the visible and readable text. For example, a particular abusive online post may reference, implicitly or explicitly, another earlier topic or social occasion offline and offscreen, positive or negative, for one, both, or more parties, which would not be decipherable by an uninvolved party or viewer. Specific instances of IBSA may be part of a chain of events, occurrences, times, and places beyond itself. Posting explicit images or videos along with offensive text can be accompanied by abusive emails, 'tag-team-style pile-ons' in Internet forums and personal attacks in blog and newspaper article comment sections (Svoboda, 2014, p. 48). This brings us to a further and fundamental form of blurring boundaries – that between gender and technology themselves.

Gender-technologisation

The framings introduced thus far – of gender-based violence and gender-sexual practices, and then technologisation, affordances and blurring boundaries – might be suggestive of some false separations. On the contrary, among the important insights from what is variously labelled technofeminism, feminist technology studies, and feminist technoscience, bringing together feminism and STS (science and technology studies) (Faulkner, 2001; Wajcman, 2004, 2010), are that gender and technology, or perhaps more accurately *gender-technologisation*, are constructed by each other. Thus, both need to be understood in broader ways than are often discussed. In the case of gender, this means recognising gender as much more than fixed gendered, and indeed gender-binary, bodies, and in the case of technology it means seeing technologies as ubiquitous not limited to relatively few often specific, large-scale, and advanced forms of technology, labelled with a capital T, still sometimes seen as relatively autonomous, separated off from society and culture.

The intermingling of gender-technology might be seen as a closely reciprocal and simultaneous process, especially when viewed in more micro-terms, or operating at the more macro-level perhaps through some time lag, either way. There is a host of ways in which technofeminist scholars trouble the strict separation of gender and technology, as well as kindred dualisms, such as the technical/social dualism (Faulkner 2000, 2001), gender in/authenticity, and in/visibility paradox (Faulkner, 2009). Gender and technology are socially constructed, and it is not only that technology is gendered, but gender is technologised across the human/machine, human/non-human boundaries (Haraway, 1991). In keeping with insights of technofeminism, DGSVs can be seen as both gendered-sexual phenomena and socio-technological phenomena, operating across those boundaries (Henry, Flynn & Powell, 2020; Salter, 2018; Shelby, 2020;).

The key set of questions raised by and for technofeminist scholars thus becomes not so much *is* technology gendered, but *how is* technology gendered?[3] Moreover we can ask how are DGSVs both and simultaneously gendered and technologised? Examples of this simultaneous gendering and technologising include the following:

- The *key specialist actors* of DGSV, including in the design of technological artefacts and systems for DGSV *are predominantly men.*
- The *technological artefacts used in DGSV, such as web platforms and covert camera devices, can be gendered,* materially and symbolically, even with the considerable interpretative flexibility and variation in their use.
- Technology is likely to be an important element in the *gender identities of men who use, work, and play with DGSV.*

Technology is far from neutral in terms of intersectional gendered power, but embodies intersectional gendered power relations already 'built-in'

---

3 In addressing these questions, Faulkner (2001, pp. 89–90) provides an extremely useful summary of key points:

   a) Technology is gendered because *key specialist actors* – especially in the design of new technological artefacts and systems – *are predominantly men.*

   b) There are strong *gender divisions of labour around technology*, based in part on an equation between masculinity and technical skill.

   c) *Technological artefacts can be gendered*, both materially and symbolically, although there often remains considerable interpretative flexibility in their use.

   d) *Cultural images of technology are strongly associated with hegemonic masculinity*, although there is a huge mismatch between image and practice.

   e) *The very detail of technical knowledge and practice is gendered*, albeit in complex and contradictory ways.

   f) *Styles of technical work may be gendered somewhat*, although there are strong normative pressures to conform.

   g) Technology is an important element in the *gender identities of men who work and play with technologies*. (italics in the original).

into its structures, functions, and deployments (Wamala-Larsson & Stark, 2019). More specifically, the roots of some platforms are in men's abuse of women. For example, Oliver (2016) reminds us that social media technology was borne out of sexist attitudes and practices towards women on college campuses. Mark Zuckerberg invented Facebook "to post pictures of girls for his college friends to rate and berate" (p. 8), when he was in a fraternity; Evan Siegel, inventor of Snapchat, sent messages "referring to women as 'bitches', 'sororisluts', to be 'peed on' and discussed getting girls drunk to have sex with them" (p. 8); and Sean Rad and Justin Mateen, founders of Tinder which was introduced on colleges campuses, were involved in a sexual harassment complaint in which Mateen was accused of sending the President of Marketing "sexist messages calling her 'slut', 'gold-digger' and a 'whore'" (p. 32).

Pornographisation

We continue our discussion of different forms of situatedness with the more focused question of visuality and DGSV. This has been one of the main ways in which DGSV has become known and even prominent in public discourse and debate, and also one of the main forms that we have investigated (see Chapter 7). To begin with, DGSV can, at least in some cases, be seen as yet another form of *pornographisation*. More precisely, it can be understood as a relatively new form or genre of pornography that is not privately but is above all publicly displayed. Seen as such, DGSV can thus be understood as part of the explosion of (online) pornography (Dines, 2010; Hearn, 2006; Hughes, 2002; Jeffreys, 2013), and more general pornografication, pornographisation (Attwood, 2009), or 'mainstreamification' of pornography in and across societies (Empel, 2011).

In this sense, DGSV can be located within a very long historical development of different elaborations of pornography, in part affected through different technological affordances (Rahman & Jackson, 2010). We can compare, for example, the move to video pornography, with the invention of that technology. This way of seeing DGSV, IBSA, NCII, 'revenge porn' and the like resurfaces some very entrenched debates on such questions as the distinctions between pornography and erotica; the ethics of pornography; the effects of pornography on behaviour (cf. Itzin, 1993; Segal & McIntosh, 1993); its relation to prostitution and the sex trade more generally and the semiotics, and indeed textual conventions, of pornography (Boyle, 2010; Paasanen, 2011).

According to Hoff (1989, p. 17), the contemporary manifestation of pornography has "come so quickly out of the shadows of antiquity into today's headlines" that we tend to presume that previous incarnations are mirrored in modern pornographies. Arguably, changing forms and meanings of pornography can themselves be placed within societal moves from sex in a narrow and limited behavioural sense to broader understandings of sexuality and its institutionalisation with and through a proliferation of discourses, including sexuality as an identity. From public ritual to private personal relationships, women have tended to be positioned as submissive and men as dominant and powerful. Hoff (1989, p. 1) argues that liberalism in the form of freedom of speech and sexual liberation is one of the key factors in porn becoming mainstream – the pornografication, pornographisation (Attwood, 2009), mainstreamification of pornography (Empel, 2011) and the sexualisation of culture, especially in Western, Japanese, and South Korean societies (Dines, 2010; Durham, 2009; Levin & Kilbourne, 2009; Paasanen, Nikunen & Saarenmaa, 2007).

What these terms refer to is the sense that some societies are becoming different, sexually different, by virtue of the mass of sexual representations and discourses, with pornography increasingly influential and porous, permeating contemporary culture, and even blurring the lines between sexuality and non-sexuality (Hearn, 2018). The mainstreaming, and increasing visibility of sex, in modern Western societies can be seen in a many further arenas. Attwood (2009, pp. xiii–xv) lists several of these, some of which include the following: porn stars now write books, advise lifestyle magazines and star in lad magazines; porn is now more visible in art, film, television, and the press, as well as in music videos and advertising, including in various mainstream forms. There has been a significant growth of so-called gentlemen's clubs featuring pole and lap dancing; the popularity of sexual paraphernalia can be seen in the growth and more general public approval of lingerie, toys, and erotica shops such as Ann Summers; there is an increasing trend to have Brazilian waxing and other forms of pubic hair removal and growing numbers of people are making, and circulating, homemade sexual images on mobile devices, as with 'sexting' (Hasinoff, 2015), and videos that can be uploaded onto specific pornography websites such as Cliphunter, Xvidoes, and PornHub. Indeed, many of these activities have become 'respectabilised'. For example, pole dancing is now promoted as mainstream corporate entertainment or fitness activity (Ringrose et al., 2012).

Pornography is both foregrounded and backgrounded in mainstream popular television entertainment:

> Pornography and related phenomena may become normalised as part of the background "visual wallpaper" of television and its viewing. This includes specifically its *intermittent* viewing. In this sense, the "design" of programmes as "meant" for a certain age group or for another real or imaginary viewing category is not necessarily the most significant issue. Pornographisation, as background or "wallpaper" can proceed even if it does not figure directly in those programmes that are designed for young people or even primarily viewed by them. Indeed, perhaps this process operates even more powerfully by virtue of its incompleteness.
>
> (Hearn & Jyrkinen, 2007, pp. 48–49)

Thus, while the use of technology for sexual purposes is at least as old as the printing press, what differentiates the modern world is the near-universal availability of porn on the Internet and technological devices for accessing it, as well as the speed in which it can be accessed (Attwood, 2009). Gone are the days of the dominance of top shelf porn magazines and sex cinemas for consuming sex; consumption now tends to take place in the comfort of one's own home. The ability to privately view and make porn both at home and in public, and the relative anonymity of doing so afforded by new technological developments has led to an explosion of online pornography (Dines, 2010; Hearn, 2006; Hughes, 2002).

Arguably, in the explosion in pornographisation, new forms of pornography through such modes as sexting, cybersex, and deepfakes have emerged. For example, some of the 100 female A-listers targeted and objectified in the so-called 'The Fappening' – leaked private naked photos – had their images superimposed on images of other people's naked bodies engaged in explicit images of sexual acts (Sanghani, 2014). While some forms of electronic pornography such as sexting may be considered consensual, Ringrose et al.'s (2012) interview and focus group study of sexting show it is often coercive and is often linked to peer-pressure, harassment, bullying, and even violence. What they also found was that these phenomena predominantly affect girls and women who are often pressured into sending images of their naked bodies, and in time may become the victim-survivors of revenge porn when relationships end. Interestingly, some of the long academic and political debate 'for' and 'against' pornography has to some extent been reframed in those research studies which attend to the particular and variable social uses and social practices of pornography, and its display and invocation, both directly and indirectly (Thomson, 1999).[4] Here, however, we situate IBSA and similar forms of DGSV as a contemporary social problem and social practice to intentionally inflict harm. Accordingly, we now turn to consider DGSV from the perspective of digital hate, misogyny, and the manosphere.

Digital hate, misogyny, and the manosphere

Misogyny has a long history but use of the term, to mean hatred of women, has increased since its use by radical feminists in the 1970s and the publication of Andrea Dworkin's consideration of pornography as *Woman Hating* in 1974. More recently, 'misogyny' has been the term used to describe a range of sexist, abusive, hateful behaviours perpetrated by men against women and girls, online and offline. Thus, another frame for understanding DGSV is through the lens of *digital hate, misogyny and the manosphere*. While it is difficult to ascertain whether there has been an increase in such behaviours (before the Internet they would have been more localised and therefore less

---

4 Indeed, some scholars (Johansson & Hammarén, 2007; Weitzer, 2011) have argued that not all pornography is harmful, as long as both parties consent (Gordon-Messer et al., 2013), thus offering continuity with a long line of pro-pornography commentators whether within the sex industry or outside it (Segal & McIntosh, 1993).

visible), it is clear that the advent of Web 2.0 and development of social media have amplified them and that amplification, together with women's activism, have raised and extended public awareness of online misogyny.

The concepts of digital hate and misogyny refer to the motives and intentions of the perpetrator. However, it can be difficult to determine the perpetrators' emotions and intentions associated with these acts, as they may not be reliable witnesses (see Hearn, 1998, for example) and may insist that they engage in these behaviours 'for a laugh' rather than to express hate. So, it is also valuable to analyse the words and expressions used as well as the ways in which they are experienced. Jane's (2014) work is useful for determining the hateful online expressions directed at women. Insisting (Jane, 2014, p. 81) that the 'ebile' directed towards women online "must be spoken in its unexpurgated entirety", she provides numerous examples of threatening, abusive online messages which demonstrate disturbing levels of hostility towards women *as women*. To understand how these messages are experienced, research that engages with recipients is useful. Lewis, Rowe and Wiper (2019) report that feminist women who experience online abuse may categorise it as misogynistic and hateful, and some note that it also conveys other forms of prejudice, such as racism or homophobia. Misogyny online, then, may be intertwined with other forms of prejudiced hate.

The 'manosphere' encapsulates and metaphorically concretises this hatred of women. It is a collection of loosely associated – and sometimes well-organised – forums, blogs and other forms of online presence including men's rights activists, Incels (involuntary celibates), fathers' rights groups, MGTOW (men going their own way), TRP (the red pill), and so-called 'pick-up artists', with connections to alt-Right and far-Right groups (Horta Ribeiro et al., 2021; Winter, 2019), and aligned in their hatred of feminism (Jane, 2017). It has been associated not only with targeted mass online abuse, such as Gamergate in 2014, but also with offline events such as the shootings in Plymouth, UK, in August 2021 by a man who had been a member of an Incel group (Dodd & Weaver, 2021). A common theme on all such 'manosphere' online spaces are masculinities, which commodify women as sexual objects to be enjoyed, abused, violated, and hated (Bates, 2020; Ging, 2019).

Recent scholarship has explored the widespread extent of expressions of digital hatred towards women, girls, and feminism and highlighted its significant impacts. Online misogyny not only causes considerable impacts for individual women (such as fear, anxiety, depression – see Amnesty International, n.d.) but also for wider civil society, as it creates obstacles to women's engagement in public debate (Barker & Jurasz, 2019). Research shows that the majority of women who experience abuse reduce or restrict their engagement in online debate[5] (see, for example, Amnesty International, 2017),

---

5 However, Lewis, Rowe and Wiper (2018) show that a majority of feminists in their study who were subjected to online abuse were galvanised by the experience and committed to continue their activism against sexist oppression.

which may be part of their personal and/or professional lives; Gardiner (2018) reveals the impact on women and BAME journalists who are more likely than their male, white counterparts to be subjected to abusive comments in response to their published work. Indeed, the British Parliament has been so concerned about the negative impacts, both online and offline, of abusive discourse on civic life, that it has addressed it in the Committee on Standards in Public Life's examination of the intimidation of Parliamentary candidates (Committee on Standards in Public Life, 2017). Digital hate and its impacts were magnified when the global pandemic resulted in the transfer of many of our activities to the online space, extending further the potential for men to perpetrate misogynistic abuse.[6]

Attempts have been made to address misogyny. In 2021 in the UK, following the example of Nottinghamshire Police, the government instructed all police forces to record, on an experimental basis, crimes motivated by sex or gender (BBC, 2021). This will effectively make misogyny a hate crime. The Law Commission's *Reform of the Communications Offences* (2021) considers whether sex is a protected characteristic in hate crime legislation. While these initiatives are aimed primarily at street harassment, they will include offences committed online, potentially resulting in a tidal wave of reporting of online misogyny. Many commentators and activists herald these changes as a progressive step forward. However, some scholars (see, for example, Gill & Mason-Bish, 2013; Lewis, Rowe & Wiper, 2018) provide a more cautious commentary and highlight the potential shortcomings of this legal approach.

Activists who have challenged online misogyny through various initiatives (e.g., the global #WomenBoycottTwitter and #NotTheCost campaigns, Reclaim the Internet in the UK, #WebWithoutViolence in Germany, and the #BetterThanThis campaign in Kenya) have more recently turned their focus to platforms and employers in a bid to hold them accountable for providing online spaces free of abuse (Ging & Siapera, 2018). In 2021, Facebook, Twitter, TikTok, and Google all signed up to new commitments to address online abuse and women's safety on the web (https://webfoundation. org/2021/07/generation-equality-commitments/). However, these commitments comprise improved reporting systems and 'better ways for women to curate their safety online' (https://webfoundation.org/2021/07/generation-equality-commitments/) rather than focusing on prevention or on sanctioning perpetrators. Thus, women and girls are responsibilised for the digital hate they are subjected to, leaving the perpetrators of abuse relatively untouched and efforts to prevent abuse unexplored.

6 Women and girls are not unique in being the target of abuse; neither are men the only perpetrators. However, the research evidence by, for example, Amnesty International (https://www.amnesty.org.uk/online-abuse-women-widespread) and the Pew Research Centre (https://www.pewresearch.org/internet/2021/01/13/the-state-of-online-harassment/) shows that women and Black and Minority Ethnic people experience more abuse, and more intense abuse.

Transnationalisation

DGSVs can also be characterised as borderlessness, difficult-to-control, and transnational – in their production, consumption, interventions to counter it, and very existence as a new online-offline configuration (Hearn & Hall, 2021). A transnational perspective foregrounds two key elements: first, the *nation* or *national boundaries*, and, second, '*trans*' (across) relations, as opposed to 'inter', 'supra', or 'intra' relations (Hearn, 2004). Thus, *the nation is simultaneously affirmed and deconstructed* in that national borders and nation-based governance and controls may become less powerful. Moreover, the second element of 'trans' in transnational can be understood as referring, initially at least, to both *moving between* nations, as in hosting and posting DGSV in one country, on a platform located elsewhere, for transnational transfer, consumption, viewing, and homosocial audiences and exchange, but also in the sense of *moving beyond* the nation-state, as in new or changing transnational gender-sexual cultures and sexual violations across and beyond national borders and in some ways making those borders redundant or at least less impactful. Both of these interpretations are highly relevant for understanding online sexual violation and attempts to counter it. A third meaning of the transnational concerns the formation of *new transnational social configurations and phenomena* (Hearn & Blagojević, 2013); in this context, new transnational gender-sexually violating configurations that work online-offline simultaneously. Such online-offline configurations are integral to the transnational circulation and consumption of online violations, and transnational mobilisation and reproduction of patriarchal power and heterosexual norms.

A fundamental issue in analysing transnational processes is the dispersion, transfer, and deployment of a variety of both material resources – finance, people, things – and virtual resources. In the latter case, dispersion is often reproduced symbolically, through and in the contexts of ICTs, with complex and evolving forms of virtualisation. Transnational processes thus concern both the physical, material movement of people and bodies, as in migration, and goods and services, as in trading, and also virtual, immaterial movements of money, data, cultural references, messages, and visual images. While sexualities are typically thought of as embodied, online sexualities, sexual cultures, and sexual violations also entail national and transnational movement of text, images, and violations.

The harmful effects of DGSVs can also be transnational, for example, with threats and damage to well-being, bodily integrity and reputation, and pressures for hypervigilance, both personally and institutionally, extending across national borders and sexual cultures. An important, if still largely unexamined, issue concerns the intersectional diversity of members signed in on homosocial platforms, their location, racialisation, ethnicity, and religion, and that of their targeted victim-survivors, and how this connects with the content generated, nationally and transnationally. For example, some forms of non-consensual sharing and distribution of sexual images and text clearly invoke (transnational) exoticisation, orientalism, and racism. A relevant case here is that of Mia Khalifa, a Lebanese US-American. While her former career in the pornography industry was short-lived, with her most famous scene showing her performing sex acts whilst wearing a hijab, after leaving the industry images of her became and remain widely circulated, and she herself campaigns against their use and against pornography more generally (BBC, 2019). Subsequently, this process attracted condemnation, especially from women, and titillation, especially for some men, transnationally, in both Islamic and non-Islamic regions.

The dynamic between borderless Internet/e-spaces and the transnationalisation of DGSV has several further implications. First, the normalisation of sex on the Internet, via sexual selfies, sexting, sexual posting, and cyberintimacy, all provide multiple resources for further non-consensual harassment, bullying, exploitation, violation, and 'revenge porn' in borderless e-spaces: "… with each new tech development – such as the option to live-broadcast on social media – comes the possibility of new forms of cyber violence" (Williams, 2017). Second, blurring and co-occurrence of offline and online means there is a greater potential for (sexual) violence, abuse, and harassment to occur together, online-offline. And, third, the publicness of previously private spaces has the potential for multiple impacts, often repeatedly, where victim-survivors have less opportunity to defend themselves against or hide from what may exist in perpetuity. These new configurations involve complex intersections of online sexual violations and abuses with direct physical violation. The theoretical and political problematic of online sexual violation can also assist in rethinking transnational processes more generally, and in multiple ways – in production, consumption, and interventions, between and beyond nations, and in the creation of new configurations and phenomena online-offline.

Publicisation and online narratives

The discussion on and concern with both the manosphere and transationalisations leads us on to the wider question of the reformulation of the public sphere online, and the approach to DGSVs through a focus on processes of publicisation. DGSVs have come to be an object of public *interest and concern for some mass media and governmental actors, including in new forms of public space,* notably among mass media, social media, governmental and policy actors, and activists. These publicisations (Brown, 1981) often also invoke demands for more legal or regulatory controls. In this perspective, the notion of 'moral panic' (Cohen, 1972) may be useful, without any playing down of the likely intentions to harm and violate, and the likely associated experiences of harm of those victimised. Mass media interest in DGSV has been elaborated through the reporting of the hacking and online posting of naked photographs of female celebrities, such as the high-profile film star of *Hunger Games* Jennifer Lawrence (Glenza, 2014).

This mediatisation perspective might also be seen as an example of a complex, unstable, and rhizomic nexus of postings, violations, media interest, law and regulation, further postings and violations, and so on. The elaboration of such governmentality may take different forms in different national and societal contexts, depending on wider framings of sexuality and violence. These networks of publicisations may broadly and in the longer run work to either promote or oppose various form of online violation. The topic and contents of, for example, revenge pornography, image-based abuse and kindred DGSVs circulate between and across these various forums in the online/offline public domains.

More broadly still, some forms of DGSVs, such as revenge porn can be seen as forms of online narratives, and thus compared with and related to the recent, or not so recent, phenomenon of 'autofiction', a term coined by the French writer, Serge Doubrovsky, in 1977, with some parallels to the genre of faction. In some examples of this genre, writers supposedly 'tell all' about their everyday lives, friends, partners, family, and acquaintances, and sometimes call it a novel or some other composite production, sometimes with spectacular personal consequences. Perhaps the most famous protagonist here is Karl Ove Knausgård, the Norwegian author of six autobiographical autofictional novels. This form of writing can be a means of saying all without recourse to responsibility for others, at times as a form of revenge social porn.

Concluding comments

There are no doubt other productive approaches for examining DGSV, for example, as accounts of the psychological dynamics of shameful and shaming actions of self or others (Bradshaw, 1995; Kaufman, 1996), as conspicuous consumption of women (Hunter, 2011), as part of intimate or formerly intimate social relations (Delphy, 1976), and so on, but the perspectives above suffice here for present purposes. Indeed, in this book we see DGSV as both the combination of these perspectives, while more specifically focusing in our analysis on the online practices and interactions of men and women, and masculinities and femininities. We discuss these in more detail in our empirical analysis Chapters 5 to 8.

References

Amnesty International. (2017). Retrieved from: https://www.amnesty.org/en/latest/news/2017/11/amnesty-reveals-alarming-impact-of-online-abuse-against-women/

Amnesty International. (n.d.). Retrieved from: https://www.amnesty.org.uk/online-abuse-women-widespread

Attwood, F. (Ed.). (2009). *Mainstreaming sex: The sexualization of Western sex.* London: I.B. Tauris.

Barker, K., & Jurasz, O. (2019). Online misogyny. *Journal of International Affairs,* 72(2), 95–114.

Bates, L. (2020). *Men who hate women: From incels to pickup artists, the truth about extreme misogyny and how it affects us all*. London: Simon & Schuster.

BBC. (2021). *Police to record crimes motivated by sex or gender on 'experimental basis'*. 17 March. Retrieved from: https://www.bbc.com/news/uk-politics-56435550

BBC. (2019). Mia Khalifa: Porn contracts 'prey on vulnerable girls' [online]. *Newsbeat*. 13 August. Retrieved from: https://www.bbc.com/news/newsbeat-4933040

Benokraitis, N. J. (1998). *Subtle sexism*. Thousand Oaks, CA: Sage.

Blumenstein, L., & Jasinski, J. L. (2015). Intimate partner assault and structural-level correlates of crime: Exploring the relationship between contextual factors and intimate partner violence. *Criminal Justice Studies*, *28*(2), 186–210.

Bourdieu, P. (1998). *Masculine domination*. Cambridge: Polity.

Boyle, K. (2014). Feminism and pornography. In M. Evans, C. Hemmings, M. Henry, H. Johnstone, et al. (Eds.), *Handbook of feminist theory* (pp. 215–231). London: Sage.

Boyle, K. (2019). What's in a name? Theorising the Inter-relationships of gender and violence. *Feminist Theory*, *20*(1), 19–36.

Boyle, K. (Ed.). (2010). *Everyday pornography*. London: Routledge.

Bradshaw, J. (1995). *Family secrets*. London: Piatkus.

Brown, C. (1981). Mothers, fathers, and children: From private to public patriarchy. In L. Sargent (Ed.), *Women and revolution: The unhappy marriage of marxism and feminism* (pp. 239–267). New York/London: Maple/Pluto.

Buiten, D., & Naidoo, K. (2020). Laying claim to a name: Towards a sociology of "gender-based violence. *South African Review of Sociology*, *51*(11), 1–8.

Cockburn, C. (2004). The continuum of violence: A gender perspective on war and peace. In W. M. Giles, & J. Hyndman (Eds.), *Sites of violence: Gender and conflict zones* (pp. 24–44). Los Angeles: University of California Press.

Cockburn, C. (2014). A continuum of violence: Gender, war and peace. In R. Jamieson (Ed.), *The criminology of war* (pp. 357–375). London: Aldgate.

Cohen, S. (1972). *Folk devils and moral panics*. London: Paladin.

Committee on Standards in Public Life. (2017). *Intimidation in public life: A review by the Committee on Standards in Public Life*.

Connell, R. (1995). *Masculinities*. Cambridge: Polity.

Delphy, C. (1976). Continuities and discontinuities in marriage and divorce. In D. Leonard Barker & S. Allen (Eds.), *Sexual divisions and society: Process and change* (pp. 76–89). London: Tavistock.

Dines, G. (2010). *Pornland: How porn has hijacked our sexuality*. Boston: Beacon.

Dodd, V., & Weaver, M. (2021). Plymouth shooting: Police focus on 'incel' links as shop CCTV tape emerges. *The Guardian*. 17 August. Retrieved from: https://www.theguardian.com/uk-news/2021/aug/17/plymouth-shooting-police-focus-on-incel-links-as-shop-cctv-tape-emerges

Durham, M. G. (2009). *The Lolita effect: The media sexualization of young girls and what we can do about it*. London: Duckworth Overlook.

Dworkin, A. (1974). *Woman hating*. New York: Dutton.

Empel, E. (2011). (XXX) potential impact: The future of the commercial sex industry in 2030. *Manoa: Journal for Fried and Half Fried Ideas (About the Future)*. December. Retrieved from: www.friedjournal.com/xxxpotential-impact-the-future-of-the-commercial-sex-industry-in-2030

Faulkner, W. (2000). Dualisms, hierarchies, and gender in engineering. *Social Studies of Science*, *30*(5), 759–792.

Faulkner, W. (2001). The technology question in feminism: A view from feminist technology studies. *Women's Studies International Forum, 24*(1), 79–95.

Faulkner, W. (2009). Doing gender in engineering workplace cultures: II. Gender in/authenticity and the in/visibility paradox. *Engineering Studies, 1*(3), 169–189.

Gardiner, B. (2018). "It's a terrible way to go to work": What 70 million readers' comments on the Guardian revealed about hostility to women and minorities online. *Feminist Media Studies, 18*(4), 592–608.

Gentry, C. E., Shepherd, L. J., & Sjoberg, L. (Eds.). (2018). *Routledge handbook of gender and security*. Abingdon: Routledge.

Gilbert, J. (2013). Materialities of text: Between the codex and the net. *New Formations: A Journal of Culture/Theory/Politics, 78*(1), 5–6.

Gill, A. K., & Mason-Bish, H. (2013). Addressing violence against women as a form of hate crime: Limitations and possibilities, *Feminist Review, 105,* 1–20.

Ging, D. (2019). Alphas, Betas, and Incels: Theorizing the masculinities of the Manosphere. *Men and Masculinities 22*(4), 638–657. https://doi.org/10.1177/1097184X17706401

Ging, D., & Siapera, E. (2018). Introduction: Special issue on online misogyny. *Feminist Media Studies, 18*(4), 515–524.

Glenza, J. (2014). Jennifer Lawrence denounces nude photos hack as 'sex crime'. *The Guardian.* 7 October. Retrieved from: www.theguardian.com/film/2014/oct/07/jennifer-lawrence-nude-photo-hack-sex-crime

Gordon-Messer, D., Bauermeister, J. A., Grodzinski, A., & Zimmerman, M. (2013). Sexting among young adults. *Journal of Adolescent Health, 52*(3), 301–306.

Graaff, K. (2021). The implications of a narrow understanding of gender-based violence. *Feminist Encounters: A Journal of Critical Studies in Culture and Politics, 5*(1), 12. Retrived from: https://doi.org/10.20897/femenc/9749

Hagemann-White, C., Gloor, D., Hanmer, J., Humphreys, C., Kelly, L., Logar, R., Martinez, M., May-Chahal, C., Novikova, I., Pringle, K., Puchert, R., & Schröttle, M. (2008). *Gendering human rights violations: The case of interpersonal violence*. Brussels: European Commission.

Hanmer, J., & Itzin, C. (Eds.). (2000). *Home truths about domestic violence: Feminist influences on policy and practice: A reader*. London: Routledge.

Haraway, D. J. (1991). *Simians, cyborgs and women: The reinvention of nature*. New York: Routledge.

Hasinoff, A. A. (2015). *Sexting panic: Rethinking criminalization, privacy, and consent*. Champaign: University of Illinois Press.

Hearn, J. (1998). *The violences of men*. London: Sage.

Hearn, J. (2004). 'Tracking 'the transnational': studying transnational organizations and managements, and the management of cohesion. *Culture and Organization, 10*(4), 273–290.

Hearn, J. (2006). The implications of information and communication technologies for sexualities and sexualized violences: Contradictions of sexual citizenships. *Political Geography, 25*(8), 944–963.

Hearn, J. (2018). Where are the boundaries of sexuality? Hovering in a zone of uncertainty between sexualities and non-sexualities. *Sexualities, 21*(8), 1368–1373.

Hearn, J., & Blagojević, M. (2013). Introducing and rethinking transnational men. In: J. Hearn, M. Blagojevic & K. Harrison (Eds.), *Rethinking transnational men: Beyond, between and within nations* (pp. 1–24). New York: Routledge.

Hearn, J., & Hall, M. (2021). The transnationalization of online sexual violation: The case of "revenge pornography" as a theoretical and political problematic. In Y. R. Zhou, C. Sinding & D. Goellnicht (Eds.), *Sexualities, transnationalism, and globalization: New perspectives* (pp. 92–106). New York: Routledge.

Hearn, J., & Jyrkinen, M. (2007). "I could be talking about a porn flick": Television-internet media companies' policies and practices, young people and pornographisation. In *Unge, kjoenn og pornografi i Norden – Mediestudier [Young people, gender and pornography in the Nordic region – media studies]* (pp. 11–155). Copenhagen: Nordic Council of Ministers. TemaNord 2006, 544. Retrieved from: www.norden.org/da/publikationer/publikationer/2006-544

Hearn, J., Strid, S., Humbert, A. L., Balkmar, D., & Delaunay, M. (2020). From gender regimes to violence regimes: Re-thinking the position of violence. *Social Politics: International Studies in Gender, State and Society*. doi: org/10.1093/sp/jxaa022.

Hearn, J., Strid, S., Humbert, A. L., & Balkmar, D. (2022). Violence regimes: A useful concept for social politics, social analysis, and social theory. *Theory & Society*. Retrieved from: https://link.springer.com/article/10.1007/s11186-022-09474-4

Henry, N., Flynn, A., & Powell, A. (2020). Technology-facilitated domestic and sexual violence: A review'. *Violence Against Women, 26*(15–16), 1828–1854.

Hoff, J. (1989). Why is there no history of pornography? In S. Gubar & J. Hoff (Eds.), *For adult users only: The dilemma of violent pornography* (pp. 17–46). Bloomington: Indiana University Press.

Horta Ribeiro, M., Blackburn, J., Bradlyn, B., De Cristofaro, E., Stringhini, G., Long, S., Greenberg, S., & Zannettou, S. (2021). The evolution of the manosphere across the web. *Proceedings of the International AAAI Conference on Web and Social Media, 15*(1), 196–207. Retrieved from https://ojs.aaai.org/index.php/ICWSM/article/view/18053

Hughes, D. (2002). The use of new communication and information technologies for the sexual exploitation of women and children. *Hastings Women's Law Journal, 13*(1), 127–146.

Hunter, M. (2011). Shake it baby, shake it: Consumption and the new gender relation in hip-hop. *Sociological Perspectives, 54*(1), 15–36.

Itzin, C. (Ed.). (1993). *Pornography: Women, violence and civil liberties: A radical new view.* Oxford: Oxford University Press.

Jane E. A. (2014). 'Back to the kitchen, cunt': Speaking the unspeakable about online misogyny. *Continuum, 28*(4), 558–570.

Jane, E. A. (2017). Systemic misogyny exposed: Translating Rapeglish from the Manosphere with a Random Rape Threat Generator. *International Journal of Cultural Studies, 21*(6), 661–680.

Jeffreys, S. (2013). The 'agency' of men: Male buyers in the global sex industry. In J. Hearn, M. Blagojević, & K. Harrison (Eds.), *Rethinking transnational men: Beyond, between and within nations* (pp. 59–75). New York: Routledge.

Johansson, T., & Hammarén, N. (2007). Hegemonic masculinity and pornography: Young people's attitudes toward and relations to pornography. *Journal of Men's Studies, 15*(1), 57–71.

Kaufman, G. (1996). *The psychology of shame* (2nd ed.). New York: Springer.

Kelly, L. (1988). *Surviving sexual violence.* Cambridge: Polity.

Lacey, B. (2007). *Social aggression: A study of internet harassment,* Unpublished Doctoral Dissertation, Long Island University.

Law Commission. (2021). *Reform of the Communications Offences*. Retrieved from: https://www.lawcom.gov.uk/project/reform-of-the-communications-offences/

Levin, D. E., & Kilbourne, J. (2009). *So sexy so soon: The new sexualized childhood and what parents can do to protect their kids*. New York: Ballantine.

Lewis, R., Rowe, M., & Wiper, C. (2017). Online abuse of feminists as an emerging form of violence against women and girls. *British Journal of Criminology, 57*(6), 1462–1481.

Lewis, R., Rowe, M., & Wiper, C. (2018). Misogyny online: Extending the boundaries of hate crime. *Journal of gender-based violence, 2*(3), 519–536.

Lewis, R., Rowe, M., & Wiper, C. (2019). Online/offline continuities: Exploring misogyny and hate in online abuse of feminists. In K. Lumsden & E. Harmer (Eds.), *Online othering: Exploring digital violence and discrimination on the web* (pp. 121–143). Cham: Palgrave Macmillan.

McGlynn, C., Rackley, E., & Houghton, R. (2017). Beyond "revenge porn": The continuum of image-based sexual abuse. *Feminist Legal Studies, 25*(1), 25–46.

Meger, S. (2016). *Rape loot pillage: The political economy of sexual violence in armed conflict*. New York: Oxford University Press.

Nixon, R. (2011). *Slow violence and the environmentalism of the poor*. London: Harvard University Press.

Oliver, K. (2016). Rape as spectator sport and *Creepshot* entertainment: Social media and the valorisation of lack of consent. *American Studies Journal, 61,* 1–16. doi: 10.18422/61–02.

Paasanen, S. (2011). *Carnal resonance: Affect and online pornography*. Cambridge, MA: MIT Press.

Paasanen, S., Nikunen, K., & Saarenmaa, L. (Eds.). (2007). *Pornification: Sex and sexuality in media culture*. Oxford and New York: Berg.

Rahman, M., & Jackson, S. (2010). *Gender & sexuality: Sociological approaches*. Cambridge: Polity.

Ringrose, J., Gill, R., Livingston, S., & Harvey, L. (2012). A qualitative study of children, young people and sexting. *NSPCC*. Retrieved from: www.nspcc.org.uk/globalassets/documents/research-reports/qualitative-study-children-young-people-sexting-report.pdf.

Salter, M. (2018). From geek masculinity to Gamergate: the technological rationality of online abuse. *Crime, Media, Culture 14*(2), 247–264.

Sanghani, R. (2014). Jennifer Lawrence photo leak: Let's stop calling this hacking 'the fappening'. *The Telegraph*. 2 September. Retrieved from: www.telegraph.co.uk/women/womens-life/11069829/Jennifer-Lawrence-photo-leak-Lets-stop-calling-this-hacking-The-Fappening.html

Schwalbe, M. (2013). *Manhood acts*. Boulder, CO: Paradigm.

Segal, L., & McIntosh, M. (1993). *Sex exposed: Sexuality and the pornography debate*. New Brunswick, NJ: Rutgers University Press.

Shelby, R.M. (2020). Techno-physical feminism: Anti-rape technology, gender, and corporeal surveillance. *Feminist Media Studies 20*(8), 1088–1109.

Slonje, R., Smith, P. K., & Frisén, A. (2013). The nature of cyberbullying, and strategies for prevention. *Computers in Human Behavior, 29*(1), 26–32.

Stark, E. (2007). *Coercive control: How men entrap women in personal life*. New York: Oxford University Press.

Svoboda, E. (2014). Virtual assault. *Scientific American Mind, 25*(6), 46–53.

Thomson, R. (1999). 'It was the way we were watching it': Young men negotiate pornography. In J. Hearn & S. Roseneil (Eds.), *Consuming cultures: Power and resistance* (pp. 178–198). London: Palgrave Macmillan.

Tilly, C. (1990). *Coercion, capital, and European states, A.D. 990–1990*. Oxford: Blackwell.

True, J. (2012). *The political economy of violence against women*. Oxford: Oxford University Press.

Wajcman, J. (2004). *Technofeminism*. Cambridge: Polity.

Wajcman, J. (2010). Feminist theories of technology. *Cambridge Journal of Economics*, *34*(1), 143–152.

Walby, S., Towers, J., Balderston, S. Corradi, C., Francis, B., Heiskanen, M., Helweg-Larsen, K., Mergaert, L., Olive, P., Palmer, E., Stockl, H., & Strid, S. (2017). *The concept and measurement of violence against women and men*, Bristol: Policy Press.

Wamala-Larsson, C., & Stark, L. (Eds.). (2019). *Gendered power and mobile technology: Intersections in the Global South*. London: Routledge.

Webfoundation. (2021). Retrieved from: https://webfoundation.org/2021/07/generation-equality-commitments/

Weitzer, R. (2011). Review essay: Pornography's effects: The need for solid evidence: A review essay of everyday pornography, edited by K. Boyle (New York: Routledge, 2010) and Pornland: How porn has Hijacked our sexuality, by G. Dines (Boston: Beacon, 2010). *Violence Against Women*, *17*(5), 666–675.

Wellman, B. (2001). Physical space and cyberspace: The rise of personalized networking. *International Journal of Urban and Regional Research*, *25*(2), 227–252.

Whisnant, R. (2010). From Jekyll to Hyde: The grooming of male pornography consumers. In K. Boyle (Ed.), *Everyday pornography* (pp. 114–133). London: Routledge.

Williams, C. (2017). Young women mobilise against 'revenge porn' and online abuse [online]. *Open Democracy*. 20 October. Retrieved from: https://www.opendemocracy.net/en/5050/young-women-mobilise-against-revenge-porn-online-abuse/

Winter, A. (2019). Online hate: From the far-right to the 'alt-right' and from the margins to the mainstream. In K. Lumsden & E. Harmer (Eds.), *Online othering: Exploring digital violence and discrimination on the web* (pp. 39–64). Cham: Palgrave Macmillan.

World Health Organisation. (2021). *Violence against women*. 9 March. Retrieved from: https://www.who.int/news-room/fact-sheets/detail/violence-against-women

Yadav, P., & Horn, D. (2021). Continuums of violence: Feminist peace research and gender-based violence. In T. Väyrynen, S. Parashar, É. Feron, & C. C. Confortini (Eds.), *Routledge handbook of feminist peace research* (pp. 105–114). London: Routledge.

Žižek, S. (2008). *Violence*. London: Profile.

3   Online interactions

Internet usage

The growth, popularity, and speed of worldwide interconnections between individual networks operated by governments, industry, academia, and private parties, or rather the Internet, is quite remarkable. Its growth since 2000 has been a staggering 1,331.9%, and it is regularly used by 65.6% of the world's population, or more than 5 billion people worldwide (Internet World Stats, 31 March 2021: https://www.internetworldstats.com/stats.htm). The percentage of people connected to the Internet now ranges from 43.2% in Africa up to 93.3% in North America. Unsurprisingly, growth burgeoned in 2020 with pandemic lockdowns and a 70% surge in Internet usage. The Deutsche Commercial Internet Exchange (DE-CIX) in Frankfurt recording a new world record of more than 9 Terabits per second of data (The Internet Society, 2020).

The Internet provides almost instantaneous and near universal access with 3G-5G (6G expected early 2030s; Doust, 2020) mobile broadband, with superfast, and more recently ultrafast broadband, becoming increasingly common (OFCOM, 2021), providing faster online access to various online resources. The Internet is used for a multitude of purposes. As well as being essential for many work environments, popular usage varies from sending emails, information searches, banking, watching films and live television, social networking, news reading, shopping, booking holidays, listening to music and many more. According to the Office of Communications' (OFCOM, 2021, p. 2) *The Communications Market Report: United Kingdom,*

> People in the UK watched an average of 3 hours and 12 minutes of broadcaster television (live, recorded and catch-up) each day in 2020. As well as watching TV, UK internet users on average spend 3 hours and 37 minutes online.

While the highest rate of use is by the 16–29 years of age bracket, around half of those older than 29 years of age in the more developed regions of the word also regularly use the Internet (Internet World Stats, 31 March 2021: https://www.internetworldstats.com/stats.htm). The portability of devices to

DOI: 10.4324/9781003138273-5

access the Internet – smartphones, laptops, tablets – means the Internet can be accessed almost anywhere and at any time of day (The Internet Society, 2020). This has implications for DGSVs.

Forms of online interaction

In broad terms, ICTs and related technologies provide the means for technological control, virtual reproducibility, conditional communality, and unfinished undecidability (Hearn, 2014). More specifically, they "… provide means for sharing and control, monitoring and surveillance of personal/ intimate information, geographical location, and sexual practices, including both the exploitative, such as the sexual evaluation of women, and the resistant" (Hearn, 2006, p. 958). They also create opportunities to organise virtual communities of interest, whether around, for, or against particular sexualities or sexualised violences; they may appear to offer a safe and trustworthy arena for support, and indeed this may be so in some cases (Hearn, 2006, p. 957).

Laurillard (2002) examined the various ways Internet platforms are designed to interact with viewers. She identified five levels of viewer interaction with electronic media. The most basic form of interaction is the 'narrative' level in which the viewer is a passive receiver of information. Examples of this are some news websites and watching videos. The second level is 'interactive', which allows the viewer to actively explore the website and decide what to view. The viewer, however, cannot change the online content. Visitors to DGSV websites can explore the images, videos, and accompanying text of the numerous victim-survivors, view adverts, and visit external websites via hyperlinks. The next level is 'communicative'. This level includes online media that allows viewers to participate in discussions or interact with the material they encounter. For example, people can engage with each other in Internet forums and with each other through comments to news articles, videos, DGSV material, and so on. This is a common facility on DGSV websites; it is often used as a means for viewers to anonymously abuse, insult, sexualise, and commodify the victim-survivor, and engage with the perpetrator and other specified and non-specified others. The fourth is the 'adaptive' level, which includes media that allows the viewer to communicate with the moderator. Moderators are often the first to provide commentary on the victim-survivor, presumably to encourage viewers to respond, thus maximising the impact of any DGSV. While skewed towards the victim-survivor, the perpetrator is not immune to negative commentary, especially if the victim-survivor is deemed not visually pleasing and sexually desirable. The final level is the 'productive' level. This includes media that allows viewers to demonstrate their understanding of the information provided and may include writing stories or creating a garment. This final and highest level is becoming more common and available with deepfake pornography and augmented reality pornography.

Communicating online, managing identity

Given the vast array of ways people can engage with online sources and each other via computer-mediated forms of communication, it should not be surprising to learn that these have impacted on individual, and indeed collective, identities (White, 2020) including how people present themselves to others when surfing the web. These have important implications for the study of DGSV which allows us to see who commits DGSV – (ex-)partners, hackers, unknown others – and what motivates them, for example, peer-status, sexual gratification, remuneration, revenge, entertainment, excitement, and so on. Focusing on the construction of online identities, we look at self-presentation, identity deception, and the co-construction of the online self.

Self-presentation

According to Goffman (1959, p. 9), "When an individual plays a part, he [sic] implicitly requests his observers?to take seriously the impression that is fostered before them". Goffman argued that people manage their own self-image in their everyday interactions, which are akin to performances. Performances are aimed at creating a definitive impression to an audience at a given time in a specific context. As such, performances are dependent on the occasion in which they take place. So, for example, one may wish to create the appearance of frivolity and sexual appeal while partying with friends, yet present oneself as a high achiever, exacting, and a talented individual and/or team player while at a job interview. Such performances consist of both verbal and non-verbal cues. Verbal cues might include intonations, pauses, openings, greetings, insertion repairs (halting the talk-in-progress to go back and add something else before resuming), and so on (Maloney, Freeman & Wohn, 2020). Non-verbal cues could range from basic facial expressions like smiles and frowns or body movements, posture, dress sense, and hairstyles to more subtle cues, such as eye tracks, smells, twitches, and so on (Goffman, 1959).

Communication in cyberspace environments is, in part, different to in-real-life (IRL) since many of these cues are absent. For example, a simple non-photographic or location status update on Facebook is devoid of visual and verbal cues. 'Facebook friends' are instead left to gain additional details from the content of the post; from word selection, grammar, word capitalisation, vernaculars, emojis, GIFs, positioning, and orientations. This means that spatial characteristics of virtual environments are often considerably different to those of physical environments (see Bargh & McKenna, 2004; McKenna & Bargh, 2000, for reviews). For instance, in a discussion forum one can remain anonymous with a tag, avatar, or pseudonym, which may not bear any resemblance to the offline self. An additional way of maintaining anonymity is communicating in the Deep Web. Web users can surf anonymously using The Onion Router (TOR). TOR is a network of virtual tunnels that allows people to avoid being tracked by other websites and their identity revealed through 'traffic analysis' – that is, identifying users from their data payload and their header. As a consequence, anonymity in online communication has the potential to facilitate deceptive (and criminal) behaviour or allow individuals to reveal or construct an aspect of a real or desired identity which may be deemed taboo or difficult in their offline life such as, for those with disabilities, their sexual desires, and preferences (Hall, 2018). Yet, the presentation of the self in an online setting is often infused with what we want to reveal and that which we might not. As Turkle (2013, p. 154) points out:

> When part of your life is lived in virtual places – it can be Second Life, a computer game, a social networking site – a vexed relationship develops between what is true and what is 'true here', true in simulation. In games where we expect to play an avatar, we end up being ourselves in the most revealing ways; on social-networking sites such as Facebook, we think we will be presenting our-selves, but our profile ends up as somebody else – often the fantasy of who we want to be.

So, what are the contexts in which people choose to be (un)intentionally deceptive or create fantasy selves, or simply reveal their 'true' or 'real' offline identities?

Online deception

Online deception is now a commonplace. Many police forces across the globe now have specific Internet units that solely target cybercrimes such as identity, copyright and financial theft, hacking, stalking, bullying, and child and adult sexual abuse. Headlines such as 'Man jailed for rape after grooming women on social media' (Colwill, *Somerset Live*, November 12, 2021) seem all too common as are headlines about fraudsters, hackers, and trolls 'Taking its troll: I was told to 'end my life' & called 'disgusting' after posting bikini pics which flashed cellulite – I'm a work of art' (Roberts, *Irish Sun*, October 31, 2021). Sadly, such forms of illegal deception may have fatal consequences (John et al., 2018).

Legal and more mundane levels of deception have been reported in various Internet computer-mediated communication channels such as résumé sites like LinkedIn (Guillory & Hancock, 2012) and online dating sites (Sharabi & Caughlin, 2019). The growth of online dating has been exponential. It is an industry worth more than US$3 billion worldwide (Statistica, 2021) with some companies such as Lovestruck experiencing a growth rate of 2658% (Deloitte, 2021). Members can create a profile of themselves (photos are optional) including indicating partner preferences, which the dating website then sends to suitable matches based on the information provided. Members then review others' profiles and decide whether to make contact through the dating website. If communication is reciprocated, offline communication may follow. However, research suggests that some users of these sites present unrealistic or deceptive images of themselves (Guadagno, Okdie & Kruse,

2012; Lamphere & Lucas, 2019). Lamphere and Lucas (2019) point out that online identities are unreliable, since there is a greater potential for creating a 'mask' as in 'catfishing'.[1] Individuals and groups are able to do this because they are in a position to control the flow of information that others receive (Hollingshead, 2001). The granting or denying of access to 'real' information means that online identities can be wholly manufactured, as in the world of gaming or a combination of 'real', exaggerated, fantasy, and intentionally deceptive. These identity constructions have been reported not only in online dating, but also in social media, professional, curriculum vitae, and other Internet sites that require the user to construct a visible identity profile (Ismailov, Tsikerdekis & Zeadally, 2020).

DGSV websites also offer further potential for online deception. For example, a UK woman, Helen Mort, had holiday, pregnancy, and teenage photos stolen from her private social media accounts, turned into deepfake pornography and uploaded to pornographic websites, where viewers were also encouraging others to use her images to create violent pornographic content (Hao, 2021). This example shows how easy it is for perpetrators to undertake DGSV anonymously with almost anyone's images, and turn them into explicit images. One could remain anonymous with a tag, avatar, or pseudonym, which may not bear any resemblance to the offline self on any of the forms of DGSV websites, pornography websites, social media, or any other website that allows for the uploading of explicit images. As we noted earlier, this can be facilitated by communicating in the Deep Web via platforms such as The Onion Router (TOR), Anonymouse, ProxFree, HideMe, and others. However, that is not to say that every person who posts any form of DGSV posts anonymously because they may seek peer recognition and status, and others, including the person in the image, and their family, friends, work colleagues, and acquaintances, may know who has committed the act even if they hide behind a tag, avatar, or pseudonym. Where an (ex-)partner has posted explicit images in so-called revenge porn, the victim-survivor is likely to know who took them and who is likely to have posted them, especially if the accompanying text claims, for example, 'This is my ex', although this is not the case where hackers are involved.

Revealing oneself

The Internet also provides ample and enhanced opportunities for making oneself 'known' to others. According to Lundy and Drouin (2016), the Internet serves several social benefits that include maintaining social connections and ties with family and friends that may previously have proved difficult

---

1 Catfishing refers to the creation of a fictional persona or fake identity on a social networking service to target a specific victim-survivor for financial gain, to harm, for entertainment, or to compromise them in some way such as through dissemination of personal data.

due to geographical location, work and life commitments, and so on. It can also provide a relatively safe place to build relationships for those people who find forming face-to-face relationships challenging due to social anxieties, shyness, or lack of necessary social skills.

A relatively non-threatening environment is important for the development of various types of communities, especially those in which membership is a social taboo, such as a cult or sexual fantasy group, or those which are social minorities, such as gender or sexual minorities. It may simply be someone wanting to discuss a socially or personally delicate topic such as sex, sexuality, illness, disability, and political and religious persuasion, to name just a few. Such epistemic, associational, or communities of practice and persuasion tend to be reinforced and facilitated by a shared language of experience (Hall, Grogan & Gough, 2015; Thelwall & Vaughan, 2004). Greer (2012) suggests that this language of experience is identifiable when examining how such communities go about constructing their group identity. Online shared experiences rely on the same references to spaces, embodiment, time, and emotional and social bonds. Many of these features have been identified in health-related forums for depression, anxiety, obesity, cancer (Tanis, 2010), those affected by suicide (Horne & Wiggins, 2009), eating disorders (McCaig et al., 2019), and sexual abuse (Noack-Lundberg et al., 2020). These communities were seen to be disclosing shared experiences and stories, knowledge, meanings, and social positions with those who have membership entitlement within the same electronic space. While the majority of responses to DGSV are gendered and sexualised, some perpetrators disclose personal information about themselves, for example, personal likes/dislikes, and shared meanings, stories, and experiences.

Online communities can provide a variety of benefits to members, which can help to develop stronger and deeper relationships with other members (Nimrod, 2014). Greer (2012) suggests that members benefit from increased self-esteem, respect, and community status. For example, those who post DGSV may boast about the sexual acts they claim to have done to (rarely with) the victim-survivor, or gain community respect and status for collecting quality and 'risky' images without the victim-survivor being aware, as in spycamming or upskirting. We show these in more detail in our analytical chapters later in the book. Social support in online communities, as elsewhere, can be instrumental, informational, and emotional, although instrumental (physical) support is less likely.[2] In terms of those perpetrating DGSV, informational support, typically homosocial, can be incredibly important in sharing practical information about legal issues related to DGSV, victim-survivor's personal details, other DGSV websites, and so on. As Tanis

---

2 It may seem strange to speak of social support in this way, but mutual social support between perpetrators is what it is (DeKeseredy & Schwartz, 2016; Hearn, 1998). Similarly, those in online communities opposing DGSV can also gain mutual benefit from each other.

(2010) points out, this type of knowledge-based support allows others to gain additional control over their current situation, reducing uncertainty and facilitating decision-making. Emotional support, on the other hand, involves shared understanding of feelings displayed through empathy, compassion, comforting, and commitment. This can often take the form of simply talking about the issue and knowing that someone is willing to listen without passing judgement. While both of these forms of social support can be beneficial in reducing anxieties and stress, exposing one's vulnerabilities may also have its setbacks. That is, the wrong advice and information, however well intended, could have serious consequences. Indeed, as we pointed out earlier, trolls take pleasure in deliberately upsetting others (Roberts, 2021) and DGSV viewers may also post responses intended to upset the poster, that is, the person who posts the initial messages or visuals.

The co-construction of identity

We show in our analytical chapters that during conversation, interactants may orientate to a particular identity or identities depending on who the other interactants are, the context of the interaction, and what the interactants are trying to achieve. So, for example, in a conversation with one's line manager one may be attempting to construct an identity of a loyal, hard-working employee who is committed to the organisation, with the objective of seeking better working conditions and a pay rise, whereas the line manager might be attempting to work up an identity of the employer who is strapped for cash and so unable to grant such requests. In a different context, for example, when being addressed by a street fundraiser, one may try to work up an identity of someone who is too busy to stop, or who already donates to several charities on a regular basis. One may also wish to disidentify with others but not feel comfortable enough to do so publicly because social taboos exist for this identity. Of particular interest for this book is how the identities of perpetrators of DGSV, and their bounded-activities and characteristics, are managed, specifically, how those identities are co-constructed during interactions with viewers. These social 'facts', as we show in our analytical chapters, can be observed and studied through available data on talk and action. With the advent of the Internet, this includes online electronic forms of communication.

Online privacy

Given the negative aspects of some online communications, it might not be surprising to learn that a significant number of people report being concerned about their online privacy (Jiang, Heng & Choi, 2013). Buchanan et al. (2007) note several multidimensional definitions of privacy. *Informational privacy* relates to a person's right to determine how, when, and to what extent their information is released to others. *Accessibility privacy* relates to a person's right to determine how, when, and to what extent their information is accessible to others. This overlaps *informational privacy* where the acquisition or attempted acquisition of information involves gaining access to that person. It overlaps also with the *physical dimension of privacy*. The *physical dimension of privacy* is the degree to which a person is physically accessible to others. Thus, *accessibility privacy* overlaps with the *physical dimension* where physical access is at stake (intrusions by spam mail, computer viruses, accessing personal information). The final dimension of privacy is *expressive privacy*. This provides a person with the opportunity to continue or to modify identity-related behaviours from interferences, pressure, and coercion from others, for example, trolls. Of course, central to these dimensions is the person's ability to control the information that others can access and use. Thus, the level of privacy depends on the individual's choices and actions based on their personal values.

Clearly, the various forms of DGSV breach victim-survivors' privacy on all four levels. The taking and posting of explicit images of another without their consent infringes victim-survivors' right to determine who sees their body. DGSV images are often accompanied by victim-survivors' personal information such as full name, home, work and email addresses, details of family, friends, and colleagues, and the social media sites the victim-survivor used. The objective in some forms of DGSV like revenge pornography is to humiliate the victim-survivor to as many people whom they come into contact with as possible. Victim-survivors therefore also lose the opportunity to continue or to modify identity-related behaviours.

What is clear is that the perpetrator is able to determine their own levels of online privacy. Having the means to post anonymously and via online privacy platforms, such as The Onion Router (TOR), perpetrators are able to determine what information about themselves they provide to others. They are also able to determine how their information is accessible to others, if at all – for example, disclosure to those who know the victim-survivor, or police forces. Given some forms of DGSV are illegal in some countries, perpetrators of revenge pornography, for example, walk a fine line between providing enough information so that the victim-survivor knows who is responsible but not so much that they incriminate themselves. Some of this information is visible in the study of perpetrators' online text.

Concluding comments

Online identities clearly have the potential to be more fluid than offline identities, as hiding behind a computer screen, surfing the Web relatively anonymously, and interacting with others are not subject to the same offline visual, social, and contextual markers. Whilst many people's online and offline identities are likely to be similar, the ability to remain anonymous and create fake online identities is exploited by perpetrators of DGSV – that is, through hacking and stealing images, grooming people to send explicit images of themselves, posting and/or creating explicit images of others, textual abuses, and interacting with posted/created explicit DGSV content. We explore some of these later in our analytical chapters. However, although perpetrators can remain anonymous and create fake online identities, their online interactions still allow us to see their motivations, and how they account for their actions. The forms of data we collected, and our analytical methods are the topic of the following chapter.

References

Bargh, J. A., & McKenna, K. Y. A. (2004). The internet and social life. *Annual Review Psychology, 55*, 573–590.

Buchanan, T., Paine, C., Joinson, A. N., & Reips, U. D. (2007). Development of measures of online privacy concern and protection for use on the Internet. *Journal of the American Society for Information Science and Technology, 58*(2), 157–165.

Colwill, J. (2021). Man jailed for rape after grooming women on social media. *Somerset Live*. 12 November. Retrieved from: https://www.somersetlive.co.uk/news/somerset-news/man-jailed-rape-after-grooming-6201210

Deloitte (2021). *Perspective on Britain's Fastest Growing Tech Companies: Innovation for Growth*. Retrieved from: https://www.deloitte.co.uk/fast50/interface/pdf/deloitte-perspectives-on-britains-fastest-growing-technology-companies.pdf

DeKeseredy, W. S., & Schwartz, M. (2016). Thinking sociologically about image-based sexual abuse: The contribution of male peer support theory. *Sexualization, Media and Society*. doi: 10.1177/2374623816684692

Doust, A. (2020). 3G, 4G, 5G and beyond: The quest for mobile connectivity and speed. *Forbes*. 18 December. Retrieved from: https://www.forbes.com/sites/forbestechcouncil/2020/12/18/3g-4g-5g-and-beyond-the-quest-for-mobile-connectivity-and-speed/?sh=bd14b8b6c670

Goffman, E. (1959). *The presentation of self in everyday life*. Garden City, NY: Doubleday.

Greer, G. (2012). *Online communities of practice: Current information systems research*. Create Space Independent Publishing Platform.

Guadagno, E. R., Okdie, B. M., & Kruse, S. A. (2012). Dating deception: Gender, online dating, and exaggerated self-presentation. *Computers in Human Behavior, 28*(2), 642–647.

Guillory, J., & Hancock, J. T. (2012). The effect of Linkedin on deception in resumes. *Cyberpsychology, Behavior, and Social Networking, 15*(3), 135–140.

Hall, M. (2018). Disability, discourse and desire: Analyzing online talk by people with disabilities. *Sexualities, 21*(3), 379–392.

Hall, M., Grogan, S., & Gough, B. (2015). Bodybuilders' accounts of synthol use: The construction of lay expertise. *The Journal of Health Psychology, 21*(9), 1939–1948.

Hao, K. (2021). Deepfake porn is ruining women's lives. Now the law may finally ban it. *Technology Review*. 12 February. Retrieved from: https://www.technology-review.com/2021/02/12/1018222/deepfake-revenge-porn-coming-ban/

Hearn, J. (1998). 'Men will be men: The ambiguity of men's support for men who have been violent to known women. In J. Popay, J. Hearn & J. Edwards (Eds.), *Men, gender divisions and welfare* (pp. 147–180). London: Routledge.

Hearn, J. (2006). The implications of information and communication technologies for sexualities and sexualised violences: Contradictions of sexual citizenship. *Political Geography, 25*(8), 944–963.

Hearn, J. (2014). Sexualities, organizations and organization sexualities: Future scenarios and the impact of socio-technologies (A transnational perspective from the global "North"). *Organization: The Critical Journal of Organization, Theory and Society, 21*(3), 400–420.

Hollingshead, A. B. (2001). Communication technologies, the internet and group research. In M. A. Hogg & R. S. Tindale (Eds.), *Blackwell handbook of social psychology: Group processes* (pp. 221–235). London: Sage.

Horne, J., & Wiggins, S. (2009). Doing being 'on the edge': Managing the dilemma of being authentically suicidal in an online forum. *Sociology of Health & Illness, 31*(2), 170–184.

Internet Society. (2020). Impact report: The internet is a lifeline. Retrieved from: https://www.internetsociety.org/impact-report/2020/

Internet World Stats. (2021). Internet usage statistics. *Miniwatts Marketing Group.* 31 March. Retrieved from: https://www.internetworldstats.com/stats.htm

Ismailov, M., Tsikerdekis, M., & Zeadally, S. (2020). Vulnerabilities to online social network identity Deception detection research and recommendations for mitigation. Future Internet, *12*(9), 148.

Jiang, Z., Heng, C. S., & Choi, B. C. (2013). Research note—Privacy concerns and privacy-protective behavior in synchronous online social interactions. *Information Systems Research, 24*(3), 579–595.

John A, Glendenning, A.C., Marchant, A., Montgomery, P., Stewart, A., Wood, S., Lloyd, K., & Hawton K. (2018). Self-harm, suicidal behaviours, and cyberbullying in children and young people: Systematic review. *Journal of Medical Internet Research, 20*(4), e129.

Lamphere, R. D., & Lucas, K. T. (2019). Online romance in the 21st century. In I. E. Chiluwa & S. A. Samoilenko (Eds.), *Deception, fake news, and misinformation online* (pp. 475–488). Hershey, PA: IGI Global.

Laurillard, D. (2002). *Rethinking university teaching: A conversational framework for the effective use of learning technologies.* New York: Routledge Falmer.

Lundy, B. L., & Drouin, M. (2016). From social anxiety to interpersonal connectedness: Relationship building within face-to-face, phone and instant messaging mediums. *Computers in Human Behavior, 54*, 271–277.

Maloney, D., Freeman, G., & Wohn, D. Y. (2020). "Talking without a voice": Understanding nonverbal communication in social virtual reality. *Proceedings of the ACM on Human-Computer Interaction, 4*(Article 175), 1–25. doi: 10.1145/3415246.

McCaig, D., Elliot, M. T., Prnjak, K., Walasek, L., & Meyer, C. (2019). Engagement with MyFitnessPal in eating disorders: Qualitative insights from online forums. International *Journal of Eating Disorders, 53*(3), 404–411.

McKenna, K. Y. A., & Bargh, J. A. (2000). Plan 9 from cyberspace: The implications of the internet for the personality and social psychology. *Personality and Social Psychology Review, 4*, 57–75.

Nimrod, G. (2014). The benefits of and constraints to participation in seniors' online communities. *Leisure Studies, 33*(3), 247–266

Noack-Lundberg, K., Liamputtong, P., Marjadi, B., Ussher, J., Perz, J., Schmied, V., Dune, T., & Brook, E. (2020). Sexual violence and safety: The narratives of transwomen in online forums. *Culture, Health & Sexuality, 22*(6), 646–659.

Office of Communications. (2021). *The communications market report: United Kingdom.* 22 July. Retrieved from: https://www.ofcom.org.uk/__data/assets/pdf_file/0011/222401/communications-market-report-2021.pdf

Roberts, A. (2021). Taking its troll: I was told to 'end my life' & called 'disgusting' after posting bikini pics which flashed cellulite – I'm a work of art. *Irish Sun*. 31 October. Retrieved from: https://www.thesun.ie/fabulous/7838199/trolled-blogger-karina/

Sharabi, L. L., & Caughlin, J. P. (2019). Deception in online dating: Significance and implications for the first offline date. *New Media & Society*, *21*(1), 229–247.

Statistica (2021). *Online dating*. Retrieved from: https://www.statista.com/outlook/dmo/eservices/dating-services/online-dating/worldwide

Tanis, M. (2010). Online social support groups. In A. N. Joinson, K. McKenna, T. Posters, & U. Reips (Eds.), *The Oxford handbook of internet psychology* (pp. 139–153). Oxford: Oxford University Press.

Thelwall, M., & Vaughan, L. (2004). Webometrics: An introduction to the special issue. *Journal of the American Society for Information Science and Technology*, *55*(14), 1213–1215.

Turkle, S. (2013). *Alone together: Why we expect more from technology and less from each other*. New York: Basic Books.

White, M. (2020). Online identities and gender norms. In K. Ross, I. Bachmann, V. Cardo, S. Moorti & C. M. Scarcelli (Eds.), *The international encyclopedia of gender, media, and communication*. New Jersey: Wiley Blackwell.

4 Data and methods of analysis

Introduction

In this chapter, we briefly discuss our datasets and our data selection, collection, and analytical methods in order to provide the reader with background contexts and information to analytical chapters. We begin by providing a brief overview of Thematic Analysis (Braun & Clarke, 2012), which we deployed in Chapters 5[1] and 6,[2] followed by a brief overview of the methods and data in Chapter 5 – women who debate feminist politics – and Chapter 6, The Candid Zone. We highlight the key elements of the form of Discourse Analysis (Potter, 1996) we deployed in Chapter 7,[3] along with some further outline of the methods and background context to our data from former Internet website, MyEx.com. We conclude this chapter with some important ethical considerations related to those who work with DGSV data and analysis.

Thematic analysis

We used Thematic Analysis (Braun & Clarke, 2012; Nowell, et al., 2017) with the online survey data and the in-depth interview data about online textual abuse from women who debate feminist politics (presented in Chapter 5), and separately to analyse the electronic talk accompanying posts about 'upskirted' women and girls on The Candid Zone (presented in Chapter 6). We drew upon Thematic Analysis because it is a flexible method of analysis that allowed us to systematically identify patterns of meaning (themes) in, and across, these different datasets. We were able to identify themes across the survey responses and interviews, but also highlight the

---

1 The data collection and analysis of online abuse experienced by women who debate feminist politics was conducted by Lewis and her colleagues at Northumbria University, Mike Rowe and Clare Wiper.
2 The data collection and analysis of The Candid Zone was conducted by Hall, Hearn, and Lewis.
3 The data collection and analysis of MyEx.com was conducted by Hall and Hearn.

DOI: 10.4324/9781003138273-6

common themes within the electronic talk on The Candid Zone. Thematic Analysis' flexibility was also useful because it allowed the analysis of themes from top-down analyst category-driven pre-given definitions of types of on-line textual abuse, such as sexual harassment, stalking and threats of physical violence, as well as themes from bottom-up, participant-driven experiences (Chapter 5). In a different context, Thematic Analysis allowed us to identify the patterns of meaning that are commonly used by posters to the forum thread we analysed in Chapter 6.

Although Thematic Analysis has assisted the recognition of the central and sub-themes in our datasets, these themes may not necessarily be shared and understood by the participants, but only by us as analysts and others familiar with the topic area. For example, in our analysis of data from The Candid Zone, we refer to the two central themes as 'homosociality' and 'craft*man*-ship'. However, our sub-themes such as 'respect' and 'camera angle' (see Table 4.1) are likely to be more common currency for forum participants.

We followed Braun and Clarke's (2012) six stages of analysis for the analysis of the data in Chapters 5 and 6. Although we were already familiar with these particular forms of DGSV, we began by familiarising ourselves with the data by reading and re-reading the survey responses and interview transcripts, and similarly the electronic forum data, making notes on interesting items. We then generated preliminary codes based on the specific features within the data such as ways of interacting (e.g., Chapter 5, types of abuse). Preliminary themes were then generated, before re-reading the textual data, and discuss-ing the themes between us, in order to review and refine the themes, such as descriptive themes and conceptual themes (see following section), and also tabulate them, as we do in Table 4.1. The relevant themes for each chapter are discussed in more detail below and in each analytical chapter.

The online abuse of feminists

The national UK study about the experiences of online abuse among women who debate feminist politics used two data collection strategies: 1) an online survey (*n*=226 valid responses) with multiple choice and open questions and 2) in-depth interviews (*n*=17). The online survey contained multiple-choice and open questions about: the use of social media for feminist debate; the nature, frequency, duration, and volume of abuse; forms of social media used to communicate abuse; the topics being discussed when the abuse began; what made the communications feel abusive; whether any aspects of identity (such as gender, sexuality, ethnicity, or disability) were targeted; how many perpetrators were involved and whether they were known to the respondent; whether the abuse was linked to offline experiences; emotional and offline impacts; responses to the abuse; reporting behaviour; and satisfactions with responses from others. Respondents were asked detailed questions about their experiences of ten types of online abuse, and the following definitions were provided:

- Harassment: repeated unsolicited communications and/or violations of privacy
- Sexual harassment: repeated unsolicited communications of a sexual nature, including unwanted sexual images
- Threats of physical violence
- Threats of sexual violence
- Stalking: someone sought and compiled information about you and used it to harass, threaten, and/or intimidate you
- Flaming, and trolling: posting deliberately inflammatory or off-topic material to humiliate and/or provoke a response or emotional reaction from you
- Electronic sabotage: e.g., spamming or viruses sent by someone
- Impersonation, defamation: your identity was stolen
- Inciting others to abuse or threaten

Respondents were asked about their experiences, in general, as well as the most recent occurrence, in order to capture the range and specificity of their experiences without skewing the data towards the 'worst', most memorable incident. Open-ended questions generated surprisingly fulsome responses, creating an extensive qualitative dataset.

Respondents were recruited by circulating the online survey (during June to October, 2015) initially to about 60 women's organisations and about 30 individual feminist activists, academics, and journalists, as well as five organisers of feminist events concurrent with the research, who were asked to circulate the survey more widely. During this initial approach, care was taken to ensure the survey was sent to groups and individuals from a range of political perspectives, to avoid a sample dominated by radical feminists or those focusing on violence against women, for example. High-profile feminists, some of whom experience extremely high volumes of abuse, were not deliberately targeted to avoid skewing the data to these extreme levels of abuse, although, because of anonymity, it cannot be determined whether some did complete the survey. This recruitment approach enabled snowball sampling, reducing the impact of initial selection bias and reaching a greater number and range of participants.

To avoid the survey being sabotaged through trolling or cyberattacks, concerns about security were central to designing the methodology. The questionnaire was hosted on SurveyMonkey which was deemed to provide sufficient data security and some protection against sabotage by preventing more than one response per IP address. These strategies proved effective; only 14 responses were deemed to be inauthentic because they included irrelevant, extensive, and/or sexualised responses. Excluding these 14 responses, 226 valid survey responses were received. Of these, 220 self-identified as women, nine as men, six as 'other', and none as 'transgender'. Eighty-eight percent were white, the majority were between 26 and 45 years of age and heterosexual, with sizeable samples of bisexual (24%) and lesbian (17%) women.

The second data strategy was a set of 17 in-depth interviews exploring emergent themes from the survey data. Interviewees were recruited through the survey and further snowballing. Interviews were conducted electronically, by telephone or in person, typically lasted an hour, and were recorded and transcribed. Seventy-five percent of interviewees were white, 54 percent were heterosexual, 23 per cent bisexual, and 15 per cent lesbian.

Quantitative survey data were analysed using SPSS to identify patterns of experiences of those who use social media to engage with feminism extensively (three or more hours per day), moderately (one to two hours per day), or minimally (less than one hour per day). As the research did not use a random sample, inferential statistics such as chi-square could not be used to generalise to the wider population, so bivariate relationships between variables were examined to establish patterns within the sample.

Qualitative survey and interview data were analysed thematically through a collaborative process of reading and re-reading the data, discussing emerging themes, and then coding the data. As the study was exploratory and aimed to understand a wide range of issues related to the nature, prevalence and impact of the abuse, as well as how the respondents made sense of the abuse, a large set of 25 themes was identified. These included, for example, descriptive themes such as 'nature of abuse' and 'emotional and other impacts', and more conceptual themes such as 'normalisation', 'silencing', and 'online/offline crossover'. A selection of qualitative data is presented in Chapter 5 where we discuss the dynamics, experiences, and implications of online abuse towards feminists.

The Candid Zone

This dataset is drawn from the dedicated 'upskirting' and voyeurism website The Candid Zone, which presents as one of the largest, containing more than 30,000 specific threads with more than half a million posts (as of January 2022). The posting of images can garner peer-status. Members are categorised by the Candid Zone as either: Lurker (someone who views but does not post); Contributor (someone who posts images and/or posts comments); and Shooters/Legend (those members who took the photos and videos considered to be the best). Popular and more successful posters were placed on the leader board alongside past leaders and top-rated members. Leaders were awarded points for the number of 'thumbs up' or 'thumbs down', content views from fellow members, and the number and 'quality' of the images and videos posted. However, since December 2019, the site's creator banned 'lurkers' and illegal or stolen content and paid 'shooters', presumably to rebrand the website as superior and distinguish it from other similar website or pornographic online platforms.

Posters from across the globe can begin a thread with the photographs and video recordings they capture posting in any of the main forum threads which curate women into body parts: Leggings & Yoga Pants; Downblouse & Boobs;

Beach & Bikini; Upskirt; Dresses & Skirts; Shorts; Tight Jeans; Uncategorised; and Requests (see Thompson & Wood, 2018, for a consideration of "how online creepshot websites represent a new form of consuming and classifying women's bodies" (p. 561) through categorisation and organisation, or "folk-sonomies of misogyny" (p. 566)). In addition to these threads, members can provide, and get advice and guidance on, the best equipment to use and how to capture the 'best' photographs and specific photographic techniques. For example, there were discussions on camera angles, types of cameras and video recording devices, such as shoe cameras, the best places to photo 'upskirts', such as on the escalator or in a shoe shop, and many others. The Candid Zone provides both posters and viewers with the ability to engage with the material they encounter through the computer-mediated communication channel, namely comments, which offer richer insights into this phenomenon.

According to The Candid Zone, members must follow some general rules for posting which included: "Too Old/Young, Not Attractive - Let's keep this website full of hot girls", "Personal Info - Please check the picture and make sure no personal information, such as the girl's full name, school name, social media account, etc. is included", "No Porn", "Not in Public - No voyeur content (Bathroom, toilet, changing room etc.)", and "CP ['child pornography'] - No sexual or suggestive content involving minors". However, the vast majority of images were sexualised for others to enjoy, taken in public spaces, and a significant number of these were claimed to be of teenage girls, for example, "Juicy Teen Pink Skirt Uppie (OC)" and "Highschool Upskirt, Visible Thong & Pussy Lips".

Imagery of child sexual abuse is illegal in the UK under the Protection of Children Act 1978 and section 160 of the Criminal Justice Act 1988 (UK Crown Prosecution Service, 2020). Given that a significant amount of the forum threads appears to involve minors, we made every effort to confine the research to text and related images where it was claimed that the victim was over 18 years of age, and also where the victim appeared so. Given The Candid Forum appeared to contain sexualised images of underage girls, we approached a member of the UK police force for advice, and referred the website to the Internet Watch Foundation, a registered UK charity with a remit to trace the origin of images of child sexual abuse and work with police around the globe to bring prosecutions.

On the Candid Zone, here were a number of threads containing several hundred unique respondents. The first author read through the ten most popular to identify the thread that aligned to our research question: "How do perpetrators of 'upskirting' account for their actions?" (Holtz, Kronberger & Wagner, 2012). Whilst reading through these threads, preliminary codes were created to identify common ways in which perpetrators accounted for their actions, such as blaming the victim, as has been widely shown for perpetrators of other forms of violence and abuse (e.g., Hearn, 1998), and providing a service to other men, which links with understandings of approaches to violence against women through male peer support (e.g., DeKeseredy,

1990; also see DeKeseredy & Schwartz, 2016). However, in this process the sub-themes suggested homosociality and craftsmanship were key themes in the thread titled '++ (OC) YOU MAY WANT TO SIT DOWN FOR THIS ONE!! ++'. In this thread, the original post was an upskirting video of two women walking near a beach, which received 1,101 replies, and 34,583 views from February 2–August 17, 2019. Given the additional richness of this data, we focused on this thread.

We downloaded all the comments on this thread and cleaned the data by removing hyperlinks and adverts. Having downloaded and cleaned our dataset all three authors read through our data identifying the central themes. Through discussion between the authors about these themes, further sub-themes emerged, which we contrasted and refined with others ('constant comparison' process). Once we agreed codes to encapsulate these themes, the data were systematically coded, line-by-line, using NVivo. We identified a list of initial themes, which we later identified as sub-themes to the main themes (see Table 4.1).

We present the analysis of these themes in Chapter 6. But whilst Thematic Analysis allowed us to see the commonalities in the experiences amongst feminists who had been abused online, and amongst the homosocial inter-actions between posters and viewers of upskirting, Discourse Analysis was deemed a more suitable analytical approach for exploring micro-textual ways in which perpetrators of 'revenge pornography' account for their actions. We discuss this approach in the following section.

Discourse analysis

In order to explore perpetrators' motivations and how they account for their actions, we conducted a discourse analysis of the electronic text accompanying perpetrators' postings of sexually explicit material on a dedicated revenge pornography website, since closed. This approach was deployed in Chapter 7. Broadly speaking, Discourse Analysis aims to explore how 'versions of world, of society, events, and inner psychological worlds are produced in discourse' and so there is 'a concern with participants' constructions and

Table 4.1 Central and sub-themes

Central themes	Sub-themes	Occurrences
Homosociality	gratitude	952
	respect	763
	advice seeking	298
	courage	239
	Envy	165
Craftmanship	subject	642
	camera angle	94
	lighting	76

how they are accomplished and undermined' (Potter, 1996, p. 146). In other words, versions of the world are worked up during conversational interaction, including online electronic talk. The relevant version(s) of the world depend on the topic of conversation (for example, revenge or risk taking), who one is conversing with (for example, (un)known others), the context (for example, someone claiming to have been the victim of infidelity, or admiration of beauty and body shape), location (for example, internet platforms such as MyEx.com), and time (for example, current interests and trends).

There is a vast number of ways one can construct and bolster what one is claiming in order to minimise potential challenges from others. Central to these constructions is the categorisation of the object or event being talked about. Categorisations tend to have specific properties (Potter, 1996, p. 111). The object or event can then be presented positively or negatively and supported by recourse to social norms. Such norms included categories' characteristics and associated activities (Sacks, 1992). For example, in Western societies heterosexual relationships are presumed normative for most people. Therefore, in heterosexual/heterosexist environments, categorising someone as gay or lesbian can be a term of abuse, although perhaps less so now than in previous years. These are the (un)spoken rules of social conduct in everyday interactions, which also include conversational norms such as turn-taking and providing reasons for decisions such as photographing or recording sexually explicit material of another person and posting this in a public place. These common features of talk are evident in analysis. To see such features, analysts collect naturally occurring communication data such as electronic conversation.

During analysis of the data, Edwards and Potter (1992) argue that to avoid analyst-led interpretations of real-world phenomena, analysts should instead read the interactions, that is, only what is made relevant, by the participants involved. This point is one of the major differences between discourse analysis and other discursive methodologies, such as critical discourse analysis (Fairclough, 2001) and Foucauldian analysis (Foucault, 1978, 1980). When discursive methodologies such as these also become interpretative commentaries, they attempt to make links between what emerges from the micro-analysis and macro-issues, such as the operation of power, ideology, and persuasion. Discourse analysts (such as Potter, 1996) argue that macro-structures (and truth claims) can only be commented on if the participants in the interaction make them relevant. If not, such references to macro-structures are simply analyst's commentary. It is these features of Discourse Analysis that we use in the examination of the MyEx.com data, discussed below and analysed in Chapter 7, where the subject is what is culturally often called 'revenge pornography', but more formally labelled as image-based sexual abuse.

MyEx.com

Before the US Federal Trade Commission and the State of Nevada closed MyEx.com in 2018, the dedicated revenge pornography website boasted more than 14,000 explicit images and videos with accompanying text written either by the poster, viewers, or 'Casey' the website moderator. Hosted by Web Solutions, B.V, Netherlands, MyEx.com was reported to be operated by anonymous US Americans, in coordination with colleagues in the Philippines (Steinbaugh, 2014). Founded in 2013, it provided an internationally accessible platform for people to upload and share images and videos of other people anonymously. Posters were invited to provide the following details of the person to be posted: their name, nickname if the poster wished, age, country of origin, region, a title for the post, and some text about the person. Unlike other online revenge porn sites, such as Expic.net, My Fucking Ex-Girlfriend, and Revenge Net, MyEx.com facilitated both posters' and viewers' engagement with the material they encountered through the computer-mediated communication channel, namely, comments and specific search facilities.

As with other revenge porn websites, the majority of MyEx.com posts were of women by men. Although posts are anonymous, it was clear from much of our data when contributors were men. Male indexing occurred through male references ("blokes", "dude"), positioning in relation to female partners ("wife", "missus") and invoking typical masculine markers (heterosexual promiscuity: "your wife dude") (Miller, 2008). These are treatable as "male" even without this identity being "named out aloud" (Antaki & Widdicombe, 1998, p. 4).

The general aim of our data collection process was to identify the different ways in which men accounted for publicly displaying sexually explicit images, movies, and text of their ex-partner in revenge seeking. We employed the following framework and reviewed the posts according to the following stages: 1) identifying relevant texts by examining title and accompanying text; 2) text selection according to explicit inclusion and exclusion criteria (English, non-consensual, about a former intimate partner cheating, posts by those orientating to male heterosexuality; and 3) discursively analysing the data to identify, for micro-textual analysis, the different ways in which gender and sexuality were invoked by the poster in their accounting for publicly displaying sexually explicit images, videos, and text of their ex-partner. Table 4.2 shows our data selection framework and the number and types of posts.

We coded the remaining texts explicitly revenge seeking with NVivo. Numbers of codes are collated into Table 4.3.

Clearly many posts contained several, often competing, discourses. In Chapter 7, we present exemplars which highlight these discourses that were drawn on by the poster (not necessarily all in the same post). Our analytical aim was to examine how posters constructed accounts, gave descriptions, managed their stake in revenge porn, and so on, for the purpose of what they can tell us about their motives.

Ethical considerations

Ethical approval was first gained from the Arden University Research and Ethics Committee before working with MyEx.com and The Candid Zone data, and by the Northumbria University Research and Ethics Committee before collecting the interview and survey data on online abuse against feminists.

Table 4.2 Inclusion/exclusion criteria matrix

Inclusion/exclusion criteria	Number of posts	Male poster	Female poster
Written in English[a]	10,813	9,731	1,082
Non-consensual posts[b]	10,272	9,245	1,026
Other[c]	5,342	4,808	534
Heterosexual	4,903	4,418	529
Same-sex	24	19	5

[a] Approximation only based on aggregating the number of posts in the US 9,285; the UK 796; Canada 496; Australia 214; and New Zealand 22.
[b] Includes, for example, rate my wife/partner, swingers, porn stars.
[c] Includes, for example, hacker, a friend, a former ex but not for revenge, sexting, a casual acquaintance.

Table 4.3 Central discourses

Central discourses	Heterosexual men	Heterosexual women	Gay men	Lesbian
Physical assault	0	37	0	0
Relationship control	17	201	0	2
Sexual objectification	1,220	83	1	0
Infidelity	4,417	477	19	5
Prostitution	554	35	0	1
Sexual preference[a]	611	99	4	3
Sexual practices[b]	378	104	6	0
Money[c]	217	110	0	0
Parenthood[d]	58	64	0	0
Sexting	90	49	1	0
Hygiene[e]	2,573	149	0	1

[a] Heterosexual and same-sex post where the victim's sexual preference is questioned.
[b] Posts in which the victim is portrayed as interested in non-vanilla sexual practices such as bondage and discipline, dominance and submission, and sadism and masochism (BDSM).
[c] Posts in which the perpetrator reports either themselves or the victim as having pilfered money, for example, child maintenance or stolen goods and sold them.
[d] Where the perpetrator reports themselves or the victim as a poor parent, for example, loss of access to the child(ren) or missed maintenance payments.
[e] Refers to people reported to have a sexually transmitted disease or poor bodily hygiene practices. We do not include those that are reported to have had multiple unsafe sexual partners, even though this might by some be considered unhygienic. These we considered were more appropriately categorised as sexual infidelity.

Gathering data about people's experiences of violence always carries ethical challenges. Key amongst them is to minimise the harm done to those who have already experienced violence or abuse. In gathering data about feminists' experiences of online abuse, care was taken to make respondents aware of the nature of the study and to phrase and order survey and interview questions in ways that enabled respondents to control the nature and extent of what they revealed to us.

Collecting data from MyEx.com and The Candid Zone typically presents ethical challenges around respect for privacy and dignity of individuals and communities. The British Psychological Society ([BPS], 2021, p. 8) suggests that without consent "observation of public behaviour needs to take place only in public situations where those observed would expect to be observed by strangers". Whilst MyEx.com was an open access website, The Candid Zone required free membership sign-up. However, free sign-up is open to anyone, and all posts are publicly available to be viewed by 'strangers'. Given the data from both websites can be considered to be in the public domain, gaining consent was not deemed necessary (BPS, 2021, p. 10). However, we did attempt to contact respondents and site moderators, but, unsurprisingly given the nature of the data, did not get any response.

Yet privacy issues are still applicable for those whose images are posted on MyEx.com and The Candid Zone and similar sites. We, therefore, only draw on the text, and not the images, and we have anonymised our dataset as far as possible, removing any in-text personal details, vernaculars, or references. We also do not draw upon, or reproduce, any of the visual material since we do not want to further compromise the dignity of those pictured. This approach restricts the analysis in some cases because meanings are conveyed through the interaction of visual material and written text.

In line with British Psychological Society guidelines on use of online data (BPS, 2021), we anonymised the datasets (e.g., omitting biographical data, replacing names with A1 [Anonymous 1], A2, etc.). We present the extracts of written talk in full as they appear on The Candid Zone including spelling and grammatical mistakes, and colloquial language.

Researching digital gender-sexual violations

Doing research on DGSV is not only about using different methods and approaches, and following ethical practice. It also involves the researchers themselves, and their relations to each other, and to the material in question, often deeply disturbing material. Dealing with this, analysing this, and processing this material is demanding. Doing so is also likely to be different, though not in a determined way, depending on the social, political, and personal positioning of the researcher(s). Researching is theoretical, political, and personal.

In particular, working with digital gender-sexual violations data can often be emotionally tough. Hearn (2021, p. 93) highlights how emotions come into play at various stages of the research process in working on violence, from before researching commences, during the research, whilst analysing, writing, and presenting findings, to the emotions in other necessary tasks associated with the project. We use this framework to highlight our own emotional journey in researching and writing this book.

Hall recalled his emotive responses listening to victim-survivors' experiences of 'revenge pornography' on the radio travelling home from work.

Then, in 2014 when he first embarked on this particular journey, there was relatively little non-legal scholarly activity on what was then commonly and culturally called 'revenge pornography'. Following an early morning taxi ride conversation to Iceland's Keflavik Airport, Hall and Hearn agreed to try and understand perpetrator motivations; the focus of our first book *Revenge pornography; Gender, sexuality, and motivations*, and this book. This agreement to work together built on earlier work by Hall on the analysis of gendered online communication and images, and by Hearn on various forms of violence, especially men's violence against women and children (Hearn, 2020).

Lewis had studied men's violence for several years before a new form of this violence emerged online. Although not active on social media herself, she became aware of this abuse through her relationships with other feminists, as well as through the developing media coverage of particularly high-profile cases. While it was no surprise that this new arena was ripe for patriarchal exploitation, its manifestation was – and is – shocking and dismaying. At that time – 2015 – public and state responses to gendered online abuse matched the history of those responses to gendered offline abuse; conducting research about this new form of gendered abuse was an important way to bring attention to it, in order to seek social justice for those experiencing it.

New forms of digital gender-sexual violations seem to emerge as frequently as do new forms of digital technology. The three authors came together – from another chance meeting, or rather reunion, this time at a conference on violence in Helsinki in 2019 – to study upskirting, another new form of such violation which demanded research scrutiny in order to help provide constructive public, social, and criminal responses to it, such as awareness-raising, information sharing, educational interventions, and others discussed in Chapter 10. Collecting the data for the first book and for this extended version has been emotionally challenging. In aiming to collect empirical survey, interview, and textual data for analysis, we have sometimes heard about and witnessed some very undesirable and oppressive experiences and images. Learning about these relatively new ways in which men abuse women, and the impacts on women's safety and freedom, can provide knowledge that is, at times, overwhelming. Reading and analysing textual violations by perpetrators, viewers, and website moderators is no less emotive than hearing from victim-survivors. And, on most occasions we have no idea of the identity of the perpetrator or victim-survivor of these textual violations, which itself was emotionally draining and frustrating, leaving a sense of helplessness (Kumar & Cavallaro, 2018). We did report to the authorities some images of what appeared to be of adolescents, but organisations tasked with pursing these were never sure whether they were of 'real' adolescents or simulated. Thus, given funding shortfalls they were unwilling to pursue these further.

Emotions experienced during data collection and analysis are often not short lived. They can lead to a lower mood, lethargy, relative disengagement with loved ones, and feeling emotionally drained (Kumar & Cavallaro, 2018). We try to mitigate such feelings by talking through our experiences and reminding ourselves that our work is important. Although we think we have generally been able to manage the impact on our emotions well, as we are experienced researchers, there remain memories of things we have seen and read that we would really rather not have encountered. The authors have access to their own institutional support networks and talking openly between us and with colleagues was considered part of the self-care strategy (Kumar & Cavallaro, 2018). Furthermore, we have found giving various presentations and being part of a number of research and policy forums, together or separately, very helpful. These are important not only in gaining academic feedback, but also in showing collective strength, safety, and support in countering digital gender-sexual violations.

References

Antaki, C., & Widdicombe, S. (Eds.). (1998). *Identities in talk*. London: Sage.

Braun, V., & Clarke, V. (2012). Thematic analysis. In H. Cooper, P. M. Camic, D. L. Long, A. T. Panter, D. Rindskopf & K. J. Sher (Eds.), *APA handbook of research methods in psychology, Vol. 2. Research designs: Quantitative, qualitative, neuropsychological, and biological* (pp. 57–71). Washington, DC: American Psychological Association.

British Psychological Society. (2021). *Ethics guidelines for internet-mediated research*. 7 June. Retrieved from: https://www.bps.org.uk/news-and-policy/ethics-guidelines-internet-mediated-research

DeKeseredy, W. S. (1990). Male peer support and woman abuse: The current state of knowledge. *Sociological Focus*, *23*(2), 129–139.

DeKeseredy, W. S., & Schwartz, M. D. (2016). Thinking sociologically about image-based sexual abuse: The contribution of male peer support theory. *Sexualization, Media, & Society*, *2*(4), 1–8.

Edwards, D., & Potter, J. (1992). *Discursive psychology: Inquiries in social construction*. London: Sage.

Fairclough, N. (2001). The discourse of new labour: Critical discourse analysis. In M. Wetherell, S. Taylor & S. Yates. (Eds.), *Discourse as data: A guide for analysis* (pp. 229–266). London: Sage.

Foucault, M. (1978). *The history of sexuality, Volume 1: An introduction*. Trans. R. Hurley. New York: Vintage.

Foucault, M. (1980). *Power/knowledge*. Brighton: Harvester.

Hearn, J. (1998). *The violences of men: How men talk about and how agencies respond to men's violence to known women*. London: Sage.

Hearn, J. (2020). "A life of violence": Some theoretical/political/policy/personal accountings on 'masculinities' and 'intimate partner violence'. In L. Gottzén, M. Bjørnholt, & F. Boonzaier (Eds.), *Men, masculinities and intimate partner violence* (pp. 16–33). London: Routledge.

Hearn, J. (2021) Serious emotions: On some emotions in working on men's violences and violences to women. In M. Husso, S. Karkulehto, T. Saresma, A. Laitila, J. Eilola, & H. Siltala (Eds.), *Violence, gender and affect: Interpersonal, institutional and ideological practices* (pp. 99–110). Cham: Palgrave Macmillan.

Holtz, P., Kronberger, N., & Wagner, W. (2012). Analysing internet forums: A practical guide. *Journal of Media Psychology: Theories, Methods and Applications*, *242*(2), 55–66.

Kumar, S., & Cavallaro, L. (2018). Researcher self-care in emotionally demanding research: A proposed conceptual framework. *Qualitative Health Research*, *28*(4), 648–658.

Miller, K. (2008). Wired: Energy drinks, jock identity, masculine norms, and risk taking. *Journal of American College Health*, *56*(5), 481–490.

Nowell, L.S., Norris, J. M., White, D. E., & Moules, N. J. (2017). Thematic analysis: Striving to meet the trustworthiness criteria. *International Journal of Qualitative Methods*, *16*(1), 1–13.

Potter, J. (1996). *Representing reality: Discourse, rhetoric and social construction*. London: Sage.

Sacks, H. (1992). *Lectures on conversation*. Oxford: Blackwell.

Steinbaugh, A. (2014). *Revenge porn site MyEx.com sued for copyright infringement*. 7 March. Retrieved from: http://adamsteinbaugh.com/2014/03/07/revenge-porn-site-myex-com-sued-for-copyright-infringement/

Thompson, C., & Wood, M. A. (2018). A media archaeology of the creepshot. *Feminist Media Studies*, *18*(4), 560–574.

UK Crown Prosecution Service. (2020). *Indecent and prohibited images of children*. 30 June. Retrieved from: https://www.cps.gov.uk/legal-guidance/indecent-and-prohibited-images-children

Part 2

Empirical analyses of digital gender-sexual violations

5 Online textual abuse of feminists, *with Michael Rowe and Clare Wiper*

Introduction

Feminists are not the only people who are targeted for online abuse, but the routine, voluminous, vitriolic, and gendered abuse directed at them online tells us something important about contemporary gender relations. Feminists are subjected to all the types of abuse discussed in other chapters, so in this chapter, as well as discussing the *types* of online abuse to which they are subjected, we also discuss the *function* of that abuse directed at feminists. We consider what purpose it serves in contemporary society, its links with the anti-feminist manosphere and with violence (sometimes fatal) that occurs offline. We also draw on data from the first study of online abuse directed at feminists, by Lewis, Rowe and Wiper (2017), to consider online abuse as a political strategy to subdue or silence women's and feminists' engagement in political campaigns, discourse, and debate.

In keeping with the discussion on terminology in Chapter 1, this chapter focuses on online abuse, rather than the broader category of digital abuse. While some examples given include image-based abuse (such as sending obscene images), in general, the abuse discussed in this chapter refers to written communications sent and received on a device such as a PC or mobile phone via a form of social media such as Twitter or Facebook. The abuse described is not always explicitly sexual in nature, however it rests on ideas about sex and gendered roles, for example, that women do not 'belong' in the online world except as sexually objectified beings. Thus, although a slur such as 'shut up and get back to the kitchen' might not be sexually explicit, it invokes ideas about the acceptable behaviours of sexed bodies. The chapter uses the terms abuse and violation, with their broader definitions (as outlined in Chapter 1) rather than violence, with its connotations of physical violence. We start with a discussion about what is known about online abuse towards women, in general, including the difficulties regarding measurement of such abuse, followed by an examination of online abuse towards feminists specifically.

DOI: 10.4324/9781003138273-8

What do we know about online abuse towards women?

In recent years, research about the gendered nature of online abuse has provided knowledge about the prevalence of such abuse. Before considering online abuse directed at *feminists*, it is useful to review what we know about online abuse towards women *in general* (some of whom will, of course, be feminist). Prevalence studies about online abuse started to emerge in the early 2010s and a selection of them is reviewed below. As we do not have agreed definitions of online abuse, these studies used different measures to survey experiences. Some measure 'harassment'. For example, the PEW Centre for Research (Duggan, 2017; Vogels, 2021) measures six forms – offensive name-calling, purposeful embarrassment, physical threats, sustained harassment, stalking and sexual harassment. The European Union Agency for Fundamental Rights (FRA, 2014) measures 'cyberharassment' by two items in their survey of violence against women: 'unwanted sexually explicit emails or SMS messages' and 'inappropriate advances on social networking websites' (p. 104). Amnesty International's survey (2017) uses one measure and asks women whether they have experienced "abuse or harassment online".

These different approaches to measuring online abuse result in different prevalence rates in the range of one-tenth to three-quarters of women of different ages reporting victimisation. They also point to the need for consistent conceptual and operational definitions and approaches for measuring online abuse over time and across locations. Online abuse is, by its nature, without geographic borders; if we are to understand the experiences of women (and others) around the world and over time, we need consistency not only on a national but also on an international basis.

Leaving aside important questions about measurement, surveys tell us that online abuse is a significant issue for women – especially young women – around the world. Perhaps the first study to survey women's experiences of online abuse across different countries was the 2014 European Union study conducted by the European Union Agency for Fundamental Rights (FRA, 2014) which asked women and girls across 28 countries about their experiences of several forms of violence, including online. It found that 11% of respondents had experienced sexual online abuse. Putting to one side debates on the comparability of reports from different countries,[1] the victimisation rate was low in countries with less widespread use of social media (e.g., 5% of respondents in Romania) and higher in those with more extensive use (e.g., 18% in Sweden and Denmark). Moreover, young women in the prime age group for social media use reported higher rates of victimisation; 20% of 18–29-year-olds had experienced it. Given the growth of social media use in the last decade, we can realistically assume that victimisation rates have risen since this study reported its findings.

---

1 There is an extensive debate on the methodology and reliability of the FRA data, especially in terms of its use for comparative purposes across countries, see: European Institute for Gender Equality, 2014; and Humbert et al., 2021.

Two years later, a study of 1,053 Australian women found that almost half experienced online harassment and 76% of those under 30 experienced it (Reilly, 2016). In 2017 an Amnesty International (2017) study, that was based on a survey by IPSOS Mori of 4,000 women between 18 and 55 years in eight countries (Denmark, Italy, New Zealand, Poland, Spain, Sweden, the UK, and the US) reported that almost a quarter of these women had experienced online abuse or harassment at least once, with significant geographic variation (16% in Italy and 33% in the US). The PEW Research Centre surveyed a random sample of US women and men about their experiences of online harassment in 2017 (n=4,248) and 2021 (n= 10,093) and reported that rates of sexual harassment of women doubled in the four-year period, from 8% to 16% (Vogels, 2021). Young women were particularly targeted with 33% of women under 35 years experiencing sexual harassment in 2021. However, these rates do not include being sent unsolicited sexual images, which by most measures would be considered a form of sexual harassment. This abusive experience was not measured in 2021, but in 2017 PEW reported that 53% of women respondents aged 18 to 29 had been sent unsolicited "explicit images" (Duggan, 2017).

Focusing on online abuse directed at girls and young women aged 15–25 years, Plan International (2020) found more than half of the 14,071 girls and young women surveyed, from 22 countries around the globe have been harassed and abused online. They conclude that "[g]irls are targeted online just because they are young and female, and if they are politically outspoken, disabled, Black or identify as LGBTIQ+, it gets worse" (Plan International, 2020, p. 8).

Together, these studies show high rates of online abuse directed at women, particularly younger women, who comprise the age group that uses more social media more intensively. While men also experience high rates of online abuse, women are more likely to experience sexualised abuse, including sexual harassment and stalking online. Although the studies do not consistently provide intersectional analyses of the experience of, for example, Black and Minority Ethnic (BME) women, or BME women from a sexual minority, there are indications that BME people and sexual minorities experience racialised and sexualised abuse (see, e.g., Dhrodia, 2017; Gardiner, 2018; Lewis, Rowe & Wiper, 2017). This, then, provides the context for a more focused analysis of online abuse directed at feminists, which is the focus of the following sections.

What do we know about online abuse of feminists?

Although the online world is rife with abuse of many kinds, women who espouse feminist politics or who might be perceived to be feminist (which can, for some people, mean any woman who speaks out about her views and knowledge) seem to be particularly targeted. Research shows that this occurs across the various professional and social sectors of society.

Research by Gardiner (2018) shows the high rates and significant consequences of abuse for women journalists. Using blocked comments as a proxy for abuse, Gardiner (2018) examined abuse posted in response to *Guardian* newspaper journalists' articles and found that "articles written by women consistently attracted a significantly higher proportion of blocked comments (2.16%) than articles by men (1.62%)" (p. 598). Younger women, those writing in male-dominated sections (such as sport, technology, and film), and Black, Asian, and Minority Ethnic (BAME), Muslim, and Jewish writers were more likely to experience online abuse. The abuse was gendered in that comments directed at women journalists were significantly more likely than those directed at men to focus on women's bodies, private lives, or sexuality. Adams (2018) examined the experiences of 102 women journalists working in a male-dominated field – technology. She notes that the computer technology industry is a "bastion of male hegemony" (p. 852) which is manifested, in part, in the abuse experienced by women in the industry. While some women journalists deal with the abuse they received by normalising it and seeing it as an expected part of life as a journalist in a male-dominated sector, over a third of her sample reported that they had changed their working practices out of fear of abuse. Like Gardiner (2018), Adams (2018) found that "abuse was often aimed, not just at women, but particularly at those defending women's rights, or in other words, at feminism" (p. 857).

Feminist researchers and academics may also be targeted for abuse. Fiona Vera-Gray (2017) analyses her experience of receiving online abuse in response to her attempts to recruit participants in a study about "men's stranger intrusions in physical public space" (p. 66). People (it can be assumed they were men because of the nature of the comments left but this cannot be confirmed because identities were not revealed) left misogynistic, sexualised, aggressive and hostile comments about the research topic, the researcher, and the women research participants. She reflects on this experience to argue that feminists who research the topic of violence against women engage with Hochschild's (1983) notion of 'emotional labour' and Liz Kelly's of 'safety work' (2012) to protect themselves and their participants:

> For feminist researchers working on violence against women then, online abuse from men doubles our hidden labour. Not only is there work to be done in managing the research subject (and our own position in relation to it), but we have to conduct both work to manage our responses to our own experiences and histories of men's violence, as well as safety work, that is the work of managing one's own safety in relation to men's practices. (Vera-Gray, 2017, p. 73).

Women politicians are another professional group who have been targeted for abuse. Around the world, they have spoken out about the sexualised and, for some, racialised abuse they have experienced. In the UK, Diane Abbott, a Black Member of Parliament since 1987, earned the unwelcome headline describing her as "more abused than any other female MP during election" (Elgot, 2017).

Research by Amnesty International that examined abuse on Twitter against women MPs found that Ms Abbott received nearly half of all abusive tweets in the run-up to the 2017 General Election and that excluding her, Black and Asian women MPs received 35% more abusive tweets than white women MPs (Dhrodia, 2017). The UK political scene is not alone in being an arena for sexist abuse towards women. For example, women politicians in India, from across the political spectrum, are abused at higher rates than their counterparts in the US and the UK, according to an Amnesty International study of 114,716 tweets in the three-month period around the 2019 Indian elections (Amnesty International India, 2020). For Indian women politicians, 14% of tweets examined were abusive in comparison to 7% of tweets sent in 2017 to women politicians in the UK and the US. The growing problem of abuse – online and offline – and its chilling effects on women's participation in political life have been recognised by the independent Committee on Standards in Public Life (which advises the UK Prime Minister). However, their report on the intimidation of Parliamentary candidates (Committee on Standards in Public Life, 2017), does little to address the gendered and racialised nature of much of this abuse.

Women who engage in political debate in more informal ways are also targeted. For example, Eckert (2018) interviewed 109 women who blog in Germany, Switzerland, the UK, and the US about feminist issues and found "[w]omen who identify as feminist, regularly write about "traditional" political issues, and/or redefine what counts as political face a higher risk of online abuse than those who do not identify as feminist and/or write about or challenge "traditional" politics" (p. 1293). Similarly, feminist activists and commentators with a high public profile have been the subject of intensive, voluminous abuse. In the UK, abuse of feminists first came to wider public attention with the abuse of Caroline Criado Perez when she led a campaign to have women represented on bank notes. The campaign of abuse directed at her also led to one of the first convictions for sending abusive tweets which included references to rape as well as threats to kill (see R. v John Raymond Nimmo and Isabella Kate Sorley 2014). In this case, the offender was a woman, showing that online abusers may adopt the discourse of misogyny regardless of their gender. However, the vast majority of abuse does not result in a prosecution, neither is it perpetrated by women.

Feminists' experiences of digital abuse

It is not only high-profile women who are targeted for abuse. Research in the UK by Lewis, Rowe and Wiper[2] (2017) revealed high rates of abuse towards

---

2 The national UK study about the experiences of online abuse among women who debate feminist politics used two data collection strategies: (1) an online survey (n=226 valid responses) with multiple choice and open questions and (2) in-depth interviews (n=17). Respondents were asked detailed questions about their experiences of ten types of online abuse (definitions were provided): harassment, sexual harassment, threats of physical violence, threats of sexual violence, stalking, flaming, and trolling, electronic sabotage,

women who engage in feminist debate; 40% of the sample of 226 survey respondents said they experienced sexual harassment (including receiving unsolicited sexualised and/or pornographic images) and 37% received threats of sexual violence. Lewis, Rowe and Wiper (2017) argue that, while the more extreme, hateful, and violent abuse tends to get more attention, especially when it is directed at a woman with a high public profile, it is also important to study the abuse directed at women without high profiles whose experiences are not covered in the national media. Feminism, as a movement, a consciousness, and a politics is comprised not only of writers, commentators, and politicians who may capture public attention, but also the countless women who explore, develop, and 'do' feminism through their daily lives and daily encounters online and offline. Indeed, online forums and groups are, in Vera-Gray's words, "the new millennium's form of feminist consciousness raising" (2017, p. 65).

All the studies noted above reveal that digital online abuse towards feminists varies from the seemingly innocuous but disruptive, to the explicitly hateful, violent, sexualised, and threatening. Lewis, Rowe and Wiper (2017) use Kelly's (1987) continuum of sexual violence to describe a continuum of online abuse ranging from comparatively sporadic and less inflammatory, unpleasant, non-threatening messages to, at the other end of the spectrum, concentrated, frequent, highly threatening, and hateful (see also, Boyle, 2019, for a consideration of the value and challenges of 'continuum thinking').

The survey respondents (n=226) here gave examples of their experiences at the former end of the spectrum:

> Abusive language in private mails and on topic threads. (A92)
> I am a prominent and regular contributor to a forum. I routinely experience hostility from a number of anonymous users – seemingly for holding feminist views; for challenging men's views; for making unpopular/radical arguments or for confronting casual sexism and misogyny. Mostly this is low-level sniping and trolling but it occasionally becomes more intense. (A86)

Respondents' experiences could be considered to be at the other end of the continuum if they were threatening, obscene violent, and/or voluminous, for example:

> A known Twitter Troll threatened to cut my face off. (A142)
> Following my tweet about a feminist event, I received a tweet the next day, of three photographs from an unknown sender. The photographs

---

impersonation, defamation, inciting others to abuse or threaten. Respondents were recruited by circulating the online survey initially to about 60 women's organisations and about 30 individual feminist activists, academics, and journalists as well as 5 organisers of feminist events concurrent with the research, who were asked to circulate the survey widely. Findings are reported in Lewis, Rowe and Wiper, (2017, 2018, 2020). Extracts are reproduced here unedited.

were of a white, older, long-haired unknown naked male, bending over and stretching his hugely gaping anus open to the camera (and so, to me as the viewer), with a really horrible distorted/angry expression on his face. (A16)

I received many abusive anonymous messages […which…] were offensive and graphic, detailing how they would carry out a rape, or death threats. (A103)

Rape and death threats were common. In many cases, such threats existed in the online sphere and respondents did not indicate that they were afraid they would be fulfilled, although this does not limit their impact as they contribute to a social and cultural milieu in which violence is part of the lived experience for women. Some perpetrators extended their fantasies about violence by referencing offline violence enacted upon women which disrupted the (imagined) distinction between online and offline violence:

One of the comments 'I wish you'd fallen into the path of Peter Sutcliffe[3] and that, you know, that's grim. That's somebody who really hates women and things like that I would say are really the things that would still touch me now. (Interviewee 16)

In this way, abuse received online can have lasting impacts, whether or not the recipient fears that the threats will be enacted offline.

As already indicated in the data shown, much online abuse is explicitly sexualised, referencing actual or imagined sexual or sexually violent acts. For these respondents, their discussions about feminist concerns – such as breast feeding and menstruation – were met with sexually abusive messages:

I was abused for discussing breast feeding in public! Told that I should never breed, that he should be able to wank[4] off next to my kids and have sex next to me and my kids on a bus! (A205)

Posted a blog about menstruation and promoted and encouraged dialogue surrounding women's periods as a normal part of life. Was attacked by both male and female users and they threatened to 'find me and rip out my bloody uterus' and said I had nothing better to do with my pathetic life. (A76)

---

3 Peter Sutcliffe was convicted of murdering 13 women and attempting to murder seven others between 1997 and 1980 in Yorkshire, England. During that time, women in the area lived in fear of the unknown attacker and women around the UK were highly critical of West Yorkshire Police force for their inept investigation and their victim-blaming attitudes, particularly of prostitutes (who were some of Sutcliffe's victims); a senior police detective distinguished between prostitutes and "innocent girls" (Smith, 1993, p. 175).

4 'Wank' is an English slang term meaning masturbate.

This sexualisation of abuse took several forms. Some, such as those above, referred to sexual acts or sexual body parts. Some referred to sexual violence as a 'deserved' punishment for feminist views. Common themes in the abuse were that women hold those views because of their lack of sexual engagement with or appeal to men. Many respondents reported they had received abuse telling them they were 'too ugly to be raped': "ALWAYS ALWAYS ALWAYS appearance. 'You ugly feminists would be lucky if someone raped you'" (A156). As well as targeting women's appearance, perpetrators also targeted aspects of an individual's identity. In some cases, the perpetrator referred to acts of sexual violence that were of specific significance to the victim-survivor:

> I was sent messages on a daily basis, sometimes several times a day, on a number of platforms telling me that I was a slut and a whore, that I'm not a real lesbian because I've 'had sex' with men, despite the fact that my only experience with and around men is as a trafficking survivor. I was called a 'cum-whore', a 'bi-slut'; I was told I deserved my rapes; I was told it was 'regret not rape'. I was told that I 'enjoyed it', I was told that I must have just been a horny kid (I was trafficked from the age of 5), I was told that dykes don't like dick so I can't be a lesbian. I was told to kill myself; I was threatened with rape, I was told I like cock, I was told I loved the taste of semen. (A198).

This (apparent) targeting of significant experiences for the victim-survivor might occur because the use of rape threats is so common in online abuse, and the experience of rape is so common amongst women, that feminists who are survivors of rape are likely to receive rape threats. However, in some cases, the perpetrator mentioned specific aspects of the woman's identity, making the abuse more personalised and more personal:

> He told me I was a 'fat ugly cunt who no one would rape' (I have rape survivor in my bio). He then upped the ante and four or five people who seemed connected to him joined in. I was threatened to be raped. I was threatened to be 'boned' and thrown all sorts of insults at. (A238)

Respondents also experienced abuse which targeted other aspects of their identity. In this way, perpetrators did not specialise in sexist and sexualised abuse, but abused their intersecting identities:

> You should be put down you disabled bitch you scrounger. (A11)
> Death threats, encouragement to commit suicide, lesbophobic slurs and attacks. (A186)

Online abuse is perpetrated by individuals and groups. Some respondents had experience of being targeted by individuals, who sent either a handful of abusive messages or engaged in a more sustained campaign of abuse. For a minority of the sample, abuse came from a group. Six per cent of respondents reported there were 50 or more perpetrators in their last incident. Typically, the abuse by an individual developed into abuse by a group because the abuse was shared with large networks or because the larger network was explicitly invited to join in the perpetration of abuse. One respondent described how her post on #everydaysexism:

> …was immediately shared by GamerGate all over Twitter, Reddit, and various other sites. Within a few hours it had over 25,000 views and 650 abusive comments on Reddit not including the comments on Twitter. My picture, name, twitter handle, location, profession, were all shared. I feared for my online security as Gamergate is known to hack people's accounts. It took days before I could get moderators to remove my personal information that was shared across sites. I was threatened with rape, abuse, etc. (A126)

Instances like these, where hundreds or thousands of people – probably mostly men – 'pile on' to abuse an individual woman, bring to mind the ways in which men in groups use sexual violence to perform their masculinity for each other (Hall, Hearn & Lewis, 2021). Offline and online, men come together as a group, which may be organised (e.g., Gamergate) or spontaneous, to share in the entertainment of rape as a "spectator sport" (Oliver, 2016).

While it seems likely that the majority of online abuse towards feminists is perpetrated by men who are anti-feminist, there are also indications from Lewis et al.'s study that some of the abuse received by feminists was sent by people who might consider themselves to be feminist but who support a different feminist politics from the recipient of abuse. Debate about sex work and about trans politics can be considered to light the blue touch paper of feminist debate; respondents in Lewis et al.'s study indicated that posting about these issues were two of the most likely topics to generate abuse (along with the topic of violence against women). For example:

> I was targeted initially by one individual as I had been quoted in the media through my work. They misrepresented my views and job, broadening it out to my personal life and my appearance. They got others involved and when I tried to engage with the discussion there was a call out for others in pro sex work lobby to come and join the 'pile-on'. The abuse and insults escalated, and my twitter feed was full of verbal abuse and threats. (A45)

It can be difficult for the respondent to be sure of the identity of the perpetrator of online abuse. However, certain tropes – such as 'die in a fire' – have become so common in some of these debates, that it might be taken as an indicator that the abuse is sent by someone who identifies as feminist but who opposes the recipient's views about hot topics in feminist debate. For example:

> One person 'set' their 10k followers on me for talking about radical feminism. I was told to 'get raped' 'Die in a fire' & that I needed 'excorcised' to name but a few. (A130)

This highlights how difficult it can be to identify whether abuse towards feminists is sent by anti-feminist, misogynist men or by people who identify as a part of the feminist movement – although their self-identification as feminist is questionable, given their use of metaphors of sexual violence and misogyny to challenge other feminist views.

Impacts of online abuse on feminists

In the early days of attention to online abuse such communications were sometimes dismissed as 'only words' with limited impact. It is now clear that online abuse can have extensive, significant impacts on those who receive it, while it can also have fewer damaging impacts for some. Data from Lewis, Rowe and Wiper's (2017) victimological study revealed that just under half of their sample reported they were 'not bothered' by the abuse or 'it was just one of those things, I shrugged it off'. Although this might indicate that the abuse was not very impactful, qualitative data indicate that, for some, normalisation is a strategy used to manage the impacts. For example:

> It's something I experience quite often, and just for being a feminist. On an almost daily basis I have to deal with messages from men, many of which contain pictures or content that's sexual and unwanted. It upsets me greatly, but I've gotten used to it and I can't afford to let it upset me. (A111)
> It happens to all women so it's almost not worth mentioning as it's so unremarkable. (A232)

Some respondents 'normalised' their experiences by referring to how common online abuse is, particularly for women and particularly for feminists. Such normalisation of men's violence against women and girls is a common strategy for minimising one's experiences of sexism or "intimate intrusions" (Stanko, 1985). As well as stemming from an awareness of the prevalence of such violence and the knowledge that it is not taken seriously in society, it is also a 'coping strategy' to manage one's emotions – particularly anger and fear – in response to these intrusions. The concept of 'normalisation' is often used to refer to the widespread internalisation of patriarchal norms and the process whereby behaviours such as men's violence against women is seen, in certain circumstances, as normal, justifiable, and acceptable. As Sundaram (2018, p. 898) notes, normalisation occurs through "the legitimation of sexual harassment through discursive (normative) constructions of gender". However, amongst these feminist respondents who are aware and critical of patriarchal norms and dominant discourses of gender, we see normalisation used as a strategy to knowingly minimise the significance of the abuse they receive in order to make it more manageable. Incidentally, no respondents compared their experiences to others' in order to emphasise the greater significance of their own experiences; this process of comparison was adopted only to indicate that their experience of abuse was *less* significant.

Slightly more than half of the sample agreed with multiple choice answer options that indicated that the abuse was more impactful: 'I was upset, and it had a significant impact, but I'll get over it' and 'it was really traumatic, and I keep thinking about it even though I don't want to'. Impacts included worry, stress, anxiety and fear and other physical symptom, for example, A92 reported "I ended up being prescribed beta blockers in the short term as I would wake up in the night with palpitations". Fear was a particular impact for feminists who experienced abuse that crossed the (imagined) boundary between online and offline abuse. While some might see this fear as misplaced if the threats are made online by people who do not know the recipient's location, the online threats and abuse may add to women's everyday fear of men's violence, taught, and learned from a young age. Just as feminists in the 1980s argued that women's heightened fear of crime in comparison to men's was a "well-founded fear" (Hanmer & Saunders, 1984), so it is clear that online threats do not happen in the vacuum of the virtual world. They have material consequences and can be enacted offline. For example, A173 feared "that he would turn up at my house in the middle of the night. I know he is capable of sexual violence, but I didn't know what he'd do to me when he got here". Several respondents reported that their abusers exposed or used their locations in ways that generated fear:

> Person found out my occupation (I still don't know from where) & made claims that I was being investigated for gross misconduct & had committed a crime (neither were true). ... Also found out whereabouts I lived & said he was going to be in the area in the next 24 hours. (A211)
> Abuser tried to find out my place of work and encouraged others to do so. He posted details of the university he wrongly thought is my employer. (A3)

In some cases, the abuse amounted to stalking, whereby the abuser exploited the woman's circumstances and revealed her whereabouts in a way that increased the risk of offline violence, for example:

> [perpetrator] knew ... he knew that he was exposing my identity to an abusive ex-husband who could have done absolutely anything. (A133)

For those who experienced greater impacts, 'triggering' was an aspect of their experience of online abuse, which points, once again, to the interconnections between online and offline experiences of men's violence towards women. Given the prevalence and harm of men's violence towards women and given the social norms which mean women's experiences are rarely validated, many women experience ongoing traumatic responses. For example, this respondent referred to her "severe mental breakdown" because:

> one person was especially intent and violent and in ways that severely triggered my CPTSD;[5] this person seemed to know exactly what would trigger me the most and kept pushing at those buttons, knowing that I am a trafficking survivor and attacking me for speaking out. …The messages were a deliberate attempt to trigger my C-PTSD and to be most harmful to a trafficking survivor – and they were successful. I was nearly hospitalised. (A198)

These data reveal that online abuse towards feminists shares many of the features of online abuse towards women more generally. It ranges in nature from relatively infrequent, unpleasant, non-threatening messages to, at the other end of the spectrum, voluminous, frequent, highly threatening, and hateful. It is often sexualised, drawing on references to and threats of sexual violence, and can target aspects of feminists' intersecting identities. It is 'normalised' by some recipients as a way to manage its impacts, and it 'triggers' some. It cannot be considered to occur only in the online domain as it has clear connections to imagined, threatened and actual, violence offline. It is part of the continuum of violence against women which functions to discipline women as a group (Lewis et al., 2017), as we discuss in the next section.

Silencing and excluding: the function of online abuse to feminists

All forms of violence against women can be considered a form of discipline used to keep women 'in their place', to silence them, and to communicate to all women, not only the women targeted, that they are at risk of men's violence; Brownmiller (1975, p. 15) argued that rape "is nothing more or less than a conscious process of intimidation, by which all men keep all women in a state of fear". Online abuse has a distinctive focus on women's speech and mouths which are often the target of threatened violence. In Lewis, Rowe and Wiper's (2017) study, as well as in others (e.g., Jane 2014), many women reported that they were told to 'shut up'. For example, "Told to shut up, sworn at etc" (A15). Often attempts to make women 'shut up' took the

---

5 CPTSD refers to complex post-traumatic stress disorder.

form of demands that women 'fuck off back to the kitchen', invoking the sexist idea that women's primary role is a domestic one:

> I said something about women in science (I am a chemist). I got a barrage of abuse targeting both me and my daughter (not my sons, whose photos are also on my feed – they were never mentioned) – it was mostly variations of 'fuck off back to the kitchen'. It went on for months and every time it started up again men would encourage others to join in. (A31)

Sometimes attempts to make women 'shut up' were conveyed in the fantasy of sexual assault on the woman's mouth:

> I was quoted in a press article speaking out about violence against women. The Facebook newspaper page included (not anon individuals) comments like …'someone should shut her up by sticking a cock in her mouth'. (A94)

Many feminists who have experienced online abuse report that abusers attempt to get them to 'shut up' by interrupting their online discussions, derailing dialogue, and stalling the development of debate. For example:

> I had used a hashtag when discussing a recent news event and started to receive hostile or derailing tweets from racist and anti-feminist users who appeared to be monitoring the hashtag in order to prevent feminists having an uninterrupted discussion with each other. (A115)

A common pattern is that such abuse starts as apparently benign engagement with the topic, develops into hostile challenges and then becomes explicit abuse. Women who are less experienced in online feminist debate may be victimised by this kind of 'trolling' if they respond to a man whom they assume is genuinely interested in debating feminist issues. Such constructive, well-intentioned debate can mean the original conversation between feminists is derailed and remains undeveloped, thereby limiting the scope for feminism to flourish (also see Herring et al., 2002, for an account of this process in a feminist forum).

   In some forms of abuse, the perpetrators are explicit in their desire to silence women and to reassert patriarchal control, as reported by these respondents:

> I was Tweeting about #EverydaySexism and received emails from several men detailing how they were going to sexually abuse me to remind me who was in control in society. (A5)
> I wrote a blog about sexual consent. Men's rights activists decided I needed to be 'taken down'. A forum section was devoted to me on Reddit. I was told my son would probably kill himself, that I was a man hater,

that I deserved to die a slow and painful death (I am seriously ill). Hundreds of comments to the blog accused me of every man-hating crime under the sun. (A100)

Anecdotally, feminists indicate these attempts at silencing them and silencing feminist debate are very common. Herring et al. (2002) noted this twenty years ago:

> When women gather online, and especially when they attempt to discuss feminism, they are not uncommonly the target of negative attention from individuals, mostly men, who feel threatened by or otherwise uncomfortable with feminism (p. 373)

Are misogynist, anti-feminist abusers successful in their attempts to silence women? Plenty of research does suggest that, as a result of abuse, women withdraw from online engagement in some way. For example, in Adams' (2018) study, out of fear of abuse 39% of women journalists changed their working practices in some way (for example, stopped writing, did not engage with audiences, and avoided some topics, especially concerning gender and feminism). (See also Ferrier and Garud-Patkar (2018) and (OSCE, 2016) for discussions of the impacts of online abuse on women journalists.) Bloggers in Eckert's (2018) study similarly reduced their presence online by avoiding certain topics, keeping a low profile, toning down language or temporarily withdrawing from the blog. A minority of the girls and young women surveyed by Plan International (2020) in 22 countries around the globe reported that they self-censored as a result of abuse; 18% who face very frequent harassment stopped posting content that expresses their opinions about, for example, abortion, LGBTQI issues, and violence.

Clearly, online abuse does silence – or at least subdue – some women and girls. However, Lewis, Rowe and Wiper (2017) found that about half their respondents were, in fact, galvanised by their experiences. Fifty-four per cent agreed it made them 'more determined in your political views'. A third agreed it made them feel 'motivated to continue to engage in debate' (33 per cent) and 'motivated to do something' (34 per cent). In this study, analysis of impacts showed that, while emotions such as anger, worry, vulnerability, fear, and sadness reduced over time, feelings of being galvanised to act increased over time. This complicates the claim that online abuse 'silences' women; while it undoubtedly has that impact for some women at some times, abuse also galvanises participation in this form of civic life, presumably by demonstrating starkly the need for feminism.

Explaining the perpetration of online abuse

We can interpret online abuse in various ways. In this section we consider several framings of online abuse; feminist victim-survivors' sense-making of their experiences, the construction of online misogyny as part of the 'manosphere', as an act of terrorism and, exploring Siapera's (2019) argument, as part of a struggle for access to resources.

A feminist, victimological approach to interpreting online abuse centres the experiences and accounts of women victims-survivors. Their understanding of their experiences provides useful insight. In Lewis, Rowe and Wiper's (2017) study some respondents identified the abuse they experienced as part the feminist struggle and the anti-feminist response. Some suggested the abuse was directed at women who stepped out of the expected gender roles and behaviour, "for being a woman that talks" (A193). For example:

> Male sent emails threatening me with sexual violence because he arrogantly believed women have no right to voice their opinions if said opinions differ from women-hating males. I view such emails as threats of male sexual violence not 'abuse' because this was more than just a trivial issue it was all about men enacting their male sex right to subject women to sexual violence if we dare to challenge men. (A114)

Similarly, some respondents suggested that these perpetrators did not hate women as a group;[6] rather they directed their sexist hostility towards selected women:

> … in their pictures, that's what shocked me, that they would have arms around their own loved females whilst targeting another female and downgrading other females and calling them slags and whores and they would have their arm around the woman [they] love and then there are the other types of people that did it were sort of those forty-year old men with a baby in their arms saying, 'You slag, you need fucking raping, ladaladala'. (Interviewee 16)
>
> This is really to qualify the sex/gender aspect: I think it is not simply 'you're a woman', it's 'you're a woman who does not stay within the prescribed parameters of what women are allowed to ask for/say/experience.' (A72)

However, gender might not be the only explanation for online abuse towards feminists. Another respondent suggested that an understanding of online hostility towards feminists and feminist campaigns requires an intersectional approach, which considers not only gender but also other systems of oppression:

> This is maybe a really controversial thing to say but … when those people were sent to prison for sending those abusing tweets [to Caroline Criado Perez], I looked at the photos of those people and thought, they

---

6 This 'selective' hostility towards women may make it more difficult to use a 'hate crime' framework to deal with online misogyny (see Lewis, Rowe & Wiper, 2018, for a fuller discussion of online misogyny as a hate crime).

do not look like happy people, you know, they look like people who have had a bit of a shit life, you know, they look like people who don't enjoy the same privileges as her, and I'm not saying that makes it right what they did, at all, but I'm saying that maybe our analysis of that needs to be a bit more nuanced. And so similarly with the men who are sending me abuse, I don't know who these men are, you know, they might be teenage boys who are kind of working out their anger issues or they might be men who've been out of work for years and years and years and feel like it's the feminists who are ruining their lives and I think, you know, we have to kind of be conscious of that. We're not saying that it's ok, and I think that you have to have an intersectional analysis of it, you can't just say, 'Misogyny! Misogyny!' you know, you have to think of the relative positions of the people involved. (Interviewee 4)

We have seen that feminists in this study experienced abuse in ways that drew upon their intersecting identities. They also drew on their own intersectional feminist understanding to make sense of the abuse they experienced. However, while a feminist interpretation might help make sense of one's experiences, understanding those experiences through a feminist lens is not without difficulty:

It hurts to have my voice constantly silenced by others who think they are above me because I am a woman. (A7)

Our understanding of online abuse is aided by research that has adopted a victimological approach. By contrast, information about perpetrators of abuse towards feminists is rather sparse. The data presented earlier in this chapter indicate that abusers may be solo actors, they may act in loosely affiliated groups in the manosphere to perpetrate misogynistic abuse, and/or they may be part of anti-feminist, anti-racist groups who seek out opportunities to challenge, troll, abuse, and silence feminists. While the latter have been the subject of most media consideration, it is likely that not all perpetrators of abuse are committed to engaging with networks such as incel[7] and men's right activists (MRAs) and instead are relatively marginal bystanders to such misogyny. However, the existence and visible activity of such organised groups provide the landscape of misogyny that other men and boys may

---

7 Laura Bates describes incels as 'not a clearly defined, organised group, but rather a sprawling, disparate community of men across a network of blogs, forums, websites, private members groups, chatrooms and social media channels" (Bates, 2021, The incel movement is a form of extremism and it cannot be ignored any longer *The Guardian*, 17 August https://www.theguardian.com/commentisfree/2021/aug/17/incel-movement-extremism-internet-community-misogyny). According to Silva et al. (2021) "[t]he incel community specifically advances an ideology of male supremacy, hatred of feminism, and a general belief that men deserve sex from women'" (p. 2166)

observe uncritically, leading to them becoming emboldened to adopt and express similarly misogynistic views. Moreover, the algorithms and mechanics of social media sites mean that observing, or 'liking' (or 'disliking'), a post results in it being likely to receive even more attention along the same lines. In addition, "[t]oday's incels are also experts at finding and recruiting young men online. They do not depend on boys coming to them... They find boys where they are most ripe for exploitation, and unless we recognise this for the radicalisation it is, we will not be able to tackle it effectively" (Bates, 2021).

Men who are affiliated to misogynistic networks have come to public attention particularly as a result of mass murders in the UK, Canada, and the US (see Baele et al., 2019). In Plymouth in the UK, in August 2021, Jake Davison killed his mother, four other people who were unknown to him (two adult men, one adult women, and a three-year old girl), and himself. Examination of his social media trails revealed that he had engaged in misogynistic online communities such as incel and on Reddit, although there is some indication that he regretted such engagement because of the impacts (on his own well-being) of the fatalistic ideology (Townsend, 2021). Davison's murders add to the recent mass murders committed by men with connections to incels, highlighting the fatal offline reality of online misogyny (see Silva et al., 2021, for an examination of gender-based mass shootings). Too often, we are told such acts are a 'one-off' and do not represent a threat to women or wider publics. Too often we are told they are 'not terrorism-related' because they do not reflect an "ideological cause" (this is a key element of the UK Crown Prosecution Service definition of terrorism). But feminist commentators argue that "[e]xtreme misogyny needs to be recognised as an ideology in its own right – and one that carries an unacceptable risk of radicalising bitter young men" (Smith, 2021, n.p.). The misogynistic ideology of incels is examined by Baele et al. (2019). Their in-depth analysis of text from an incel online forum (incel.me which lasted 1 year from 8 November 2017) reveals that "the incel discussions demonstrate clear traits of an extremist worldview whereby violence is not only seen as acceptable but also as the only possible way to solve the crisis endpoint in which society is supposedly stuck" (p. 18).

In the case of Davison, the apparently clear connection between his misogynistic communications and his lethal violence has prompted a conversation about whether incel ideology should now be categorised as terrorism. Such categorisation could have several implications, both symbolic and material. It could send a symbolic message that online abuse against feminists specifically and women generally is recognised by the state and society as a serious threat. This desire for a symbolic statement about intolerance of misogyny has been a key feature of feminist campaigning around men's violence against women since the 1970s. Arguably, it has helped shift public attitudes so that violence against women is now more widely recognised as a public issue, a crime, and incompatible with the aim of gender equality, although evidence continually reveals high levels of tolerance of violence against women and girls, even in young people (see, e.g., Sundaram, 2018).

Categorisation of misogynist groups like incel as terrorist could also have the material impact of greater investigation and censor of such groups by state powers such as the European Counter Terrorism Centre, and the UK National Counter Terrorism Security Office. Such a step is not without its problems, however. Can states, which may be led by politicians who express misogynistic views (brilliantly exposed by Julia Guillard, 2020 in her 'Misogyny speech'; also see Kaul, 2021) be trusted to protect their citizens from misogyny? Can agencies which are male dominated and have histories of sexism – such as the police – adapt their cultures and practices to recognise and treat misogyny as a serious problem which comprises the rights and freedoms of citizens? (For a similar example, see Barlow et al.'s (2020) consideration of police struggles to implement new ways of thinking about gendered offences.) Can states and agencies imbued with neo-liberal philosophies, and the concomitant focus on equality and gender-blindness rather than with an understanding of how deeply patriarchal structures and cultures shape contemporary life, adopt a critical approach to the reality of misogyny? Would the recognition of online misogynistic ideologies as a form of terrorism lead to the over-policing of men from marginalised groups (because of, for example, racism and classism) and leave untouched men with more extensive resources to protect themselves while continuing their misogynistic abuse? The symbolic impacts of classifying online misogyny and abuse as a form of terrorism might be greater than the practical value of such a shift.

An alternative approach to combatting online abuse towards feminists and feminism is suggested by Siapera (2019) whose work foregrounds the functions of abuse. She calls for a materialist rather than cultural perspective, an understanding of "online misogyny as a question of distribution of material resources" (p. 22). She compares online misogyny to witch-hunting in the 16th and 17th centuries. Her argument is that the function of witch-hunting was to help restructure society from feudalism to industrial capitalism; it impelled women, through extreme violence, to conform to the requirements of emerging capitalism. In a similar way, online misogyny serves to exclude women "from accessing and controlling the means of production and from socio-economic participation in the emerging new formation … tecno-capitalism" (p. 21). At the current turn towards an economy based on technology and knowledge, "online misogyny can be seen as seeking to prevent women from participating in building the forthcoming technological future" (p. 22). Rather than focusing on the cultural manifestations of misogyny, or on the perpetrators, whether solo or organised, she argues that a materialist approach recognises the function served by online misogyny in the fundamental, materialist reshaping of society:

> misogyny and gender violence cannot be seen as epiphenomenal or incidental or a remnant of the past, but rather as playing an active role in determining and fixing women's position in society. Misogyny is, in other words, the methodology of female subjugation and exploitation.

> Its re-emergence in the current historical conjuncture must therefore be understood as symptomatic of changes in the social order, and in the political and economic domains. (Siapera, 2019, p. 37)

Siapera's argument brings to mind work about sexual harassment in the workplace which frames such harassment as a way of preserving male domains. For example, Carothers and Crull (1984) argue that sexual harassment at work is a form of hostility used by male workers against women who are seen to challenge or compete with the men for their jobs. This form of domination functions to reinforce the gendered segregation of the workplace and to preserve male-dominated work environments as spaces for men rather than women. Similarly, Wilson and Thompson (2001) argue "sexual harassment can be usefully viewed as a form of social control. …to keep a junior woman 'in her place' or to warn a more senior woman of her 'proper place', it is a controlling gesture to diminish any sense of a woman's power" (p. 76) (see also, Folke et al., 2020; Folke & Riche, 2020; Rosenberg, Perlstadt & Phillips, 1993).

The argument that online misogyny serves a function in the continuing sequestration of resources for the benefit of men as a group suggests that future research and prevention efforts should be aimed less at individual perpetrators and more at the reorientation of society away from misogyny and sexism, towards the implementation of a feminist vision of gender relations. Siapera (2019) argues that efforts by social media platforms to 'take-down' misogynistic comments – even if they were more enthusiastic than we have seen to date – will have minimal impacts. We have seen how determined misogynistic groups can be to preserve space online (see, e.g., Hargreaves, 2018) and how limited social platforms' efforts have been to challenge misogyny online. Rather than focusing on individual posts or groups online, or developing policy responses to online abuse, Siapera argues that strengthened feminist resistance and alliances between feminist women and men comprise a more effective strategy to challenge misogyny. She argues that this strategy needs to be rooted in a materialist response that recognises online abuse as an attempt to prevent women from enjoying equal access to technological resources, rather than one which see it merely as a cultural expression.

Valuable as Siapera's argument is for understanding online abuse in the wider temporal, social and economic landscape, her work tends to underplay the agency of the people who send misogynistic abuse; the abuse becomes part of a process in the larger project of social change conducted by unidentified social forces. Individual perpetrators are unseen in this account of online abuse, in keeping with the tendency in discourse about gender-based violence to render perpetrators invisible. Lamb (1991) argues we should avoid this tendency to construct "acts without agents" (p. 250) and should instead emphasise the agency of perpetrators of abuse in order to hold them accountable. This aligns with the feminist drive to hold to account the individuals who violate women and girls as well as the organisations that enable such violation to flourish. However, this has been implemented in a rather narrow way, through a reliance on the criminal justice system to redress the harms of gender-based violence. Perhaps a more fruitful strategy for addressing the harms of online abuse would be to use a fuller range of resources; in addition to criminal justice systems, and social media platforms, we might also engage with public health, education at all levels, and workers' rights organisations, for example, to both prevent online abuse and respond to it when it occurs. We discuss potential responses to online abuse in more detail in Part Three.

Conclusion

While feminists are by no means the only people or groups to be targeted for abuse, and feminism is not the only politics to be attacked online, such abuse reveals the extent of misogyny online and offline. As we have shown in this chapter, some abuse is explicitly targeted at feminists because of their feminist politics. It seems clear that such abuse aims, consciously or not on the part of the perpetrator, to subdue or silence feminist debate. There is some evidence that it does indeed have this effect. But there is also evidence of attempts to challenge such abuse and to enable feminism to thrive online. Preserving this space for feminist debate is important because the online world is an important – but not the only – environment for the development of a feminist politics and a feminist consciousness. This online space serves a particularly important purpose for younger generations of feminists, and for all generations during Covid-19 restrictions when alternative forms of organising were proscribed and when online abuse increased (Glitch UK and End Violence Against Women, 2020). Together with such online activism, campaigns, initiatives, networks, and actions that occur in the offline world to challenge the material and cultural manifestations of patriarchy have an important role to play in ending online abuse.

References

Adams, C. (2018). "They go for gender first" The nature and effect of sexist abuse of female technology journalists. *Journalism Practice*, *12*(7), 850–869.

Amnesty International. (2017). *Amnesty reveals alarming impacts of online abuse against women*. 20 November. Retrieved from: https://www.amnesty.org/en/latest/press-release/2017/11/amnesty-reveals-alarming-impact-of-online-abuse-against-women/

Amnesty International India. (2020). *Troll patrol India: Exposing online abuse faced by women politicians in India*. Bengaluru: Indians for Amnesty International Trust. No date. Retrieved from: https://decoders.amnesty.org/projects/troll-patrol-india

Baele, S. J., Brace, L., & Coan, T. G. (2019). From 'Incel' to 'Saint': Analyzing the violent worldview behind the 2018 Toronto attack. *Terrorism and Political Violence*, *33*(8), 1667–1691.

Barlow, C., Johnson, K., Walklate, S., & Humphreys, L. (2020). Putting coercive control into practice: Problems and possibilities. *The British Journal of Criminology*, *60*(1), 160–179.

Bates, L. (2021). The incel movement is a form of extremism and it cannot be ignored any longer. *The Guardian*. 17 August. Retrieved from: https://www.theguardian.com/commentisfree/2021/aug/17/incel-movement-extremism-internet-community-misogyny

Boyle, K. (2019). What's in a name? Theorising the inter-relationships of gender and violence. *Feminist Theory, 20*(1), 19–36.

Brownmiller, S. (1975) *Against Our will: Men, women and rape*. New York: Balantine.

Carothers, S. C., & Crull, P. (1984) Contrasting sexual harassment in female- and male- dominated occupations. In K. Brodkin-Sacha & D. Remy (Eds.), *My troubles are going to have trouble with me* (pp. 219–227). New Brunswick, NJ: Rutgers University Press.

Committee on Standards in Public Life (2017). *Intimidation in public life: A review by the committee on standards in public life*. 13 December. Retrieved from: https://assets.publishing.service.gov.uk/government/uploads/system/uploads/attachment_data/file/666927/6.3637_CO_v6_061217_Web3.1__2_.pdf

Dhrodia, (2017). *Unsocial Media: Tracking Twitter Abuse against Women MPs*. 4 September. Retrieved from: https://medium.com/@AmnestyInsights/unsocial-media-tracking-twitter-abuse-against-women-mps-fc28aeca498a

Duggan, M. (2017). *Online Harassment 2017*. 11 July. Retrieved from: http://assets.pewresearch.org/wp-content/uploads/sites/14/2017/07/10151519/ PI_2017.07.11_Online-Harassment_FINAL.pdf

Eckert, S. (2018). Fighting for recognition: Online abuse of women bloggers in Germany, Switzerland, the United Kingdom, and the United States. *New Media & Society, 20*(4), 1282–1302.

Elgot, J. (2017) Diane Abbott more abused than any other female MP during election. *The Guardian*. 5 September. Retrieved from: https://www.theguardian.com/politics/2017/sep/05/diane-abbott-more-abused-than-any-other-mps-during-election

European Institute for Gender Equality. (2014). *Estimating the costs of gender-based violence in the European Union*. Luxembourg: Publications Office of the European Union.

Ferrier, M., & Garud-Patkar, N. (2018). TrollBusters: Fighting digital harassment of women journalists. In *Mediating Misogyny* (pp. 311–332). Cham: Palgrave Macmillan.

Folke, O. & Rickne, J. (2020). *Sexual harassment and gender inequality in the labor market*. CEPR Discussion Paper No. DP14737. Social Science Research Network, 28 May. Retrieved from: https://papers.ssrn.com/sol3/papers.cfm?abstract_id=3603968

Folke, O, Rickne, J., Tanaka, S., & Tateishi, Y. (2020), Sexual harassment of women leaders. *Daedalus, 149*(1), 180–197.

FRA. (2014). *Violence against women: an EU-wide survey. Main results report*. Retrieved from: https://fra.europa.eu/en/publication/2014/violence-against-women-eu-wide-survey-main-results-report

Gardiner, B. (2018) "It's a terrible way to go to work:" what 70 million readers' comments on the Guardian revealed about hostility to women and minorities digital, *Feminist Media Studies, 18*(4), 592–608.

Glitch UK and End Violence Against Women. (2020). *The ripple effect: Covid-19 and the epidemic of online abuse*. Retrieved from: https://www.endviolenceagainstwomen.org.uk/wp-content/uploads/Glitch-and-EVAW-The-Ripple-Effect-Online-abuse-during-COVID-19-Sept-2020.pdf

Hall, M., Hearn, J., & Lewis, R. (2021). "Upskirting," homosociality, and craftmanship: A thematic analysis of perpetrator and viewer interactions. *Violence against women, 28*(2), 532–550.

Hanmer, J. & Saunders, S. (1984) *Well-founded fear: A community study of violence to women.* Explorations in Feminism Collective: Women's Research and Resources Centre. London: Hutchinson.

Hargreaves, S. (2018). 'I'm a creep, i'm a weirdo': Street photography in the service of the male gaze. In B. Clayton Newell, T. Timan & B.-J. Koops (Eds.), *Surveillance, privacy and public space* (pp. 179–198). Abingdon: Routledge.

Herring, S., Job-Sluder, K., Scheckler, R., & Barab, S. (2002). Searching for safety online: Managing "trolling" in a feminist forum. *The Information Society, 18*(5), 371–384.

Hochschild, A. R. (1983). *The managed heart: Commercialization of human feeling.* Berkeley: University of California Press.

Humbert, A. L., Strid, S., Hearn, J., & Balkmar, D. (2021). Undoing the 'Nordic Paradox': Factors affecting rates of disclosed violence against women across the EU. *PLOS ONE, 16*(5). https://journals.plos.org/plosone/article?id=10.1371/journal.pone.0249693

Jane, E. A. (2014). Back to the kitchen, cunt': Speaking the unspeakable about digital misogyny. *Continuum: Journal of Media and Cultural Studies, 28*(4), 558–570.

Kaul, N. (2021). The misogyny of authoritarians in contemporary democracies. *International Studies Review,* 23(4), 1619–1645.

Kelly, L. (2012). Standing the test of time? Reflections on the concept of the continuum of sexual violence. In J. Brown & S. Walklate (Eds.), *Handbook on sexual violence* (pp. xvii–xxvi). London: Routledge.

Kelly, L. (1987). The continuum of sexual violence. In J. Hanmer & M. Maynard (Eds.), *Women, violence and social control* (pp. 46–60). Basingstoke: Macmillan.

Lamb, S. (1991). Acts without agents: An analysis of linguistic avoidance in journal articles on men who batter women. *American Journal of Orthopsychiatry, 61*(2), 250–257.

Lewis, R., Rowe, M., & Wiper, C. (2017). Online abuse of feminists as an emerging form of violence against women and girls. *British Journal of Criminology, 57*(6), 462–1481.

Lewis, R., Rowe, M., & Wiper, C. (2018). Misogyny online: Extending the boundaries of hate crime. *Journal of Gender Based Violence, 2*(3), 519–536.

Lewis, R., Rowe, M., & Wiper, C. (2020). Online/offline continuities: Exploring hate in online abuse of feminists. In K. Lumsden & E. Harmer (Eds.), *Online othering: Exploring digital violence and discrimination on the web* (pp. 145–164). Basingstoke: Palgrave Macmillan.

Oliver, K. (2016). Rape as spectator sport and creepshot entertainment: Social media and the valorization of lack of consent. *American Studies Journal, 61.* doi: 10.18422/61–02.

OSCE. (2016). *New challenges to freedom of expression: Countering online abuse of female journalists.* Vienna: Office of The Representative on Freedom and the Media. Retrieved from: https://www.osce.org/files/f/documents/c/3/220411.pdf

Plan International. (2020). *Free to be online? Girls' and young women's experiences of digital harassment.* Retrieved from: https://plan-international.org/publications/free-to-be-online/

R. v John Raymond Nimmo and Isabella Kate Sorley. (2014). Retrieved from: https://www.judiciary.gov.uk/wp-content/uploads/JCO/Documents/Judgments/r-v-nimmo-and-sorley.pdf

Reilly, C. (2016). 'Not just words': Online harassment of women an 'epidemic'. *C/net.* 7 March. Retrieved from: https://www.cnet.com/tech/services-and-software/not-just-words-online-harassment-of-women-epidemic-norton-research/

Rickne, J., & Folke, O. (2020). Discrimination in work conditions: The case of sexual harassment, *VoxEU/CEPR.* 21 May. Retrieved from: https://voxeu.org/article/discrimination-work-conditions-case-sexual-harassment

Rosenberg, J., Perlstadt, H., & Phillips, W. R. (1993). Now that we are here: Discrimination, disparagement, and harassment at work and the experience of women lawyers. *Gender & Society,* 7(3), 415–433.

Siapera E. (2019). Digital misogyny as witch hunt: Primitive accumulation in the age of techno-capitalism. In D. Ging, & E. Siapera (Eds.), *Gender hate digital* (pp. 21–43). New York: Springer.

Silva, J. R., Capellan, J. A., Schmuhl, M. A., & Mills, C. E. (2021). Gender-based mass shootings: an examination of attacks motivated by grievances against women. *Violence against Women,* 27(12–13), 2163–2186.

Smith, J. (2021). If extreme misogyny is an ideology, doesn't that make Plymouth killer a terrorist? *The Guardian.* 15 August. Retrieved from: https://www.theguardian.com/commentisfree/2021/aug/15/extreme-misogyny-ideaology-plymouth-killer-terrorist

Smith, J. (1993). *Misogynies.* London: Faber and Faber.

Stanko, E. (1985). *Intimate intrusions: women's experience of male violence.* London: Routledge.

Sundaram, V. (2018). A continuum of acceptability: Understanding young people's views on gender-based violence'. In S. Anitha & R. Lewis (Eds.), *Gender based violence in university communities: Policy, prevention and educational initiatives* (pp. 23–40). Bristol: Policy.

Townsend, M. (2021). Plymouth gunman ranted digital that 'women are arrogant' days before rampage. *The Guardian.* 14 August. Retrieved from: https://www.theguardian.com/world/2021/aug/14/plymouth-gunman-ranted-digital-that-women-are-arrogant-days-before-rampage

Vera-Gray, F. (2017). *Men's intrusion, women's embodiment: A critical analysis of street harassment.* Abingdon: Routledge.

Vogels, E. A. (2021). *The state of online harassment.* 13 January. Retrieved from: https://www.pewresearch.org/internet/2021/01/13/the-state-of-online-harassment/

Wilson, F., & Thompson, P. (2001). Sexual harassment as an exercise of power. *Gender, Work & Organization,* 8(1), 61–83.

6 Upskirting, homosociality, and craft*man*ship

Introduction

'Upskirting' refers to the act of taking photographs or recordings from underneath someone's skirt or dress of their buttocks, crotch, genitals, underwear, or legs, without their consent and usually without their knowledge. The images are generally taken in public, such as on public transport, in the street, in shops and shopping centres, in schools and colleges, as well as in offices, workplaces, and leisure spaces. It is one form of image-based sexual abuse (McGlynn & Rackley, 2017), and cyberviolence more broadly, and, from the emerging research evidence, is overwhelmingly perpetrated by men against women (Oppenheim, 2019; Thompson, 2019). There have been increasing legal responses internationally, with many laws addressing 'upskirting' defined as a form of voyeurism, in Australia, Canada, Hong Kong, Ireland, New Zealand, and the US, for example (seeMcCann et al., 2018; New Zealand Law Commission, 2004; Thompson, 2020; Whiteman, 2019). However, the global policy response is still uneven and contested, not least because of the difficulties of creating laws capable of regulating some technologies (Bennett Moses, 2013).

In April 2019 'upskirting' became an offence in England and Wales as voyeurism under the Sexual Offences Act 2003, punishable by up to 2 years imprisonment with more serious cases added to the Violent and Sex Offender Register (Gov.UK, 2019). Whilst there have been reports of victim-survivors as young as 7 years old and senior citizens (see Oppenheim, 2019), there appears to be little comprehensive data showing the full extent of the problem and the abuse.

Although 'upskirting' has received a lot of media attention as an apparently new activity, it has a long history in voyeurism and associated photographic activities.[1] With the aid of technological advances, which have produced

---

1 There is long history of (mainly) men making use of technological innovations to represent sex and sexuality and promote voyeurism. Pornographers, in particular, have done so in a more or less organized ways. Rosen (2010) examines how pornography and technology have enjoyed a symbiotic relationship. Increasingly complex technologies have developed

DOI: 10.4324/9781003138273-9

recording devices such as smartphone cameras, pen or shoe cameras, Google Glasses,[2] and other forms of spyware equipment, offering various forms of elaborated affordances, today's voyeurs can take photos or recordings of people in public places unobtrusively and surreptitiously.

A key element of the abusiveness of 'upskirting' is that the images are not only *taken* without the woman's or girl's consent but are also *shared* without her consent. It is thus a double abuse. The images may be shared via social media within friendship or other groups or via websites dedicated to hosting non-consensual upskirt images. This non-consensual sharing of non-consensual images generates significant harms. McGlynn and Rackley (2017) point to the "profound" (p. 545) and "deeply gendered" (p. 544) harms of image-based sexual assault that can include severe distress and anxiety, mental health effects, and impacts, for younger people, on educational and emotional development. Moreover, its effects are wider, as it contributes to the more general sexual objectification of women and their commodification for sexual consumption by men across societies. Indeed, the dissemination of this misogynistic material on social media platforms and dedicated websites such as The Candid Forum celebrates and reinforces these practices as acceptable, through viewing and sharing, and the proud use of labels like 'upskirter'. Such online platforms also allow for a new form of the storage, classification, curation, and consumption of women's bodies (or parts of), through multi-users tagging images, which fosters and reinforces harmful sexist attitudes (Thompson & Wood, 2018). These socio-technologies make the possibility for the sexualisation and abuse of women's bodies easily available, instantaneous, mobile, and thus ubiquitous.

In this chapter, we analyse 'upskirting' as a form of gender-based violence and a form of online men's homosociality. We examine a selection of data taken from postings on The Candid Zone, a website dedicated to surreptitiously taken photos of women's bodies. Those postings reveal that 'upskirting' is construed by posters as a form of 'craftsmanship'[3] which uses photographic skills and filmmaking skills. First, we discuss the importance of misogyny, and craftsmanship in the construction of homosociality.

Homosociality and misogyny

Although upskirt images may be taken by solitary men, the consumption of the images is very often a social act. Dedicated websites, such as The Candid

---

from the peep show, photography, film and video. Early filmmakers were quick to exploit voyeurism and sexual display on the screen, with sexual themes figuring in clear conscious, and sometimes less conscious, ways (Hearn, 1992, ch. 8; also see Kittler, 2010; Thompson & Wood, 2018).

2 Google Glasses were launched in 2014 and removed from circulation the same year.

3 We have emphasised 'man' in crafts*man*ship because our dataset only contained 'men', and many of these presented or commented on 'upskirting' as a skilled activity.

Zone, provide a platform for men to view and comment on – "rate and be-rate" (Oliver, 2016, p. 8) – each other's pictures. In this respect, 'upskirting' can be considered as a performance of masculinity which (re)produces and is (re)produced by homosocial bonds. Homosociality refers to the (explicitly) non-sexual attraction and mutual valuing between those of the same sex and is often used to refer to heterosexual male social bonds (Lipman-Blumen, 1976). Bird (1996) argued that this sort of homosocial interaction contributes to the maintenance of more dominant forms of masculinity through the affirmation of idealised male identity norms. Hammarén and Johansson (2014) state a further key feature of homosociality is men's (and boys') competition with each other to gain approval and status. Competitiveness may be performed through occupational status, wealth, physical strength, sporting achievements, sexual prowess, and so on. Those with lesser status may seek advice and guidance from their peers, and thereby celebrate peer successes.

Homosociality thrives online. Pioneering studies in this respect include Kendall's 2002 study of the so-called 'virtual pub', Olson's (2012) study of online homosociality in the hacker organisation, Anonymous, and Whisnant's (2010) study of imagined homosocial audiences in viewing pornography online. More recently, there is now an increasing range of studies on different aspects of (largely younger) men and masculinities online, such as those on incels, MGTOW (Men Going Their Own Way), and the Manosphere (Bates, 2021; Ding, 2019; Horta Ribeiro et al., 2021; Mogensen & Helding Rand, 2019), along with more focused studies pointing to the harmful and homosocial behaviours of perpetrators (DeKeseredy, 1990; DeKeseredy & Schwartz, 2016; Hall & Hearn, 2017; Henry & Flynn, 2019; Henry et al., 2017; Thompson & Wood, 2018).

A wide variety of studies has shown how homosocial bonds can be predicated on misogynistic attitudes and shape men's relations with women, their sexual attitudes, and behaviours (Bird, 1996; Connell, 1987; Flood, 2008; Sedgwick, 2015). In many different, though certainly not all, social contexts, some men's friendships have been characterised as highly stoic and constrained and policed by personal and social homophobia, thus permitting very limited emotional or physical expression (Magrath & Scoats, 2019). Typically, such friendships might be based on shared activities – around, for example, drinking, gambling, sport, 'womanising', and humour. Some research shows that some contemporary forms of younger masculinities and friendships are more fluid, varied and emotionally expressive (Magrath & Scoats, 2019; McCormack, 2011; Robinson et al., 2018). However, scholarship also indicates that these developments do not equate to a detachment from sexist attitudes and behaviours. Arxer (2011) notes that the 'hybrid masculinity' expressed by the men he studied includes *both* more intimate emotionality *and* the sexual objectification of women, which is one of the "hallmark strategies used in homosocial interaction among men to promote patriarchy" (p. 399).

Engagements between men around 'upskirting' and other forms of sexual violence and abuse indicate that misogynistic attitudes are still expressed as a form of homosocial bonding in which humour and 'banter' are integral. For example, Oliver (2016) examines the ways in which, amongst some young men, rape is constructed as a "spectator sport". For example, when high school footballers in Steubenville, Ohio, in the US raped a young woman in 2012, their offences became widely known in that community and beyond because some of the young men involved had filmed and photographed the assault and shared images and celebratory comments on Instagram and Twitter (Levy, 2013; Scheper-Hughes & Bourgois, 2013). Levy describes this online communication, which includes victim-blaming, deeply derogatory sexualised comments about the victim-survivor specifically and women, in general, denial that the men's acts constituted rape (even though the victim-survivor was inebriated to the point of unconsciousness and incapable of giving consent), and 'jokes' about the offence. One video showed a young man, "drunkenly holding forth about the evening … [he] keeps on riffing, and his audience keeps on laughing, for more than twelve minutes" (Levy, 2013). The recordings and knowledge of the sexually violent acts were used amongst groups of young men to bond and share their apparent humour and delight at the abusive behaviours of these men.

Another high-profile case, this one in the UK, reveals the ways in which some young men can bond over sexual violence. At Warwick University a group of young male students was exposed for engaging over the course of more than a year in what came to be known as 'rape chat' – sexually violent (as well as racist) comments on a Facebook 'group chat' about young women in their friendship group. The so-called chat contained references to gang rape, genital mutilation, and abducting and chaining a woman to a bed. The men had changed their online names to those of notorious serial killers and rapists. It was dismissed by at least one of the men involved as a joke and "how boys talk" (Lee & Kennelly, 2019).

These two recent high-profile examples illustrate how some men use social media to share and generate delight in misogynistic, sexually violent ideas and activity in the name of 'chat' or 'banter'. Concepts of masculinity and masculine friendships also relate to ideas about craftsmanship, skill, and competition, which we discus below.

Homosociality and craftsmanship

Craftsmanship can be one way to maintain, deepen and engrain homosociality. Moreover, craftsmanship, and the associated pride that can accompany it, has long been associated with the skilful manipulation of tools, with particular significance for working-class men (Balkmar, 2012; Law, 2001; Mellström, 1999, 2004), but this positioning has been taken up, perhaps appropriated, by men with various different class backgrounds, as, for example, in some manifestations of the hipster movement. Craftsmanship involves the valuing of conspicuous interpersonal or collective display, earned through hard and skilled workmanship, usually with tools and technologies, rather than simply direct individualistic bragging. Performance is largely individual but is also directed to what is seen as a potentially appreciative collective audience.

Willis's (1990) notion of symbolic creativity – highlighting how commodities are actively appropriated in processes of identity construction – is of relevance here. The concept of symbolic creativity adds the dimension of craft and the manipulation of things as key in the active process of purposeful image-making (Willis, 1990, pp. 84–89). With some forms of craftmanship, there should be no signs of mess or of forced or untidy presentation (Balkmar, 2012). In *The Craftsman*, Sennett (2009, p. 258) notes how getting things into perfect shape can mean removing traces and evidence of previous work or work in progress: "[p]erfection of this cleaned-up sort is a static condition; the object does not hint at the narrative of its making" (Sennett, 2009, p. 258). When such evidence is eliminated, the object appears pristine and well crafted. 'Upskirting' is a material hands-on cultural practice, women's bodies are the currency between men, tools, and material objects (Law, 2001). As we show below, notions of craftsmanship are employed by men who comment on online fora dedicated to 'upskirting' images.

Exemplars of homosociality and craftsmanship

In the analysis of a selection of data on The Candid Zone website, homosociality and craftmanship were the two key themes identified, along with a number of sub-themes. The posters' extracts that we present here, unedited and with original punctuation and spelling mistakes, are exemplars of the specific themes we identified through data analysis. We begin by presenting the analysis of the text that accompanied the video and photographic stills.[4] The video creator (VC) was held in high esteem by all respondents, although in differing ways. As Sacks (1992) pointed out, those who speak first provide the context in which all other responses should be read:

> VC
> I don't really ever do skirts and uppies, but I mean look at this amazing beauty. She has to be a model, right? Anyway, I don't shoot dresses and skirts because I don't think they shape the ass the way I like. But, this is an exception! The dress kept riding up which is why she was constantly pulling it down. It was a really windy day so I'm sure it was really drafty up in there. It was also fairly cold which is why she had serious goosebumps on those long legs for days. I was doing a follow[5] and felt like I was

---

4 The photographs were single frames from the video of the victim-survivors' genitalia, presumably for closer examination by viewers.
5 The use of the term, a follow, is especially interesting in conveying a supposed professionalism, by way of nominalisation, that is, conversion (zero derivation) of a verb to a noun. Other examples might include converting 'to ask' to 'an ask' or 'to report' to 'reports', meaning people who report to someone. The reverse process, verbification, of changing a

getting way too obvious so I went out in front and stopped at this vendor table and just hoped they would also stop... and they did! I couldn't believe my good fortune. They gave me all kinds of opportunity to get close ups. The denim girl was a bonus...

A number of things in VC's text stand out. First, the victim-survivor(s)[6] is objectified "this amazing beauty. She has to be a model, right?" We were surprised that, in general, comments about the women whose images were taken tended to focus on their attractiveness and that there were relatively few disparaging, abusive comments (although there were some). Instead, men who engaged on the Candid Zone took their sexual objectification of the subjects (women and girls) seriously in itself, with no reflexive reference to the abusive or objectionable nature of their activities.

Relatedly, the objectification and filming of the victim is also presented as an opportunity, as in "I don't really ever do skirts and uppies, but I mean look at this amazing beauty". This statement 'justifies' his actions within the peer-group (Sweeney, 2014). In other words, it is presumed that any member of the group would have taken the opportunity in this situation.

Second, what is also evident is that the victim is presented as complicit; "They gave me all kinds of opportunity to get close ups". In other words, she is deemed to have invited attention by choosing to wear a "dress" on a "windy day", which "kept riding up". Berkowitz and Cornell (2005) argue victim-blaming protects the perpetrator against self-destructive impulses such as guilt, so that any risk of internal harm can be externalised. Indeed, victim-blaming was common in all The Candid Zone forums, as, for example, in other posts in the thread, "Women always find a reason to bend over", "this attention whore".

It also became apparent in our analysis that VC's craftmanship bolstered his peer-status. Mikorski and Szymanski's (2017) online survey research with 329 heterosexually identified undergraduate males found that male peer group status was interlinked with their sexual objectification of women and girls. Those who had intimate interactions with women deemed attractive by their peers enjoyed higher esteem. This was also evident in our dataset, and we return to this later.

The final point to notice is that VC invokes 'risk'; "I was doing a follow [physically following a woman/en with a view to do upskirting photography] and felt like I was getting way too obvious". Smiler's (2006) survey research with 688 heterosexual US adults aged 1882 years old (340 men), found men's risk-taking and dominance of women were the only two consistent correlations with presumed masculine traits. By presenting the filming as risky, VC invokes his masculine credentials as a means to increase his status within the group.

---

noun to a verb, as in 'to task' or 'to action' can also carry connotations of managerialism (see Poole, 2013). Both processes are examples of antimeria.

6 Two women were caught on camera, but the main focus was on one in particular.

Presenting his video 'work' of the objectified "amazing beauty" as skilled and 'risky', VC lays out his homosocial credentials. However, it is only homosocial approval and recognition that will determine his peer-group status (Kimmel, 1994). In the following section, we present a range of responses: gratitude, respect, courage, envy, advice-seeking, and admiration for his video skills (craftsmanship).

Gratitude

A1

Very nice work on this one. I thought they'd catch on to you with how "interested" you were in the bracelets, but you did your thing. Awesome post and thanks for sharing!

A2

Good god that is just fantastic work!!!! Very nicely done, and another big thanks for the share.

People experience gratitude when they receive something beneficial or when somebody else does something kind or helpful (Emmons, 2004). Gratitude can be experienced through several different means such as recognition of a sacrifice, giving, compliments, showing appreciation, and acknowledgement of skills and talents. Kashdan et al. (2009) point out that although on the whole women and girls tend to benefit more than men and boys from receiving gratitude and find it easier to show gratitude, in some contexts (e.g., male communities, teams), the men concerned may derive similar advantages. Thus, in these exemplars it is clear that A1 and A2 both show gratitude.

Often gratitude is accompanied by respect. In the following two posts we can see both A3 and A4 showing respect although in different ways:

Respect

A3

Standing ovation for you sir! Very well done! Hundreds of ups[7] for you

A4

Bravo – absolutely superb work. The quality of the subject and the video is outstanding!! Well done, and thank you so much for this amazing contribution, it will go down in history as one of the greats!

---

7 Short for thumbs up.

Here we see A3 showing masculine respect for VC's abilities, qualities, and achievements "Standing ovation for you sir!" The use of "sir" in this context is readable as a highly gendered term used by men of disparate backgrounds to confer respect and homosocial bonding. Notice also that A3 normalises his respect, aligning it with others in the forum through noting the number of 'thumbs up'[8] VC has received "Hundreds of ups for you". Ample research identifies the significant relationships between masculinity and respect from male peers in areas such as sports (Wheaton, 2000), education (Harris, 2010), and alcohol consumption (Hunt, Mackenzie & Joe-Laider, 2005). Hammarén and Johansson (2014) argue that respect may be performed through recognition of, for example, occupational status, wealth, and sexual prowess.

Although A4 also shows respect, what is also noticeable is that A4 invokes VC's crafts*man*ship – "Bravo – absolutely superb work. The quality of the subject and the video is outstanding!!" – a point we return to later.

Respect for VC's abilities, qualities, and achievements was expressed as envy for some viewers.

Envy

A5
This is dream stuff, talk about right place, right time, you lucky bastard 😀 epic cap[9] and thanks for sharing 👏

A6
If only this happened to me sir!

Although not explicitly stated, one might presume that A5 and A6 envy VC's status with other male viewers given VC's was the most popular thread on the website. But what both responses show is envy for VC being in the "right place" at the "right time" as A5 "This is dream stuff...you lucky bastard" and A6 "If only this happened to me sir!" make explicit. Envy is a complex and powerful feeling where the person has a desire for another's qualities or advantage. Studies such as Guignard (2018) argue that women tend to report envy when comparing their own attractiveness to other women, while men tend to report envying other men with greater financial resources, skills, and status with other men.

Invoking envy, gratitude and respect help to elevate VC's status within this community of viewers in this particular context. In the following two

8 Thumbs up or down 👍👎 are a means for viewers to rate posts, and are common on many social media platforms.
9 Short for capture.

exemplar posts, the posters recycle the 'risk' element in the video that VC referred to in his accompanying text:

Risk

A7

VC I sauté[10] you!! That was an awesome and fearless follow of a stunning subject! Thank you

A8

You are really a brave man

We showed earlier how VC invoked risk through 'risk taking' "I was doing a follow and felt like I was getting way too obvious". This was repeated by many posters similarly to A7 and A8 "That was…fearless", "You are a really brave man". These exemplars clearly demonstrate how the recognition of risk-taking – being caught, especially as 'upskirting' is illegal in many countries – increases the person's masculine peer group status, as made explicit by A7 at the outset "I sauté you!!" (see Smiler, 2006).

So far, we have presented elements of homosocial approval and recognition (Kimmel, 1994). However, in the remaining exemplar posts, we see how recognition of VC's technical skills – crafts*man*ship – bolster his homosocial status. We begin with advice-seeking which also refers to camera skills and video content.

Advice-seeking

A9

This is superb mate. How did you record that? Can you mention about this? Your techniques? I want to do that but i dont know. Because people could see me if i try to video recording with my camera. i will be waiting for your answer! Thanks.

A10

awesome content! and nice ass camera too btw, really good. what did you use?

A9 and A10 seek advice, respectively, on recording techniques and appropriate equipment to avoid being caught. Many posters sought advice and guidance on how to film videos and take photographs, what equipment to

---

10 Presumably a misspelling for 'salute' or a mixing of 'salute' and 'santé'.

use, where to film or photograph and so on. Given the illegality of this activity in many countries, knowledge about how to execute the activity is not widely shared. Epstein's (1995) study of AIDS activism demonstrated that where there is an absence of specialist knowledge this gap is often filled with lay expertise. We can see in these posts that advice-seeking positions VC as a lay expert (Hammarén & Johansson, 2014).

As we have argued, homosocial peer status may be maintained and elevated through specific actions deemed as having exceptional quality. We have shown the specific ways in which homosocial status is displayed through gratitude, respect, courage, envy, and advice-seeking. A further way that homosocial status may be bolstered is through peer recognition of technical skills: craft*man*ship. The following exemplars show how VC's skills – subject, camera angle, and lighting – contribute to his homosocial status. We begin with the subject in the video.

Photographic skills

A11

Good God i thought I was sitting down. Excellent capture of a perfect body and perfect beauty. A+

A12

Simply superb piece of work from you!!!
    This truly is one of the best OC[11] works here.
    She was the perfect subject...fit hot body....long legs...awesome wide thigh gap and the shortest of skirts!! And the view of her bare ass and her tiny thongs was mind blowing hot!!!
    Looking forward to more contris[12] like this from you.
    Thanks for sharing

We can see in A11's and A12's posts their admiration for the quality of the subject in the film. For example, A11 refers to the subject's physical and facial attractiveness. Jefferson (1991) showed the presence of items on a list adds clarity and weight to arguments and points being made.

References to the subject's physical and facial features were common in our dataset and clearly constitute sexual objectification of the woman in the video. As Arxer (2011) notes sexual objectification can be seen as a hallmark of homosocial interaction, and, in particular, recognition of the VC's video skills. Although the posters sexually objectify the subject, they also focus on the quality of VC's photographic skills

---

11 Presumably shorthand for 'original content'.
12 Presumably shorthand for 'contributions'.

A13

wow you hit pure gold. Great subject, great angle, and great lighting. A big thanks for this one.

A14

She's such a pretty girl with nice long legs. The dress is an exceptional choice on that body. HQ[13] video work here! Great angles, clear views of face and her sweet ass. Six minutes isn't nearly long enough.

Amateur films and photographs, now frequently posted on social media platforms, are often compared to professional standards. That is not to say that viewers expect the same standards of amateur videos and photos, but the quality or likeability may be compared to commercially produced material (Zimmerman, 1988). Jacobs (2004) highlights a similar relationship between commercial pornographic production and amateur pornography recorded on mobile devices.

Dines' (2010) study of pornography highlights how commercially produced pornographic films and images are highly edited in order to make the subject appear more aesthetically pleasing than perhaps they would appear in 'real life'. This is often done with lighting, specific camera angles, makeup, pubic hair grooming/removal and so on. Such practices have become mainstream in society and in amateur home movies and photos, and are an element of what has been termed the pornografication, pornographisation (Attwood, 2009) or 'mainstreamification' of pornography (Empel, 2011).

Because commercially produced porn acts as a benchmark by which to compare amateur produced videos and images, those of high quality are often celebrated through positive audience responses or by the viewer clicking on the thumbs up icon found on most pornographic websites. We see this in A11–14's responses. All gave VC a thumbs up and praised his video (e.g., "wow you hit pure gold", "you nailed with this one!!!!", "absolutely superb work") and specific photographic skills (e.g., "Great subject, great angle, and great lighting", "the angles are simply incredible!", "great camerawork", "The quality of the subject and the video is outstanding!!". "looks like a professional photo session"). These comments invoke elements of craftsmanship, bolstering homosocial status.

Discussion

'Upskirting' is certainly a form of gendered violation, both initially in real life (IRL) and then subsequently as Internet-based. As we have shown, the dissemination of this misogynistic material celebrates and reinforces these

---

13 Presumably shorthand for 'high quality'.

practices as acceptable and the classification of practices into 'upskirting', 'downblousing', and so on can be seen as misogynistic, as they foster and reinforce harmful sexist attitudes (Thompson & Wood, 2018). This raises some rather more complex, somewhat nuanced issues in normalising sexual objectification of women than is the case with more obvious and direct forms of violence and misogyny.

In the form in which it is currently constituted, 'upskirting' is a relatively recent phenomenon – even if, historically, there are continuities with, for example, the so-called 'peeping tom', 'what the butler saw', and other forms of voyeurism. It also continues the trajectory of the collection of photographic pin-ups and the isolation of body parts in pornography, but now such that they are self-made and self-distributed, as with DIY pornography, thereby extending the production of pornography from a specialist industry to the wider (male) public. In a different way, it also constitutes stalking, both IRL and online. It enacts the male gaze, as in narrative, photography, and film (Mulvey, 1975), with such visual power extended through the widely available and linked technological prosthetics of cameras and the Internet. Abuse of women's bodies is by stealth; it can be instant if asynchronous, mobile, collected, and collective, and ubiquitous to the extent that women cannot know the extent of their sexualised surveillance in the present or the future.

We were surprised to find less highly sexualised and overtly gross textual commentary than we expected (although there was certainly some), and more comments about and 'appreciation' of the 'beauty' of the women's and girls' physical appearance. The commentaries to the visuals include, *in their own terms*, evaluative appreciations of the woman *as beauty and body*, while the homosocial appreciation by the man positions him *as expert in visuality*, that is, in terms of his expertise in representing the woman as body. There is a close overlapping and blurring here between: first, patriarchal and sexist assessments of woman, body, beauty, appearance, clothing and indeed detailed transgression thereof (Kaite, 1988); second, the homosocial evaluation of technical expertise, skill and technique; and, third, the process of representing (Hearn & Melechi, 1992), men making 'women'– all within a specific "visual ontology" (Oyěwùmí, 1997).

'Upskirting' is constituted in and by homosocial masculinity, drawing on notions of craftsmanship. The homosocial element is created through creating in-group identity, which is bolstered by positioning the activity as risky and requiring courage. Also, unlike, say, 'revenge porn', 'upskirting' largely seems to involve strangers or relative strangers; indeed, the non-consensual intrusion into the woman's personal and body space seems to be part of the attraction, in both senses, for many of the men. Homosocial misogyny is reproduced through women as currency, initially close up, then at a relative distance, in a dispersed way amongst an online community of men who are probably strangers to the woman.

More specifically, 'upskirting' entails both reinforcing and breaking gender norms, dehumanising women, transgressing social boundaries with invasive action into women's space and world, along with (supposedly) polite, serious, crafted, studied normalisation of misogyny. We call this latter aspect, polite misogyny, in contrast to more gross forms of misogyny, which are more commonly recognised as misogyny, involving the explicit degradation and abuse of women. This polite misogyny may appear to have some common-ality with what some see as notions of chivalrous, gentlemanly behaviour whereby the male gaze appraises and 'appreciates' the female body, as if it were an object, an antique vase or a fine wine. The appraiser is imbued with a sense of skillful, knowledgeable judgement, the 'upskirter' becomes a skilled craftsman, taking pride in his pursuit, rather than a perverted 'peeping tom'. There is at the same time a parallel here with the practice of hunting and killing animals as prey, where the display of such trophies is appreciated and admired, by some, as evidence of courage, skill, even bizarrely 'civilisation', even while the 'capture' involves abusive violation (Thompson & Wood, 2018). Violence and violation bring their own, sometimes paradoxical, aes-thetics and styles (Appelbaum, 2017; Bennett, 2005; Burr & Hearn, 2008).

While there is no doubt a place for policy and legal interventions in re-sponse to 'upskirting', formal regulations do not provide an easy solution and regulation of anonymous public postings is mired in complexity. At the same time, attention needs to be given to the ways in which masculinities are reproduced online and offline to create homosocial environments which use objectification of women as currency between men, and how cultural and social structures, norms and practices enable these environments to flourish.

References

Appelbaum, R. (2017). *The aesthetics of violence*. London: Rowman & Littlefield.

Arxer, S. L. (2011). Hybrid masculine power: Reconceptualizing the relationship between homosociality and hegemonic masculinity. *Humanity & Society, 35*(4), 390–422.

Attwood, F. (2009). Introduction: The sexualization of culture. In F. Attwood (Ed.), *Mainstreaming sex: The sexualization of Western culture*. London: I.B.Tauris.

Balkmar, D. (2012). *On men and cars: An ethnographic study of gendered, risky and danger-ous relations*. Linköping: Linköping University Electronic Press.

Bates, L. (2021). *Men who hate women: From incels to pickup artists: The truth about extreme misogyny and how it affects us all*. London: Simon Schuster.

Bennett, J. (2005). *Empathic vision: Affect, trauma, and contemporary art*. Stanford, CA: Stanford University Press.

Bennett Moses, L. (2013). How to think about law, regulation and technology: Problems with 'technology' as a regulatory target. *Law, Innovation and Technology, 5*(1), 1–20.

Berkowitz, R., & Cornell, D. (2005). Parables of revenge and masculinity in Clint Eastwood's Mystic River. *Law, Culture and the Humanities, 1*(3), 316–332.

Bird, S. R. (1996). Welcome to the men's club: Homosociality and the maintenance of hegemonic masculinity. *Gender & Society, 10*(2), 120–132.

Burr, V., & Hearn, J. (Eds.). (2008). *Sex, violence and the body: The erotics of wounding*. Houndmills: Palgrave Macmillan.

Connell, R. W. (1987). *Gender and power*. Cambridge: Polity.

DeKeseredy, W. S. (1990). Male peer support and woman abuse: The current state of knowledge. *Sociological Focus, 23*(2), 129–139.

DeKeseredy, W. S., & Schwartz, M. D. (2016). Thinking sociologically about image-based sexual abuse: The contribution of male peer support theory. *Sexualization, Media, & Society, 2*(4). doi: 10.1177/2374623816684692.

Dines, G. (2010). *Pornland: How porn has hijacked our sexuality*. Boston, MA: Beacon Press.

Ding, D. (2019). Alphas, Betas, and Incels: Theorizing the masculinities of the manosphere. *Men and Masculinities, 22*(4), 638–657.

Emmons, R. A. (2004). Gratitude. In M. E. P. Seligman & C. Peterson (Eds.), *The VIA taxonomy of human strengths and virtues* (pp. 553–568). New York: Oxford University Press.

Empel, E. (2011). *(XXX) Potential impact: The future of the commercial sex industry in 2030.* Retrieved from https://www.houstonforesight.org/wp-content/uploads/2012/04/XXXpotentialImpact_CommercialSexIndustry2030_Empel.pdf

Epstein, S. (1995). Expertise: AIDS activism and the forging of credibility in the reform of clinical trials. *Science Technology Human Values, 20*(4), 408–437.

Flood, M. (2008). Men, sex, and homosociality: How bonds between men shape their sexual relations with women. *Men and Masculinities, 10*(3), 339–359.

Guignard, F. (2018). Envy in Western society: Today and tomorrow. In R. Roth & A. Lemma (Eds.), *Envy and gratitude revisited* (2nd ed., pp. 109–123). London: Karnac.

Hall, M., & Hearn, J. (2017). *Revenge Pornography: Gender, sexuality and motivations*. London: Routledge.

Hammarén, N., & Johansson, T. (2014). Homosociality in between power and intimacy. *SAGE Open, 4*(1), 1–11.

Harris, F. (2010). College men's meanings of masculinities and contextual influences: Toward a conceptual model. *Journal of College Student Development, 51*(3), 297–318.

Hearn, J. (1992). *Men in the public eye*. London: Routledge.

Hearn, J., & Melechi, A. (1992). The Transatlantic gaze: Masculinities, youth and the American imaginary. In S. Craig (Ed.), *Men, masculinity and the media* (pp. 215–232). Newbury Park, CA: Sage.

Henry, N., & Flynn, A. (2019). Image-based sexual abuse: Online distribution channels and illicit communities of support. *Violence against women, 25*(16), 1932–1955.

Henry, N., Powell, A., & Flynn, A. (2017). *Not just 'revenge pornography': Australians' experiences of image-based abuse. A summary report*. Melbourne: RMIT University.

Horta Ribeiro, M., Blackburn, J., Bradlyn, B., De Cristofaro, E., Stringhini, G., Long, S., Greenberg, S., & Zannettou, S. (2021). The evolution of the manosphere across the web. *Proceedings of the International AAAI Conference on Web and Social Media, 15*(1), 196–207. Retrieved from https://ojs.aaai.org/index.php/ICWSM/article/view/18053

Hunt, G. P., Mackenzie, K., & Joe-Laider, K. (2005). Alcohol and masculinity: The case of ethnic youth gangs. In T. M. Wilson (Ed.), *Drinking cultures*, (pp. 225–254). Oxford: Berg.

Jacobs, C. (2004). *Interactive panoramas: techniques for digital panoramic photography* (Vol. 1). Berlin: Springer Science & Business Media.

Jefferson, G. (1991). List construction as a task and a resource. In G. Psathas (Ed.), *Interactional competence*. New York: Irvington.

Kaite, B. (1988). The pornographer's body double: Transgression is the law. In A. M. Kroker, (Ed.), *Body invaders: Sexuality and the postmodern condition* (pp. 150–168). London: Macmillan.

Kashdan, T. B., Mishra, A., Breen, W. E., & Froh, J. J. (2009). Gender differences in gratitude: Examining appraisals, narratives, the willingness to express emotions, and changes in psychological needs. *Journal of Personality*, 77(3), 691–730.

Kendall, L. (2002). *Hanging out in the virtual pub: Masculinities and relationships online.* Berkeley: University of California Press.

Kimmel, M. S. (1994). Masculinities as Homophobia: Fear, shame, and silence in the construction of gender identity. Theorizing masculinities. In P. F. Murphy (Ed.), *Feminism & masculinities. Oxford readings in feminism* (pp. 182–199). Oxford: Oxford University Press.

Kittler, F. A. (2010). *Optical media.* Cambridge: Polity.

Law, J. (2001). *Machinic pleasures and interpellations.* Centre for Science Studies, Lancaster University, UK.

Lee, D., & Kennelly, L. (2019). Inside the Warwick University rape chat scandal *BBC News.* Retrieved from: https://www.bbc.co.uk/news/uk-48366835

Levy, A. (2013). Trial by Twitter: After high-school football stars were accused of rape, online vigilantes demanded that justice be served. Was it? *The New Yorker,* 5 August. Retrieved from: https://www.newyorker.com/magazine/2013/08/05/trial-by-twitter?subId1=xid:fr1576604404259cgd

Lipman-Blumen, J. (1976). Toward a homosocial theory of sex roles: An explanation of the sex segregation of social institutions. *Signs: Journal of Women and Culture and Society,* 1(3), 15–31.

Magrath, R., & Scoats, R. (2019). Young men's friendships: Inclusive masculinities in a post-university setting. *Journal of Gender Studies,* 28(1), 45–56.

McCann, W., Pedneault, A., Stohr, M. K., & Hemmens, C. (2018). Upskirting: A statutory analysis of legislative responses to video Voyeurism 10 years down the road. *Criminal Justice Review,* 43(4), 399–418.

McCormack, M. (2011). Hierarchy without hegemony: Locating boys in an inclusive school setting. *Sociological Perspectives,* 54(1), 83–101.

McGlynn, C., & Rackley, E. (2017). Image-based sexual abuse. *Oxford Journal of Legal Studies,* 37(3), 534–561.

Mellström, U. (1999). Technology and masculinity: Men and their machines. In S. Ervø & T. Johansson (Eds.), *Moulding masculinities* (pp. 118–135). Oxon: Ashgate.

Mellström, U. (2004). Machines and masculine subjectivity: Technology as an integral part of men's life experiences. *Men and Masculinities,* 6(4), 368–382.

Mogensen, C., & Helding Rand, S. (2019). *Vrede Unge Maend.* Copenhagen: Center for Digital Pædagogik.

Mikorski, R., & Szymanski, D. M. (2017). Masculine norms, peer group, pornography, facebook, and men's sexual objectification of women. *Psychology of Men & Masculinity,* 18(4), 257–267.

Mulvey, L. (1975). Visual pleasure and narrative cinema. *Screen,* 16(3), 6–18.

New Zealand Law Commission. (2004). *Intimate covert filming.* Study Paper 15. NZLC SP15. Retrieved from: http://www.nzlii.org/nz/other/nzlc/sp/SP15/

Oliver, K. (2016). Rape as spectator sport and creepshot entertainment: Social media and the valorization of lack of consent. *American Studies Journal,* 61(2016), 2. Web. 10 April 2020. doi: 10.18422/61–02.

Olson, P. (2012). *We are anonymous.* New York: Little, Brown.

Oppenheim, M. (2019). Victims aged seven to 70 subject to upskirting last year, police figures show. *The Independent.* 12 April. Retrieved from: https://www.independent.co.uk/news/uk/home-news/upskirting-victims-age-police-figures-2018-year-gina-martin-a8865746.html

Oyěwùmí, O. (1997). *The invention of women: Making an African sense of Western gender discourses.* Minneapolis: University of Minnesota Press.

Poole, S. (2013). *Who touched base in my thought shower? A treasury of unbearable office jargon.* London: Sceptre.

Robinson, S., Anderson, E., & White, A. (2018). The bromance: Undergraduate male friendships and the expansion of contemporary homosocial boundaries. *Sex Roles, 78*(1–2), 94–106.

Rosen, R. (2010). *Beaver street: A history of modern pornography: From the birth of phone sex to the skin mag in cyberspace: An investigative memoir.* London: Headpress.

Sacks, H. (1992). *Lectures on conversation: Volume I.* Malden, MA: Blackwell. doi:10.1002/9781444328301

Scheper-Hughes, N., & Bourgois, P. I. (2013). *Violence in war and peace.* Hoboken, NJ: Wiley.

Sedgwick, E. K. (2015). *Between men: English literature and male homosocial desire.* New York: Columbia University Press.

Sennett, R. (2009). *The craftsman.* New Haven, CT: Yale University Press.

Smiler, A. P. (2006). Conforming to masculine norms: Evidence for validity among adult men and women. *Sex Roles, 54*(11–12), 767–775.

Sweeney, B. N. (2014). Sorting women sexually: Masculine status, sexual performance, and the sexual stigmatization of women. *Symbolic Interaction, 37*(3), 369–390.

Thompson, C. (2019). *Everyday misogyny: On 'upskirting' as image-based sexual abuse,* PhD Thesis, University of Melbourne.

Thompson, C. (2020). Skirting around the issue: Misdirection and linguistic avoidance in parliamentary discourses on upskirting. *Violence Against Women, 26*(11), 1403–1422.

Thompson, C., & Wood, M. A. (2018). A media archaeology of the creepshot. *Feminist Media Studies, 18*(4), 560–574.

UK Government. (2019). *'Upskirting' law comes into force.* 12 April. Retrieved from: https://www.gov.uk/government/news/upskirting-law-comes-into-force

Wheaton, B. (2000). "New lads?" Masculinities and the new sport participant. *Men & Masculinities, 2*(4), 436–458.

Whisnant, R. (2010). From Jekyll to Hyde: The grooming of male pornography consumers. In K. Boyle (Ed.), *Everyday pornography* (pp. 114–133). London: Routledge.

Whiteman, M. (2019). Upskirting, bitcoin, and crime, oh my: Judicial resistance to apply old laws to new crimes-what is a legislature to Do? *Indiana Law Journal Supplement, 95,* 66.

Willis, P. (1990). *Common culture: Symbolic work at play in the everyday cultures of the young.* Milton Keynes: Open University Press.

Zimmerman, R. (1998). Photo finish. *Sciences, 38*(6), 16–18.

7   Revenge pornography

Introduction

Colloquially, revenge pornography refers to intentionally or being coerced to send, receive, or forward sexually explicit images of oneself or another via mobile devices such as smartphones and tablets. In our previous book (Hall & Hearn, 2017), with the same title as this chapter, we analysed data from the former revenge porn large and dedicated website, MyEx.com. In four separate chapters, we analysed perpetrator responses to show the various ways in which gender and sexuality were invoked by perpetrators to account for their actions. In this chapter, these perpetrator responses are presented in the posts as different poster-postee permutations: male-to-female; female-to-make; male-to-male; female-to-female. As a consequence of broadening the scope of this book, we have combined those four chapters into one. This has necessitated selecting only a limited number of perpetrator extracts and our analysis from each of those previous four chapter as exemplars to give the reader a sense of the array of ways gender and sexuality are invoked in perpetrator accounts. We direct the reader who wishes to view the full range of perpetrators accounts to our book, *Revenge pornography: gender, sexuality, and motivations* (Hall & Hearn, 2017).

We should mention at this point that MyEx.com has since been closed by the US Federal Trade Commission and the State of Nevada in 2018. Whilst there is a number of other revenge porn dedicated websites still in existence, we are not aware of any that provide perpetrators and viewers with the same response opportunities. MyEX.com had a moderator (named 'Casey') who facilitated poster-viewer communications, and this appeared to have incited further electronic textual abuse of the victim-survivor on the website. Poster-viewer responses on other similar websites we are aware of do not have such comprehensive interactions that are as conducive to a discourse analysis. We see this a unique and rich dataset providing a valuable insight into the mind, attitudes and practices of the perpetrators and worthy of reproduction, if in part.

The term 'revenge pornography' (hereafter, revenge porn) is typically understood as the online, sometimes offline, non-consensual distribution, or sharing, of explicit images by ex-partners, partners, others, or hackers

DOI: 10.4324/9781003138273-10

seeking revenge or entertainment. In our book, *Revenge pornography: gender, sexuality, and motivations* (Hall & Hearn 2017), we highlighted a variety of definitions of revenge porn such as that provided by the US National Conference of State Legislature. However, with changes in legislation, the impacts of activism, and legal and social science scholars problematising the term, many governmental and non-governmental actors now do not provide definitions of 'revenge porn', and instead prefer to use other terms such as non-consensual pornography, image-based sexual abuse, non-consensual explicit image sharing, and several other variations. We refer our reader to Chapter 1 for more on the problem of terminologies, words, and concepts. Thus, although we refer to 'revenge porn' in this chapter, we do so as this was, and still is colloquially, the most well-used term to describe the phenomenon and actions examined. However, it should also be noted that because revenge porn, or its similars, is now illegal in some countries and perpetrators can be prosecuted and platforms closed down, as we have noted, explicit images and videos are still being posted online often under different titles such as 'stolen' or 'leaked sex tapes' (#NotYourPorn, n.d).

A recent study by the South West Grid for Learning (SWGfL), in combination with the University of Exeter and Revenge Porn Helpline and Online Safety Helpline (Sharratt, 2019), found that the majority of callers to the Revenge Porn Helpline were women and adolescent girls, and 97% of those reported becoming a victim-survivor of revenge porn and other DGSVs. Whilst adolescence to mid-30s is the typical age range for victim-survivors, older women have also reported becoming victim-survivors (Telegraph, 2015).

During the COVID pandemic, the number of reports of revenge porn has increased and been linked to pandemic lockdowns (e.g., Robinson, 2020: UK Safer Internet Centre). In the UK, a government-funded helpline reported an increase by 22% of revenge porn in 2020 from the previous year (Criddle, 2020). Some scholars have indicated a link between the growth of (coerced) sexting and the increase in opportunities to commit revenge porn (Englander, 2015; Hasinoff, 2015). An online survey of 1929 adults about sexting, stress, and coping by Bianchi et al. (2021) found that lockdowns seem to have exasperated sexting as people looked for other ways to either interact sexually with those they could no longer see in person, or as a way to cope with their emotions. Whilst potentially facilitating some revenge porn and other DGSV, it would be wrong to suggest sexting explains the abuse of those images in subsequent revenges and other uses.

Whilst revenge porn can be located within several broad frameworks, as highlighted in Chapter 2, we focus here on what this relatively recent digital phenomenon reveals about the dynamics of gender and sexuality, through detailed analysis of posters' texts on MyEx.com. We address how tropes around gender and sexuality are drawn upon in online spaces in accounting for actions. In particular, we examine commonalities and differences in the complex, and sometimes contradictory, ways in which gender and sexuality are invoked in posters' accounts of their motivations for revenge porn.

Exemplars of revenge porn

We begin with a heterosexual man's account of sexually discarded that invokes notions of masculinity, homosocial bragging, and humour.

Male-to-female

Sexually discarded

A1

> "(name omitted) the Hoe"
>
> Anonymous says:
>
> This waist [sic.] of Oxygen is my ex of 15 years. She has been cocked more times than John Wayne's Gun. She has been shot over more times than Bagdad [sic.]. She has seen more loads than your Mums Washing Machine. Enter at your own Risk![1]

This text is simultaneously readable as boastful talk of sexual activity but also talk about an ex-partner's sexual infidelity. The latter is immediately readable from the disparaging term applied to her in the title "Hoe" but also in the warning to others "Enter at your own Risk!" Schulz's (1975) historical analysis of derogative terms applied women and girls shows that "Hoe" (whore) is a term typically applied to heterosexually promiscuous women (see also Winkler Reid, 2014, on the construction of women as 'slags'). Combined with the warning "Enter at your own Risk!" which is readable as heterosexual, "Enter" suggests that A1 is male and is speaking to a male audience.

A1 presents as fact a three-part list (Jefferson, 1991) of sexual activities that have been done to the woman "she has been cocked", "she has been shot over" and "she has seen more loads". Jefferson (1991) showed that the presence of three or more items on a list adds clarity and weight to arguments: in other words, strength by numbers. Therefore, A1's use of listing helps strengthen his account of his ex-partner as a "Hoe" and avoid potential discord or criticism. This works also to raise his masculine status by suggesting that he is the one who has done these things to her. However, given that this post is also a warning, his masculine status might be challenged without him providing a reason for the breakdown of their "15 years'" relationship since other readers might interpret these sexual acts as done by other(s). What A1 does to try and avoid this interpretation is construct his account as 'humorous': "cocked more times than John Wayne's Gun", "shot over more times than Bagdad" and "seen more loads than your Mums Washing Machine" (see Benwell, 2004, for more on how men use humour as a deflection strategy). In other words, the sexual humour works to position him as the 'doer' of these sexual acts because it portrays him as less emotionally invested. A1's

---

1 Texts cited are verbatim, including grammatical errors, apart from changing identifiers.

deployment of 'jokey' humour also works to present him as one of the lads (albeit a more mature one since his age is referenced with his knowledge of John Wayne). That is, this is normative behaviour for men, whether they produce or consume this type of material, and so he constructs himself as blameless for such posting (Whisnant, 2010, p. 122).

In the following extract the heterosexual men's promiscuity is normalised with the addition of point scoring against another man, that is, sexual trophyism (Barbee, 1997). This linguistic device has also been used by some men in their accounts of their own violence to women (Hearn, 1998).

Sexual trophyism

A2

"Your wife dude"

Anonymous says:

> I had an affair with this lady for over two years. But her sneaky husband kept following us around, trying to take photos of us together. He threatened to expose our relationship. In the end I got so annoyed I ended it. So here you are dude your wife and the photos you never got to take. She had never given a full blowjob before she met me her husband was super uptight I left her as a cock sucking anal queen.

It is immediately clear from the title that A2 has had some form of relationship with a woman who was married to another man. In A2's description of his affair, two aspects are marked out, first, that the woman he had an affair with was a "lady". The selection of a category carries important implications for how the text is read. Edwards (1998, p. 25) argues that these categories carry "potentially useful conventional associations with age, marital status, and potential sexual availability" such that "lady" infers she is respectable (Stokoe, 2003, p. 331). It could also convey literally, ironically, or sarcastically, that she is smart, sensible or selective, or specifically not these. Second, his marker of time suggests that this was not purely sexual but that they were emotionally involved. In working up this position he is able to position himself as the 'victim' of "her sneaky husband" who "threatened to expose" them, which suggests A2 was also cheating on someone. Threatening to expose them positions the "sneaky husband" in a position of power and indeed the outcome was that the affair was "ended". A2's posting explicit images of his ex-partner is readable as a way to re-empower himself, and this can be seen in the sexual acts he claims she has done "given a full blowjob" "anal queen" with him, and not with her husband.

The graphic detail of the sexual acts also works to position him as sexually powerful (and her weak and subordinate) vis-à-vis her husband since he was able to get her to do things she might not have done with her husband, as is visible in his downgrading of her from a "lady" to a "cock sucking anal queen". Whilst the selection "lady" infers respectability and modesty, "cock sucking anal queen" implies "frivolity" and "sleaziness" (Stokoe, 2003, p. 331). This 'category, predicate and task' (Hester & Eglin, 1997) in switching from "lady" to ""cock sucking anal queen" functions to downgrade the overall victory of her husband in keeping his wife, whilst claiming victory over her husband in the sexual acts he had with his wife, a theme of cuckolding familiar to Shakespeare.

Male-to-male

Trophyism, power and victory over another man are themes by the male poster in the following extract. The intention was to humiliate a former intimate male partner by taking photos of their sexual interactions.

Sexual humiliation

A3

"Cheating ex-boyfriend exposed and totally humiliated"

Anonymous says:

This is my cheating ex-boyfriend in all his glory. I found out he was cheating, so I didn't say I knew. I just spent weeks making loads of humiliating sex snaps and vids of him! So I could expose him and get revenge after dumping him. This is what the cheating slut deserves!! I've got loads of him sucking dick, balls, licking ass, spreading his legs and being the slut he always is. I've no doubt that his new bf doesn't have any idea what he's really like, so maybe he'll come across these photos and realise. Have fun jacking off guys, and if you reblog or repost these pics please let me know so I can get a kick out of seeing them spread

Any poster who believes that their ex-partner has committed infidelity or finished the relationship is likely to be in a position of disempowerment through loss of control. One of the objectives of revenge, and the tactics for dealing with, and sometimes coping with, what may be experienced as disempowerment is to do something which is perceived as regaining control (Berkowitz & Cornell, 2005). A3 does this by stating at the outset what his intention was and what he believes he has achieved: "Cheating ex-boyfriend exposed and totally humiliated". Yet at the same time, re-empowerment is likely to have less impact unless the other person is aware of the act. A3 implies that his ex-partner is aware of him posting these images "totally humiliated", although he indicates that he would like his "ex-boyfriends'" new partner to remain unaware: "I've no doubt that his new bf doesn't have any idea what he's really like, so maybe he'll come across these photos and realise".

Yet seeking revenge through displaying explicit images of one's ex-partner may be perceived by others as purely vindictive (Johansson & Hammarén, 2007, p. 67), and, as such, the poster is compelled to provide an account of their action (Salter, 2013). Accordingly, the poster seeks to "instrumentalise double standards in sexual mores to punish an ex-partner for leaving them", blaming the victim-survivor for their exposure (Salter, 2013, p. 1). A3 accounts for this by blaming his ex-partner as "my cheating ex-boyfriend", and "I found out he was cheating". However, A3 risks being viewed by others as purely vindictive because, once he was aware of the claimed infidelity, he "spent weeks making loads of humiliating sex snaps and vids [videos] of him! … I've got loads of him sucking dick, balls, licking ass, spreading his legs". In order to avoid readers drawing this conclusion, A3 presents this as also being for readers' benefit, including for the benefit of those who are anonymous or uninvolved: "Have fun jacking off guys".

In blaming the pictured person for their exposure, producers of revenge porn are able to take the moral high ground by implying that that person's purported crime was worse, or at least equal to, having their private images made public. Consumers who enjoy this material are able to displace responsibility, since it is not they who have humiliated the pictured man. They are only looking at, or masturbating to, the images and perhaps also passing them on to others: "… if you reblog or repost these pics" (Whisnant, 2010, p. 122). Given the wealth of data on MyEx.com, both producers and consumers of this material might also point out that this practice is commonplace as so to diffuse responsibility. It is not they then who are the monsters, but other men who are posting these images or the man themselves for their purported crimes (Whisnant, 2010, p. 127). This "quieter backstory", as Whisnant (2010, pp. 126–129) points out, is about how men manage their identities as 'real', and still 'moral', men, whilst engaging with the production and consumption of revenge porn.

Although revenge for infidelity is the main theme in the following extract, it carries two warnings: risky sex, and sexual dissatisfaction.

Risky sex

A4

"Slimy Grindr[2] Creep"

Anonymous says:

[Anonymised] likes nothing more than to meet as many guys as possible from Grindr and other apps usually asking for bareback sex.[3] [Anonymised] enjoys fucking as many other desperate guys as possible behind his boyfriends back. His tiny cock doesn't leave you very satisfied.

A4 categorises this man as "Slimy" and a "Creep", along with the location of these categorisations from "Grindr". Sacks (1992) pointed out that when someone is categorised they are presumed to be the doer of particular actions

---

2 Grindr claims to be the largest and most popular all-male social network spanning 196 countries worldwide. Uses include finding a date, buddy, or friend.
3 Anal sexual intercourse without the use of condoms.

(category-bound activities) and have specific characteristics (category-bound predicates). Sacks (1992) uses the example of babies crying and requiring love and attention. Men are presumed to be sexually promiscuous, and this can be seen in the data when A4 says "meet as many guys as possible" (Varella et al., 2014). However, "Slimy" and a "Creep" alone are relatively non-descriptive categories without further qualification and justification (Jayyusi, 1984). A4's account centres on the pictured man as interested in risky sex with numerous partners, and as a person who "likes nothing more than to meet as many guys as possible", and who is "asking for bareback sex". In doing so, A4 positions himself as practising safe sex thus imply that his ex-partner sought "bareback sex" because he was unwilling to provide it. In positioning himself as such A4 works up a contrast pair (Smith, 1978); safe/unsafe sexual practices, and those that are interested in unsafe "bareback sex" are categorised as "desperate". Thus, A4's account can be seen as a warning to other men.

However, some viewers might still be interested in "bareback sex" and potentially A4's ex-partner. Indeed, Blackwell's (2008) study of same sex dating sites found that 43% of men wanting "bareback sex" used dating websites to recruit sex partners even though unprotected same-sex male intercourse is likely to place both sexual partners at a higher risk of HIV transmission.

A4 cautions interested viewers by stating that his ex-partner's penis was "tiny" which he claims, "doesn't leave you very satisfied". This appears to achieve three things. First, the reference to sexual dissatisfaction acts as potential deterrent to interested others. Second, it implies that he remained in the relationship whilst sexually unfulfilled, as well as practicing safe sex, allows him to take the moral high ground. Third, it acts as a disparagement and 'emasculation' of the man pictured.

Female-to-male

Warnings and sexual dissatisfactions were relatively common themes in our data for both men and women. In the following heterosexual woman's post, the main thrust of the extract focuses on his inability to satisfy her because she claims he does not have a "big, long, thick dick".

Sexual dissatisfaction

A5

"So small you have to look twice, to see it!"

Anonymous says:

This guy promised he had a big, long, thick dick, but boy was I in for a surprise! I was with this guy for a year, we didn't have sex until the last few months of our relationship. When I first laid eyes on his dick, I couldn't believe how small it was. I tried my best to stay with him because I really liked him. To be honest the sex was terrible, the only thing he did well was eating me out. That wasn't enough and I decided to end things with him after a yearlong relationship. I couldn't even feel it when I tried putting it in my mouth. Size really does matter, no matter what you hear!!!

Disparaging comments about the man's penis size or aesthetics are an established form of ridicule of men. Most of these comments centre on the man's penis as not straight, too small, too narrow in girth, or having an unattractive glans (relative to perceived averages) (Hall, 2015). This is not surprising, given that "in many cultures it [the penis] has come to symbolise attributes such as largeness, strength, endurance, ability, courage, intelligence, knowledge, dominance over men, possession of women; a symbol of loving and being loved", as well as fertility (Wylie & Eardley, 2007, p. 1449). What is especially interesting about this post is that it centres on what she hoped for, "a big, long, thick dick", rather than perjoratively talking about the man's penis size or aesthetics as a means to punish or hurt for a prior misdemeanor. Given the A5 poster is compelled to produce an account for her claims, she provides an account based on his deceit "promised he had a big, long, thick dick, but boy was I in for a surprise". A5 deploys a three-part list of penis attributes "big, long, thick" (Jefferson, 1991). In this context, as with A1, the three-part list works to add clarity and weight to her account of his lie. Yet readers may sympathise since penis size, without cosmetic surgery, cannot be changed significantly. Therefore, A5 also works up an account of herself as being attentive: "I tried my best", "I really liked him", and initially tolerant, "I was with this guy for a year". In other words, she "tried" her "best" but due to his "poor sexual performance" because of his genital size – "I couldn't believe how small it was" – she is compelled to terminate the relationship, "I decided to end things". In doing so, A5 takes the moral high ground similarly to A4. A5 concludes her post by correcting narratives around penis size not being a concern for women's sexual satisfaction from 'it's not the size, it's what you do with it that matters' to "Size really does matter, no matter what you hear!!!" (Veale et al., 2021).

Given the historical, cultural, sexual, and gender importance that tends to be associated with the penis it is not surprising many women who engage in revenge porn state that their ex-partner's penis and sexual performance were inadequate (Wylie & Eardley, 2007). In the following extract, although the poster discusses the man's genital size and shape, she also claims his sexual likes are dubious and potentially non-normative.

Kinky sex

A6

"JUST WANTS TO USE YOU FOR SEX"

Anonymous says:

This guy goes through women like there is no tomorrow they all must wanna feel what a square cock feel like. Then they find out he's a kinky guy into all sorts of toy play. He loves himself so much its time share the love, so here is his square cock. Plus to show how kinky he is a vid of him

Phony sexuality

A8

> "This bitch really has LOW self-esteem (Lesbian)"

Anonymous says:

> I dated this girl for a few months, at the time she was into Wicca,[4] and just about anything to upset her parents. She quickly turned into an attention whore. One day she tried to get with one of my friends and I thought it was time to call it quits. Needless to say, the breakup did not go well and she even threatened suicide on more than one occasion. I come to find out she's what we call in the lesbian community a pretesbian. She is only lesbian because she is spiteful about men who wouldn't give her the time of day when she was younger.

Several things are immediately noticeable in A8's title. First, A8 categorises her as a "bitch" – a malicious, unpleasant, selfish person, especially a woman (*Cambridge Online Dictionary*, 2022). The categorisation (Sacks, 1992) is qualified with the category-bound predicate "LOW self-esteem" emphasised with the extreme-case formulation "really" (Pomerantz, 1986) and electronic shouting "LOW" (Barrett, 2012). Significantly, A8's identification of the pictured woman as a "Lesbian" is parenthesised as opposed to saying perhaps "This lesbian bitch really has LOW self-esteem". Parenthesising "Lesbian" in this way suggests there may be some difficulty with this identity.

A8 immediately begins the main body of her text by marking the time she was in a relationship with the pictured woman, "I dated this girl for a few months". Doing so allows A8 to imply that she had less emotional investment in the former relationship, thus deflecting unwarranted claims of vindictiveness from the pictured woman's claimed attempted infidelity, "she tried to get with one of my friends". Time is also marked for the pictured woman's former interest, "she was into Wicca, and just about anything to upset her parents". The marking of time by "was" and the length of their relationship "a few months" achieves two things. First, membership of the identity category "into Wicca" is marked as rebellion "anything to upset her parents", thus suggesting to viewers that she was not a 'real' member of this sub-cultural group (Widdicombe & Woofitt, 1990), and, perhaps, presenting her as childish because focused on pleasing (or not pleasing) her parents. Second, A8 is also working up a picture of the woman as having multiple and changing identities, thus signalling instability. The pictured woman's unstable identity is further qualified by claiming that "she even threatened suicide on more than one occasion". This also suggests the pictured woman was more attached to A8 than vice versa, again positioning A8 as more powerful. In also positioning the pictured woman as unstable, A8 works up the contrast pair (Smith, 1978)

---

4 Propounded in the 1950s by the retired British civil servant Gerald Brosseau Gardner, Wicca is a modern form of paganism, witchcraft religion (Guilly, 2008).

of identities stable/unstable, which allows A8 to position herself as stable; later claiming the pictured women's membership of the "lesbian community" as 'phony' (Sacks, 1992; Schegloff, 2007) "pretesbian". As we have pointed out, those who are seen to be non-normative or not having 'real' group member-ship are often declared 'phony' or 'defective' (Sacks, 1992).

Working up a picture of the woman as a 'phony' lesbian and as mentally unstable, as suicidal, does three further things. First, the inherent disempow-erment from her ex-partner attempting to commit infidelity, "she tried to get with one of my friends", is deflected, allowing A8 to present herself as in con-trol. Indeed, A8 claimed to be the one who ended the relationship, "I thought it was time to call it quits". Second, A8 is signalling caution to viewers who might know or be interested in a relationship with this woman. Finally, A8 is also able to minimise potential claims by viewers that she is purely moti-vated by revenge. Overall, what A8's account shows is that gender and sexual identities are presumed to be stable with specific identity-bound categories and predicates. Those seen to contravene these conventions are thus labelled as 'phony' or 'defective' (Sacks, 1992; Schegloff, 2007), in transgressing con-ventional notions of gender/sexual identity boundaries.

Conclusion

As noted in Chapter 2, there are various ways of analysing DGSVs, including revenge porn, and thus particular posts and extracts, for example, in terms of the psycho-social dynamics of revenge, or the expansion and affordances of ICTs. While it is difficult to separate out different analytical frameworks, our focus here has been on gender and sexual positioning, and the use of gender and sexual meanings in the practice of and accounting for revenge porn. In particular, we have been interested in how posters of revenge porn invoke gender and sexuality to account for posting explicit images of an ex-partner, and what were the similarities and differences between different sexual framings of revenge porn in online posts: male-to-female, female-to-male, male-to-male, female-to-female. In addressing these questions, eight basic gendered-sexual themes were identified across sexual 'orientations' of poster-postee: sexually discarded; sexual trophyism; risky sex; sexual dissat-isfaction; kinky sex; sexual promiscuity; and phony sexuality. Analysis of the posts in this way highlights how the written texts[5] worked by invoking tropes about gender and sexuality in accounting for their actions.

In terms of similarities between the different sexual framings, what is clear is that the display of sexual orientation, whether heterosexual or same-sex, is through antagonism, power and control, or worse, towards those who have been, and may still be, the object of desire. The structure and direction of

5 To analyse those posts with only headlines or no or minimal written texts would entail visual analysis, with attendant ethical complications. In some cases, posters may have con-sidered that the visuals speak for themselves, and that a separate rationale was unnecessary or perhaps difficult to formulate. Such 'only visuals' or 'almost only visuals' posts might reveal, if subject to visual or multi-modal analysis, different patterns to those we addressed. There would likely be methodological challenges in translating meanings between written and visual data.

revenge porn, and its non-consensual and abusive form, parallel in text those respective forms of past or present sexual attraction. Sex, desire, and even love are structurally paralleled by (attempted) revenge, humiliation, and abuse. The intensity of desire and its disappointment or frustration provide the grounds – from the perspective of the perpetrating poster – for revenge and abuse, as said in the revenge porn text, and sometimes shown in the accompanying visuals.

This structure of affect is comparable to the dynamics of power and control in marriage continuing after separation and divorce (cf. Delphy, 1976). Revenge porn is one way of continuing the gender-sexual dynamics of gender, sexuality, power, and control post-separation into abuse, or even beginning a new phase of more explicit power, control, and abuse. For example, numerous studies of domestic violence and intimate partner violence have pointed to the risks of violence and abuse in post-separation, as summarised by Macdonald (2013, p. 3):

> Domestic violence may start or escalate at the point of separation and/or post-separation (Abrahams, 1994; Hester and Radford, 1996; Humphreys and Thiara, 2003; Richards, 2003) and the post-separation period can be a time of acute danger for women and children, where risk of homicide increases (Wilson and Daly, 2002).

For a start, there are differences in form and impact between physical, sexual, emotional, psychological, and representational violence and threats thereof. Additionally, the difference now is the extension of potential violence and abuse into the cyberworld, with its own features, such as of permanency and replicability, without total deletion, as afforded by ICTs. Specific sexual orientations may be overridden by the monological logics of desire and revenge (counter-desire), made possible in extended form by the (social) affordances of ICTs, despite their dialogical and interactive potential.

More specifically, this may involve exertion of power in relation to loss of control and/or of an (ex-)partner and/or power to wish to continue controlling an (ex-)partner or power enacted through gender and sexuality. Such revenges were generally explained by justifications rather than excuses, so that the avenged person (the passive postee) is the one to be blamed (as active) for the actions performed towards them (the active sexual poster), comparable to men's justifications for their violence to women (Bellini et al., 2020; Cavanagh et al., 2001; Hearn, 1998; Ptacek, 1988).

However, such exertion of power and control, and its justification, was not unrestrained, and here a certain contradictory complexity is apparent. What was common across all eight central themes was that the poster claimed their ex-partner had committed some misdemeanour leading to the breakdown of the relationship, and so positioned themselves as supposed victim. Claiming ex-partners had committed a misdemeanour was often not enough for the poster's claims to appear legitimate; posters frequently engaged in self-legitimation practices, probably to avoid or reduce the risks of being interpreted as having 'sour grapes' or simply being vindictive. This could suggest certain moral rules are employed, whereby to write more than a minimum required some "good reasons". If written texts were to be used, then the "logics" used needed to be credible, and thus not open to further shaming of the poster as an inadequate partner, lover, or spouse.

At the same time, there are clear differences between the different discursively constructed gender/sexual orientations and genres of the posts and posters. The precise textual devices by which revenge porn is differentially practiced, and justified, is then less about the affordances of ICTs, and more about gendered/sexual discursive positions and possibilities within dominant gender/sexual orders. For example, in the posts references to women's bodies can be used not only to exact heterosexual revenge on them directly, but also on another (male) partner of the woman concerned, and so indirectly onto her. Focusing on gender and sexuality as discursive framings in this way is not to stereotype such practices according to sexual orientation. Different sexuality positionings, such as male–female or male–male, may invoke various straight and gay conventions, respectively, as in the appeal to known or unknown other readers and audiences of assumed similar homosocial gay or straight men (cf. Heinskou, 2015; Thomson, 1999). It is through these devices, such as the appeal to similar (to the poster) others, that the differences between male-to-female, female-to-male, male-to-male, female-to-female online postings are most explicitly enacted.

To put this a little differently, men's postings of revenge porn, both straight and gay, and the discourses employed within and around them, can be examples of the dominant repertoires of those posters' positioning as men and in terms of masculinities. In this sense, they are perhaps less novel than they may appear at first sight; rather, they are often extensions and elaborations of well-charted ways of abusing others, especially in the context of the extensive sexist and misogynist texts online. On the other hand, posts by women, whether straight or lesbian, tend to involve different forms, for example, of women posters as scorned revengers, or of women postees as unfaithful or not a real lesbian. Justifications of such gender/sexual positionings often rest on external referencing, for example, to the/a man's sexual/penile inadequacy, incapability and just deserts, or the lesbian women's promiscuity or her inability to be a real and consistent lesbian, but rather a pretend lesbian, a pretesbian.

Having said that, a further word of caution is necessary, as in commenting on such positionings, we are not seeking to attribute such meanings exhaustively from specific posts, as there may well be considerable complexity and contradiction in the texts, given the nature of some of the online postings. Furthermore, we do not necessarily assume a match between online and offline personae, for example, it is possible that not all the 'lesbian postings' may be lesbian women or those identifying as lesbian or even by women at all.

Finally, we note how the mass of online revenge porn, while complex, and even contradictory, in its accounting, seems to be strongly based in binary, non-queer gender positionings. In that way, despite the potentialities of virtual sexualities,[6] it reproduces broader gender hegemony. Online revenge

6 These online potentialities have been widely documented elsewhere (e.g., Elund, 2015; O'Riordan & Phillips, 2007), and seem, currently at least, to be a separable aspect of online sexualities; this may change in the future.

porn is another site for the performance of gender hegemony, even with the variable sexual orientations said and shown. In contrast to possible blurrings of binary gender/sexuality (cf. Monro, 2005; Roseneil, 2005), revenge (porn), it seems, is not (yet) very queer.

References

Abrahams, C. (1994). *The hidden victims: Children and domestic violence.* London: NCH Action for Children.

Barrett, M. (2012). The efficacy of interviewing young drug users through online chat. *Drug and Alcohol Review, 31*(4), 566–572.

Barbee, A. P. (1997). Troubled men. *Psyccritiques, 42*(5), 420–421.

Bellini, R., Tseng, E., McDonald, N., Greenstadt, R., McCoy, D., Ristenpart, T., & Dell, N. (2020). "So-called privacy breeds evil": Narrative justifications for intimate partner surveillance in online forums. *Proceedings of the ACM on Human-Computer Interaction, 4*(CSCW), 1–27. doi: 10.1145/3432909.

Benwell, B. (2004). Ironic discourse: Evasive masculinity in British men's lifestyle magazines. *Men & Masculinities, 7*(1), 3–21.

Berkowitz, R., & Cornell, D. (2005). Parables of revenge and masculinity in Clint Eastwood's Mystic River. *Law, Culture and the Humanities, 1*(3), 316–332.

Blackwell, C. W. (2008). Men who have sex with men and recruit bareback sex partners on the internet: Implications for STI and HIV prevention and client education. *American Journal of Men's Health, 2*(4), 306–313.

Carpenter, L. M. (2015). Gender and the meaning and experience of virginity loss in the contemporary United States. *Gender & Society, 16*(3), 345–365.

Cavanagh, K., Dobash, R. E., Dobash, R. P., & Lewis, R. (2001). "Remedial work": Men's strategic responses to their violence against intimate female partners. *Sociology, 35*(3), 695–714.

Criddle, C. (2020). 'Revenge porn new normal' after cases surge in lockdown. *BBC.* 17 September. Retrieved from: https://www.bbc.com/news/technology-54149682

Delphy, C. (1976). Continuities and discontinuities in marriage and divorce. In D. Leonard Barker & S. Allen (Eds.), *Sexual divisions and society: Process and change* (pp. 76–89). London: Tavistock.

Dickerson, P. (2000). "But I'm different to them": Constructing contrasts between self and others in talk-in-interaction. *British Journal of Social Psychology, 39*(3), 381–398.

Dines, G. (2010). *Pornland: How porn has hijacked our sexuality.* Boston: Beacon.

Bianchi, D., Baiocco, R., Lonigro, A., Pompili, S., Zammuto, M., Di Tata, D., Morelli, M., Chirumbolo, A., Di Norcia, A., Cannoni, E., Longobardi, E., & Laghi, F. (2021). Love in quarantine: Sexting, stress, and coping during the COVID-19 lockdown. *Sexuality Research and Social Policy.* 23 September. doi: 10.1007/s13178-021-00645-z.

Cambridge Online Dictionary (2022). *Bitch.* Retrieved from: https://dictionary.cambridge.org/dictionary/learner-english/bitch

Edwards, D. (1998). The relevant thing about her: Social identity categories in use. In C. Antaki & S. Widdicombe (Eds.), *Identities in talk* (pp. 15–34). London: Sage.

Edwards, T. (2003). Sex, booze and fags: Masculinity, style and men's magazines. In B. Benwell (Ed.), *Masculinity and men's lifestyle magazines* (pp. 132–146). Oxford: Blackwell Publishing/Sociological Review.

Elund, J. (2015). *Subversion, sexuality and the virtual self.* New York: Palgrave Macmillan.

Englander, E. (2015). Coerced sexting and revenge porn among teens. *Bullying, Teen Aggression & Social Media, 1*(2), 19–21.

Federal Trade Commission. (2018). Emp Media Inc. (MyEx.com). Retrieved from: https://www.ftc.gov/enforcement/cases-proceedings/162-3052/emp-media-inc-myexcom

Guiley, R. E. (2008). *The encyclopedia of witches, witchcraft and wicca,* 3rd edn. New York: Facts on File Inc.

Hall, M. (2015). 'When there's no underbrush the tree looks taller': A discourse analysis of men's online groin shaving talk. *Sexualities, 18*(8), 997–1017.

Hall, M., & Hearn, J. (2017). *Revenge pornography: Gender, sexuality and motivations.* Abingdon: Routledge.

Hasinoff, A. A. (2015). *Sexting panic: Rethinking criminalization, privacy, and Consent.* Urbana: University of Illinois Press.

Hearn, J. (1998). *The violences of men.* London: Sage.

Heinskou, M. B. (2015). Sexuality in transit – Gender gaming and spaces of sexuality in late modernity. *Sexualities, 18*(7), 885–899.

Hester, M., & Radford, L. (1996). *Domestic violence and child contact arrangements in England and Denmark.* Bristol: Policy Press.

Hester, S., & Eglin, P. (Eds.), (1997). *Culture and action: Studies in membership categorization analysis.* Washington: University Press of America.

Humphreys, C., & Thiara, R. (2003). Neither justice nor protection: Women's experiences of post-separation violence. *Journal of Social Welfare and Family Law, 25*(4), 195–214.

Jayyusi, L. (1984). *Categorization and the moral order.* Boston, MA Routledge & Kegan.

Jefferson, G. (1991). List construction as a task and a resource. In G. Psathas (Ed.), *Interactional competence.* New York: Irvington Publications.

Johansson, T., & Hammarén, N. (2007). Hegemonic masculinity and pornography: Young people's attitudes toward and relations to pornography. *Journal of Men's Studies, 15*(1), 57–71.

Macdonald, G. (2013). *Domestic violence and private family court proceedings: Promotion child welfare or promoting contact?* Research Paper Series # CASP8. Bath: University of Bath.

McDonald, R. I., & Crandall, C. S. (2015). Social norms and social influence. *Current Opinion in Behavioral Sciences, 3,* 147–151.

Miller, K. (2008). Wired: Energy drinks, jock identity, masculine norms, and risk taking. *Journal of American College Health, 56*(5), 481–490.

Monro, S. (2005). *Gender politics: Activism, citizenship and sexual diversity.* London: Pluto.

Nylund, D. (2007). *Beer, babes, and balls: Masculinity and sports talk Radio.* Albany: State University New York Press.

O'Riordan, K., & Phillips, D. J. (Eds.). (2007). *Queer online: Media technology and sexuality.* New York: Peter Lang.

Pomerantz, A. (1986). Extreme case formulations: A way of legitimizing claims. *Human Studies, 9*(2), 219–229.

Ptacek, J. (1988). Why do men batter their wives? In K. Yllö & M. Bograd (Eds.), *Feminist perspectives on wife abuse* (pp. 133–157). Newbury Park, CA: Sage.

Richards, L. (2003). *Findings from the multi-agency domestic violence murder reviews in London.* London: Metropolitan Police.

Robinson, A. (2020). Revenge porn pandemic: Rise in reports shows no sign of slowing even as lockdown eases. *UK Safer Internet Centre*. 17 September. Retrieved from: https://saferinternet.org.uk/blog/revenge-porn-pandemic-rise-in-reports-shows-no-sign-of-slowing-even-as-lockdown-eases

Roseneil, S. (2005). Living and loving beyond the boundaries of the heteronorm: Personal relationships in the 21st Century. In L. Mackie, S. Cunningham-Burley & J. McKendrick (Eds.), *Families in society: Boundaries and relationships* (pp. 241–258). Bristol: Policy.

Sacks, H. (1992). *Lectures on conversation*. Oxford: Blackwell.

Salter, M. (2013) 'Responding to revenge porn: Gender, justice and online legal impunity'. Paper delivered at: Whose Justice? Conflicted Approaches to Crime and Conflict, University of Western Sydney, Sydney, 27 September.

Schegloff, E. A. (2007). A tutorial on membership categorization. *Journal of Pragmatics*, *39*(3), 462–482.

Schulz, M. (1975). The semantic derogation of women. *Language and Sex: Difference and Dominance*, *64*(75), 134–147.

Smith, D. (1978). K is Mentally Ill: The anatomy of a factual account. *Sociology*, *12*(1), 23–53.

Stokoe, E. H. (2003). Mothers, single women and sluts: Gender, morality and membership categorization in neighbour disputes. *Feminism & Psychology*, *13*(3), 317–344.

Sharratt, E. (2019). Intimate image abuse in adults and under 18s. A comparative analysis of cases dealt with by the Revenge Porn Helpline and Professionals Online Safety Helpline. *SWGfL*. Retrieved from: https://swgfl.org.uk/assets/documents/intimate-image-abuse-in-adults-and-under-18s.pdf

Telegraph. (2015). *Revenge porn victims include pensioner in 60s and girls as young as 11*. 16 July. Retrieved from: https://www.telegraph.co.uk/news/uknews/crime/11741695/Revenge-porn-victims-include-pensioner-in-60s-and-girls-as-young-as-11.html

Thomson, R. (1999). 'It was the way we were watching it': Young men negotiate pornography. In J. Hearn & S. Roseneil (Eds.), *Consuming cultures: Power and resistance* (pp. 178–198). London: Palgrave Macmillan.

Varella, M. A. C., Valentova, J. V., Pereira, K. J., & Bussab, V. S. R. (2014). Promiscuity is related to masculine and feminine body traits in both men and women: Evidence from Brazilian and Czech samples. *Behavioural Processes*, *109*(Part A), 34–39.

Veale, D., Vaidya, A., Papageorgiou, A., Foks, M., Giona, S., Hodsoll, J. Freeston, M., & Muir, G. (2021). A preliminary investigation of a novel method to manipulate penis length to measure female sexual satisfaction: A single-case experimental design. *British Medical Journal International*. 1 April. doi: 10.1111/bju.15416.

Whisnant, R. (2010). From Jekyll to Hyde: The grooming of male pornography consumers. In K. Boyle (Ed.), *Everyday pornography* (pp. 114–133). London: Routledge.

Widdicombe, S., & Woofitt, R. (1990) 'Being' versus 'doing' punk: On achieving authenticity as a member. *Journal of Language and Social Psychology*, *9*(4), 257–277.

Wilson, M., & Daly, M. (2002). *Homicide*. New York: Aldine de Gruyter.

Winkler Reid, S. (2014). 'She's not a slag because she only had sex once': Sexual ethics in a London secondary school. *Journal of Moral Education*, *43*(2), 183–197.

Wylie R. R., & Eardley, I. (2007). Penile size and the 'small penis syndrome'. *BJU International*, *99*(6), 1449–1455.

8 Some further forms of digital gender-sexual violations

Introduction

Modern information and communication technologies (ICTs) provide many open-ended and undefined possibilities for online violation, as we have highlighted in previous chapters. We have noted that ICTs bring several distinctive features to everyday life such as: time/space compression of distance and physical separation and the instantaneousness of this in real time; asynchronicity; blurring the 'real' and the 'representational'; broader bandwidth, wireless portability, and globalised connectivity; personalisation, and blurring, even abolition, of online/offline boundaries that allow for the relative ease of DGSV and their dissemination. Whilst we have examined online textual abuse of feminists, revenge pornography, and upskirting, there is however, a multiplicity of further forms of DGSV, which include, for example, online child sexual abuse rings, sex trafficking, commercial sex exploitation, online pornography – to name a few. It is beyond the scope of this book to cover all these and other forms. Indeed, the frequency in which new forms of DGSV seem to appear would mean a full comprehensive review of all forms of DGSV would challenge any researcher; indeed, we wonder if that is even possible as technologies and their social affordances develop and change as we discuss in our Afterword chapter. Therefore, in this chapter we highlight four more forms of DGSV, some of their derivatives, and some of the related issues arising: deepfake pornography, sexual spycamming, cyberflashing, and sexual happy slapping.

Deepfake pornography

The last few decades have seen a remarkable rise in the accessibility and capabilities of technologies using artificial intelligence (AI), which has been programmed to simulate human thinking processes (e.g., ridesharing apps like *Uber*; commercial flight autopilot software) (Caldwell et al., 2020). But despite the legitimate uses, this greater accessibility of AI has coincided with a rise in its use in criminal activities (e.g., evasion of image recognition, ransomware attacks). One of the fastest growing and more malevolent uses of this is reported to be the deepfake (Ajder et al., 2019).

DOI: 10.4324/9781003138273-11

The term 'deepfake' is a portmanteau of 'deep learning' and 'fake'. Deepfake is a form of synthetic media in which one person's image, video, and/or voice is swapped for another so that the substituted person appears to be the person in the image or video, and/or saying or doing what is being portrayed. AI is able to do this because it has human cognitive abilities software. That is, if presented with a problem or unfamiliar task, AI can learn and find a solution.

AI is typically categorised as either weak/narrow or strong/general. Most AI is task specific (narrow/weak) such as facial recognition, trading bots, and self-driving cars. A more developed subset of weak/narrow AI is deep learning (as opposed to machine learning). As with the human brain, deep learning algorithms can identify patterns and classify various types of information even as and when it receives new information. In this sense, computers can 'make decisions'. So, for example, deep learning AI can make classifications of people's facial and bodily features, whereas simple machine learning AI would require those classifications to be manually inputted by someone. Deepfakes are a version of deep learning because they do not need human input to identify facial or other similarities. Instead, they rely on large sets of data samples that are analysed by neural networks. AI uses these data samples to learn to mimic people's facial expressions, body movements, mannerisms, voice and so on (Westerlund, 2019).

Although deepfakes are used legitimately in, for example, film production and criminal forensics, there has also been a growing concern in their misuse in the distribution of political disinformation, blackmailing, 'sockpuppeting'[1] and pornography (Citron & Chesney, 2018). Indeed, the term deepfake was apparently coined by a Reddit user with the same pseudonym in 2017 when they used AI to manipulate pornographic images (Maddocks, 2020).

Whilst technology to create fake pornographic photos has been around for decades with the use of software such as Photoshop, what is different about AI fake pornography is that realistic images can be produced that are almost impossible to distinguish as fake just by looking at them. What is also relatively new is their increasing popularity. For an example, one only has to look at the closure of DeepNude: a recent online application that used artificial intelligence to 'undress' photos of women in order to show the viewer realistic images of what they would look like naked (Mahdawi, 2019). DeepNude's (undisclosed) developer closed the platform within four days of launching it because the volume of traffic caused the platform to keep crashing (Telford, 2019). Although now closed, various other (un)paid versions by other creators now exist to fill demand.

---

1 'Sockpuppetting' is a slang term for a fake online identity or person used to deceive (unlike 'trolls' who often do not remain anonymous). For example, 'sockpuppets' may be created in significant numbers to bolster some point of view, especially at times of elections, thus creating the impression that a candidate is more popular than the really are.

Pornographic deepfake videos, with voiceovers, are popular too. Indeed, there is a burgeoning number of deepfake pornographic videos on well-known pornographic websites such as PornHub and Xvideos (Kikerpill, 2020). Pornographic search engines such as 'The Porn Dude' also contain a number of platforms dedicated to deepfake pornography such as Adult-DeepFakes.com, Deepfakeporn.net, FamousBoard.com, SexCelebrity.net, MrDeepFakes.com, CelbJihad.com. CFake.com, and many others. Porn-Hub's *2019 Year in Review* report shows that celebrity deepfake pornography is popular. It reports that when "celebrities are in the news and on everyone's mind, they tend to drive a lot of Pornhub searches" (PornHub, 2019, p. 38), and the top five searches for 2019, generated more than 50 million searches. But whilst the vast majority of pornographic deepfakes are of female celebrities, Ajder et al. (2019) suggests that, as deepfake technologies become easier to use, pornographic deepfakes will become a greater threat to any woman.

Deepfake videos are lucrative too. For example, the development of 'bots' designed to harvest (that is, steal) explicit sexual images and videos (or turn non-explicit images and videos into explicit ones), and then post them on so-called 'parasite websites', means such websites can charge for pay-per-view, increase revenues through advertising or hyperlink signposting (Topping, 2012), and via take-down services.

Where once deepfakes technologies were largely accessible only to experts in specialised industries, with the launch of programs like FaceApp[2] it has become relatively easy for almost anyone with a basic level of IT knowledge and access to the Internet to be able to create convincing pornographic deepfake images, videos, and voiceovers of anybody's face and/or body (Öhman, 2020). Indeed, for those who experience difficulties in creating quality images and videos, some websites dedicated to pornography such as MrDeepFakes.com offer free online guides (DeepFake Creation Guide; DeepFake Making Process), tutorials (DeepFakeLab 2.0[3]), and forum support from the moderator and other platform members.

Many of the websites dedicated to pornography are based on the normalisation of unproblematic male sexual fantasies, often about female celebrities such as those listed above in PornHub's *2019 Year in Review* report. For example, AdultDeepFakes.com is promoted with the following text (as of October 8, 2021):

> Ah, Adult DeepFakes! We've all thought about this sort of content, don't lie! You know the moment when you're watching Game of Thrones and you see Emilia Clarke's tits and you're like: "Holy shit I want to see her

2 A 2019 video and image editing application produced by Wireless Lab (a Russian-based organisation) that allows the users to produce high quality and realistic, but fake, videos and images of a person's face.

3 DeepFaceLab 2.0 is the newest and most popular (as of September 21, 2021) software for creating deepfakes.

do a porno". Or even "Dude I'd fuck this bitch stupid mad". Yeah, we've all been there, buddy. We've all been there. Well, guess what. You can FINALLY see her in a real porno! Well, not Emilia Clarke but someone that looks exactly like her. We're talking about deepfakes and to present this amazing concept we have an even more amazing website call [sic.] AdultDeepFakes.com

AdultDeepFakes.com is a kind of site that looks exactly like a normal porn tube site. But believe me when I say that this place is anything but your average porn tube website. This place has some really high-quality porn to show off, and it makes sense cause if you're making porn with chicks who look like famous actresses and singers, then you're going to be all out as far as the equipment is concerned. I'm pretty sure you can find any bitch you want from Jennifer Lopez to Rihanna. Every bitch here has a deepfake of her and you can enjoy these as much as you like. It's that simple.

Male sexual fantasies are clearly presented as normative and thus pornographic deepfakes are too. This conflation is what Öhman (2020, p. 134) terms 'pervert's dilemma' which he articulates here:

i.   Creating pornographic Deepfake videos based on someone's face (without their explicit consent) is morally impermissible.
ii. Having private sexual fantasies about someone (without their explicit consent) is per se normally morally permissible.
iii. Under conditions (i) and (ii), there is no morally relevant difference between creating a Deepfake video based on someone's face and having a private sexual fantasy about someone.

In this context, it is not difficult to see how pornographic deepfakes (and other forms of DGSV) might be deemed less problematic for some and thus their significance or impact minimised, especially where celebrities are the victims (Harwell, 2018). Of course, the pornographic deepfake phenomenon is, or should be, considered morally impermissible; it is highly gendered, further contributing to reinforcing gender norms and inequalities, dehumanising, commodifying and objectifying women and girls. It is an invasive action into their space and world, whether they are aware of it or not, and so yet another means of normalising misogyny and with very few (inter)national laws for prosecution (Banet-Weiser, 2021; Öhman, 2020).

The relative absence of (inter)national laws to tackle pornographic deepfakes (like other DGSVs) has led some legal scholars, such as McGlynn in an interview with the UK broadcaster the BBC, to warn of a potential 'epidemic' in pornographic deepfakes (Selbie & Williams, 2021). According to Citron (2016, in Ajder et al., 2019, p. 6), "Deepfake technology is being weaponised against women by inserting their faces into porn. It is terrifying, embarrassing, demeaning, and silencing. Deepfake sex videos say to individuals that their bodies are not their own and can make it difficult to stay online, get or keep a job, and feel safe".

Whilst celebrities have tended to be the main target for pornographic deepfake creators, an increasing number of non-celebrity women have also become victim-survivors. Indeed, the Amsterdam-based cybersecurity company Deeptrace (2019) report found nearly 15,000 pornographic deep-fakes, almost double the previous year's number, which have been viewed around 134 million times. Ninety-six percent of these videos were of women. Other examples include a number of women in Cork, Ireland, who found their Facebook photos had been stolen and used in in pornographic deepfakes (Edwards & Roche, 2016). Solsman (2020) also reported that a Telegram AI-bot targeted more than 100,000 women, creating, and distributing daily pornographic deepfakes of images they had uploaded of themselves, family, and friends (some are reported to appear under 18-years old) which were distributed to almost 25,000 subscribers to Telegram.

Women have also spoken out about their experiences. Karen Mort, a poet and broadcaster in Sheffield, UK, became a victim when someone stole non-intimate images of her from her private social media accounts, uploaded them and invited others to make deepfake pornography with them (Hao, 2021). She is reported as saying: "It really makes you feel powerless, like you're being put in your place". "Punished for being a woman with a public voice of any kind. That's the best way I can describe it. It's saying, 'Look: we can always do this to you'" (Hao, 2021, p. 1).

The Indian investigative journalist, Rana Ayyub (2018), became a victim when she criticised nationalist Bharatiya Janata Party (BJP) on the BBC and Al Jazeera for bringing shame on itself by protecting child sex abusers after an eight-year-old Kashmiri girl had been raped. She reports that the following day fake claims on social media and pornographic videos of her started circu-lating as retribution and to silence her and others.

Although there have been some attempts to address the pornographic deepfakes with bans on their platforms (such as Reddit, Twitter), and the development of AI bots (#MeTooBots) to detect such activities, their presence in men-only spaces is pervasive, especially in the 'dark web'[4] where 96% of the Internet is unmonitored or regulated (Deyan, 2021).

It would also seem that pornographic deepfakes will evolve. For exam-ple, sex robots with the faces of actors such as Angelina Jolie and Scarlett Johansson have already been developed by a Hong Kong developer and were set for retail practiced between $2,000–3,000 (Glaser, 2016; Michael, 2016). Augmented reality pornography (AR porn) is overlapping and blurring the boundaries between animation, deepfakes, and reality(ies). Augmented

---

4 The dark web is that version of the internet where specific software is used to commu-nicate and conduct business, without divulging identifying information, such as a user's location and personal details.

reality technology allows the modification of the 'real-world' by merging it with interactive 2D and 3D virtual objects. By blending or blurring the virtual with the 'real' the user can gain some degree of control of what the animated representation of another person, or oneself, does. As technology improves it is likely that people will be able to use AI and AR to enact their sexual fantasies with any person they choose in the comfort of their own surroundings: virtual sexual abuse of anyone at any time without them necessarily being aware of it.

Sexual spycamming

Sexual spycammming is the covert photographing or filming of a person (usually girls and women) during sexual activities, naked, urinating or discharging bowels. It typically takes place at distance with tiny hidden still and/or video cameras in, for example, a clock, radio, TV, or similar devices. They can also be built into devices, such as cigarette lighters, pens, and chewing gum packets, or installed into shoes, bags, inside toilets and walls (see Gallagher, 2020; Gogarty, 2020; Van Der Meer, 2020; Wyllie, 2020). These cameras may be hidden in both public and private spaces, and include toilets, bathrooms, clothing store and sports changing rooms, bedrooms, and hotel rooms, where the perpetrator might expect the unsuspecting victim to expose themselves. For example, some guests in Airbnb properties have reported cameras in bedrooms and bathrooms and only noticed them because light reflected off the camera lens (Fussell, 2019). Sexual spycamming[5] is also known as the 'creepshot' (Thompson, 2018).

'Spycamming' might be thought of as a modern incarnation of the 'peeping tom' and like other forms of DGSV such as 'upskirting', is often normalised in culture, such as the films *Disturbia* (2007), *Under the Skin* (2014), and *The Voyeurs* (2021) (Duff, 2018). But what is different about this modern incarnation is that, with the aid of modern technology, the perpetrator can record or live stream images across the globe in real time to be viewed by anyone with access (Thompson, 2018).

It is difficult to gauge the extent of the problem (inter)nationally as datasets are sparse. Perpetrators are from all social echelons, and likely to enact other forms of DGSV (Smith, 2019). Långström and Seto (2006) argue that voyeurism is one of the most prevalent crimes globally (although quality macrodatasets on which to base this claim have not been created), and 'spycam' and 'public' are increasingly popular in PornHub (2019) search terms. In some countries such as South Korea media reports even suggest the phenomenon is at epidemic proportions (Al Jazeera, 2018).

Spycamming can be profitable with purveyors of such materials making money from selling to specialised websites such as The Candid Zone. Other

---

5 As opposed to the use of CCTV to spy on for example, one's neighbours.

platforms such as SpyArchive.com charge members £9.96 per month (as of October 7, 2021) for access, a relatively low charge. Others such as Nude-Vista.com do not appear to buy material but use a web spider programme to browse the Internet methodically for photos and video galleries of spycam victims to upload to its own website. As with platforms dedicated to 'revenge porn' and 'upskirting', viewers on these Spycamming platforms have the opportunity to comment on, and rate, the images of the unsuspecting victims. Comments from viewers of shared sexual spycam images share similarities to those we have highlighted in Chapters 5–7. Themes such as sexual commodification, promiscuity, victim-blaming, male bonding and status affirmation, and craft*man*ship are common. As with other forms of DGSV, the impacts on victim-survivors can be profound with reports of some victims taking their own life (Smith, 2019).

Cyberflashing

As with some other forms of DGSV, there is also an historical dimension to cyberflashing; Herodotus cited incidents of flashing in *The Histories* (Waterfield, 1998, p. 119). However, the modern technological incarnation of cyberflashing involves perpetrators, usually (un)known men or boys, airdropping[6] (un)solicited so-called 'dick pics', 'hog shots', 'shaft shots', 'richard pics' (see the urbanthesaurus.com, 2021 for variations) to (un)suspecting women's (and gay men's) mobile devices in public spaces such a trains, cafés, workspaces, and educational settings (Law Commission, 2021; McGlynn & Johnson, 2021). Cyberflashing may also include posting pictures of men's genitals on social media platforms such as Facebook and Twitter, on online forums websites such as Redditt, some dating websites such as Match.com, and on dedicated gay forums such as GaySpeak. Incidences of anonymised 'twat shots', 'crotch shots', 'snatch snaps' (see the urbanthesaurus.com, 2021 for variations) and 'tit pics' being posted on such platforms appear to be much rarer, and the response by many (male) viewers is largely welcoming. Whilst for some the issue of non-consent in receiving an unsolicited image of another person's genitals may not be paramount, for most the non-consent element is an infringement.

Since the pandemic lockdowns, there has been a reported increase of a similar trend in so-called sexual Zoombombing, which involves (presumably men) intentionally disrupting virtual meetings on the teleconferencing platform Zoom with lewd or sexually explicit images or videos by so-called 'Zoombies'. For example, a meeting between Italian senators was briefly interrupted by a pornographic video of characters from Final Fantasy VII[7]

---

6 Airdropping refers to the use of AirDrop, an Apple service for file transferring between similar devices.

7 Final Fantasy VII is video game developed by Square, a Japanese video game company, that allows players to role-play battles and navigate terrains in 3D on a world map.

(Kaonga, 2022). What is different about this genre is that the targets are not always girls and women, and the images are not always explicitly 'dic pics' but instead it can involve indiscriminate posting or pornography to meetings or lessons, including those involving minors. Whilst some Zoombombing is reported to be by hackers, other instances are reported to be 'inside jobs' by students and workers as Zoom codes are passed around via email, text, Twitter, and other social media platforms (Dormehl, 2021).

Although cyberflashing can include (un)solicited images of genitals to (un)suspecting others in both online and offline settings, and some cases might involve consensual or welcome sharing of images, our primary focus here is on unsolicited images being sent to unsuspecting others. As such, we highlight the violation element of this form of DGSV in contrast to those receivers of 'dic pics' reporting them as 'sexy', 'funny' or discounting their significance as 'boring' (Smith, 2017). Our focus, then, is on the ways in which this form of DGSV reinforces, and reaffirms, male-dominated, phallocentric, penile-oriented, relationships and sexuality (Ringrose & Lawrence, 2018).

The recent UK Law Commission's *Reform of the Communications Offences* report (2021) suggests it is important to distinguish cyberflashing and its various manifestations from other forms of DGSV because the victim-survivor is not the subject in the image being shared – rather that is (usually) the perpetrator. However, it does share similarities with 'upskirting' and pornographic deepfakes' in that the victim-survivor is also unlikely to know the identity of the perpetrator, whereas the victim-survivors of 'revenge pornography' and 'sexual happy slapping' are, in most cases, aware of the identity of the perpetrator(s).

Cyberflashing is reported to be common; a relatively recent YouGov, UK (Smith, 2017) survey of 2,121 women and 1,738 men (aged 18–36) of British millennials[8] found that 46% of women reported being victim-survivors. The likelihood increases to 53% for those aged 18–24 years, compared to 36% of 31–36-year-olds. Only 22% of men admitted to sending one. Many women reported receiving their first explicit image when they were under 18 years of age. Unsurprisingly, victims and perpetrators reported different experiences with women describing receiving a 'dic pic', as gross (58%) or stupid (54%), and men believing sending one was sexy (44%) or funny (51%).

Like other forms of DGSV victims-survivors may experience a range of impacts as highlighted in previous chapters (also see McGlynn & Johnson, 2021 for specific violations related to this DGSV). Although the cyberflashing perpetrator may remain anonymous they may also remain socially proximate as Airdropping may only be used between devices close enough to establish a good Wi-Fi connection, such as across several rooms, adding an additional layer of abuse and threat to the victim's personal safety (Law

8 A person who was born between the mid-1980s and 2000s and who has grown up with, and is presumed to be reliant on, the internet.

Commission, 2021). Despite the harmful impacts, many countries around the globe do not have laws that (adequately) address this issue (McGlynn & Johnson, 2021), and, as we have noted in other chapters, there is an absence of international laws to tackle transnational violations (see Hearn & Hall, 2021 for more detailed discussion of this in relation to 'revenge pornography' and image-based sexual abuse).

Sexual happy slapping

One form of DGSV that appears less common as little data exists on prevalence rates, although just as harmful, is what may be termed 'sexual happy slapping'. Sexual happy slapping can be seen as a development of happy slapping (Andersson, Thapar-Björkert & Hearn, 2011), which developed in the 2000s with videoing and online distribution of physical assaults, mainly by young men. The origins of 'happy slapping' can be traced to television programmes such as 'Jackass' aired 2002–2007 (Chan et al., 2012). Happy slapping refers to the filming of (un)known others (typically on portable devices) being assaulted and then the video is edited by adding provocative titles before being circulated on platforms such as YouTube or via mobile devices (Harrison, 2018, Vesna, 2019).

Happy slapping is transnational with reports of its occurrence in (non-) European, Asian, North America, and other regions too (Chan et al., 2012). Whilst the vast majority of 'happy slapping' tends to be less (explicitly) sexually orientated, there have been reports of sexual attacks on both adolescent and adult women and men, although it would appear that women are predominantly the victims in groping videos for example, by men on public transport and other public spaces by individuals or groups (e.g., see Cooney, 2020; *Mail on Sunday*, 2005; *Metro*, 2007). Recordings of sexual assault are posted onto pornographic websites such as the fetish pornography platform Heavy-R that claims to offer free the world's most hardcore pornography. Whilst the authenticity of all the materials on such platforms may be questionable, they would appear popular given viewing numbers reach the hundreds of thousands. In this way, this form of sexual violence is treated as a spectacle recorded live and disseminated globally for the sexual pleasure of pornography-users (Kelly, 2015), contributing, like other forms of DGSV, to the normalisation of men's violence against women.

The distribution of the video online to social media platforms and to pornographic websites such as Heavy-R allows the harm to the victim-survivor to continue in perpetuity, after any physical harms may have subsided, through insulting comments, sexual objectification, and humiliation by (un)known others (Vesna, 2019) as well as through the lack of control over one's sexual autonomy, identity, and reputation. Thus, this form of DGSV combines more traditional forms of violence with cyberbullying. Indeed, we highlight similar overlaps between the on- and offline worlds in other forms of DGSV such as 'revenge pornography' and its relationship with domestic violence (see Hadley, 2017; Hearn & Hall, 2019; Refuge, 2020; Women's Aid, 2020).

Whilst some motivations for sexual happy slapping – such as entertainment and peer/homosocial status – are similar to those for other forms of DGSV, it would appear that with this form there is a greater emphasis on men's peer popularity through their use of direct physical violence, depictions of which may reverberate on and contribute to their online homosocial status (Macur & Schweber, 2012; Vesna, 2019).

Conclusion

Clearly there are various, perhaps many, further (un)known forms of DGSV, and we have discussed only some forms, and their derivatives, here. What is common to all of these, and others, is the question of the lack of consent, whether that is in the taking, making, dissemination, or receiving of explicit images. However, as we have noted, the element of (non-)consent varies between forms of DGSV. For example, in the sending of 'dic pics' or 'sexual zoombombing' consent is implied in the taking and sending of the image unless of course, coercion is involved. In this example, consent to receive is infringed, so too if the image is forwarded. However, in the latter case while some might presume that the perpetrator gets his 'just desserts', it is likely that many might not be so concerned about that, even while the secondary receiver of the forwarded image may not have given consent. In revenge porn, consent to take the image might have been given, but where the images are publicly disseminated, consent of the victim is violated. In upskirting, sexual spycamming, and sexual happy slapping, consent to take, distribute, and forward is not given, and indeed, consent to receive is also questionable, unless perhaps on dedicated websites for the distribution of such materials. In pornographic deepfakes, consent to take becomes blurry as the taking of the image may have been in a public space and (un)know to the person. Stolen images from social media sites used in the creation of deepfake pornography may have had initial consent, but of course, not when stolen, and then made into a sexual image or video, and disseminated to others.

Questions of consent can have implications for accountability of the perpetrator or for the victim-survivor. It can also have serious implications in prosecutions, the development of legislation, monitoring of posts on social media, and so on. We discuss many of these in Chapter 10 on socio-legal-technical considerations. But first we explore the wider implications of DGSV for workplaces, organisations, and public spaces.

References

Andersson, K., Thapar-Björkert, S., & Hearn, J. (2011) Mediated communications of violence – The example of happy slapping. *Journal of Children and Media*, *5*(2), 320–324.

Ajder, H., Patrini, G., Cavalli, F., & Cullen, L. (2019). The state of the art deefakes: Landscape, threats, and impact. *Deeptrace*. September. Retrieved from: https://regmedia.co.uk/2019/10/08/deepfake_report.pdf

Al Jazeera. (2018). 'Spycam' epidemic seizes South Korea's women. 22 October. Retrieved from: https://www.aljazeera.com/news/2018/10/epidemic-seizes-south-korea-women-181022042455511.html

Ayyub, R. (2018). I was the victim of a deepfake porn plot intended to silence me. *Huffington Post*. 21 November. Retrieved from: https://www.huffingtonpost.co.uk/entry/deepfake-porn_uk_5bf2c126e4b0f32bd58ba316

Banet-Weiser, S. (2021). Misogyny and the politics of misinformation. In H. Tumber & S. Waisbord (Eds.), *The Routledge companion to media disinformation and populism* (pp. 211–220). London: Routledge.

Chan, S., Khader, M., Ang, J., Tan, E., Khoo, K., & Chin, J. (2012). Understanding 'happy slapping'. *International Journal of Police Science & Management*, *14*(1), 42–57.

Citron, D. K., & Chesney, R. (2018). Deep fakes: A looming crisis for national security, democracy and privacy? *Lawfare*. 21 February. Retrieved from: https://perma.cc/L6B5-DGNR

Caldwell, M., Andrews, J. T. A., Tanay, T., & Griffin, L. D. (2020). AI-enabled future crime. *Crime Science*, *9*, 14. doi: 10.1186/s40163-020-00123-8.

Cooney, C. (2020). 'Crime against humanity' Girl, 16, 'gang raped by 30 men as suspects filmed attack in Red Sea resort hotel'. *The Sun*. 20 August. Retrieved from: https://www.thesun.co.uk/news/12458292/girl-gang-raped-men-hotel-red-sea-resort-filmed/

Deyan, G. (2021). How much of the internet is the dark web in 2021? Tech Jury. 21 September. Retrieved from: https://techjury.net/blog/how-much-of-the-internet-is-the-dark-web/

Dormehl, L. (2021). Inside job: Why Zoombombing isn't as random as you might think. *Digital Trends*, 7 February. Retrieved from: https://www.digitaltrends.com/features/zoombombing-inside-job/

Duff, S. (2018). *Voyeurism: A case study*. London: Palgrave Pivot.

Edwards, E., & Roche, B. (2016). Use of women's Facebook pictures on porn site investigated. *Irish Times*. 14 January. Retrieved from: https://www.irishtimes.com/news/crime-and-law/use-of-women-s-facebook-pictures-on-porn-site-investigated-1.2497092

Fussell, S. (2019). Airbnb has a hidden-camera problem. *The Atlantic*. 26 March. Retrieved from: https://www.theatlantic.com/technology/archive/2019/03/what-happens-when-you-find-cameras-your-airbnb/585007/

Gallagher, D. (2020). Moment horrified university student finds male housemate's iPhone hidden inside a metal box which was secretly filming her and her friends using the bathroom. *Mail Online*. 9 July. Retrieved from: https://www.dailymail.co.uk/news/article-8505813/Lincoln-university-student-finds-male-housemates-iPhone-recording-shared-bathroom.html

Glaser, A. (2016). The Scarlett Johansson bot is the robotic future of objectifying women. *Wired*. Retrieved from: https://www.wired.com/2016/04/the-scarlett-johansson-bot-signals-some-icky-things-about-our-future/

Gogarty, C. (2020). Man used hidden camera to film people using toilet. *Bristol Live*. 16 July. Retrieved from: https://www.bristolpost.co.uk/news/bristol-news/man-used-hidden-camera-film-4334605

Hadley, L. (2017). Tackling domestic abuse in a digital age. A recommendations report on online abuse by the all-party parliamentary group on domestic violence. Bristol: Women's Aid Federation of England.

Hao, K. (2021). Deepfake porn is ruining women's lives. Now the law may finally ban it. *Technology Review*. 12 February. Retrieved from: https://www.technologyreview. com/2021/02/12/1018222/deepfake-revenge-porn-coming-ban/

Harrison, A. (2018). A complete history of happy-slapping. *Vice*. 26 February. Retrieved from: https://www.vice.com/en/article/437b9d/a-complete-history-of-happy-slapping

Harwell, D. (2018). Scarlett Johansson on fake AI-generated sex videos: 'Nothing can stop someone from cutting and pasting my image'. *Washington Post*. 31 December. Retrieved form: https://www.washingtonpost.com/technology/2018/12/31/scarlett-johansson-fake-ai-generated-sex-videos-nothing-can-stop-someone-cutting-pasting-my-image/

Hearn, J., & Hall, M. (2019). *Physical violence and online violation: Concepts, terminologies and comparison*. Retrieved from: https://www.researchgate.net/publication/334391331_Physical_violence_and_online_violation_concepts_terminologies_and_comparison

Hearn, J., & Hall, M. (2021). The transnationalization of online sexual violation: The case of 'revenge pornography' as a theoretical and political problematic. In Y. R. Zhou, C. Sinding & D. Goellnicht (Eds.), *Sexualities, transnationalism, and globalization: New perspectives* (pp. 92–106). New York: Routledge.

Herodutus (1998). *The histories* (R. Waterfield, Trans.). Oxford: Oxford University Press.

Kaonga, G. (2022). Italian Senate meeting interrupted by 'final fantasy' porn video. *Newsweek*. 20 January. Retrieved from: https://www.newsweek.com/italian-senate-meeting-zoom-final-fantasy-porn-maria-laura-mantovani-video-1671170

Kelly, O. (2015). 'Rape as spectator sport and creepshot entertainment: Social media and the valorization of lack of consent.' *American Studies Journal*, ASJ Occasional Papers no. 10, 30 September. Retrieved from: op.asjournal.org/rape-as-spectator-sport-and-creepshot- entertainment

Kikerpill, K. (2020). Choose your stars and studs: The rise of deepfake designer porn. *Porn Studies*, 7(4), 352–356.

Långström, N., & Seto, M. C. (2006). Exhibitionistic and voyeuristic behavior in a Swedish national population survey. *Archives of Sexual Behavior*, 35(4), 427–435.

Law Commission. (2021). *Reform of the communications offences*. 21 July. Retrieved from: https://s3-eu-west-2.amazonaws.com/lawcom-prod-storage-11jsxou24uy7q/uploads/2021/07/Modernising-Communications-Offences-2021-Law-Com-No-399.pdf

Macur, J., & Schweber, N. (2012). Rape case unfolds on web and splits city. *The New York Times*. 16 December. Retrieved July 18 from: http://www.umdknes.com/knes287resources/Readings/11/R03a.pdf

Maddocks, S. (2020). 'A Deepfake Porn Plot Intended to Silence Me': Exploring continuities between pornographic and 'political'deep fakes. *Porn Studies*, 7(4), 415–423.

Mail on Sunday. (2005). Girl of 11 raped in 'happy slap' attack. 18 June. Retrieved from: https://www.dailymail.co.uk/news/article-352730/Girl-11-raped-happy-slap-attack.html

Mahdawi, A. (2019). An app using AI to 'undress' women offers a terrifying glimpse into the future. *The Guardian*. 29 June. Retrieved from: https://www.theguardian.com/commentisfree/2019/jun/29/deepnude-app-week-in-patriarchy-women#:~:text=It's%20 called%20DeepNude%20and%20it,about%20DeepNude%20catalyzed%20 widespread%20outrage

McGlynn, C., & Johnson, K. (2021). *Cyberflashing: Recognising harms, reforming laws.* Bristol: Bristol University Press.

Metro. (2007). *Teenage girls in 'happy slap' sex attack.* Retrieved from: https://metro. co.uk/2007/08/09/teenage-girls-in-happy-slap-sex-attack-604507/

Michael, T. (2016). Sex robots modelled on your favourite celebs set to take over the market, expert warns. *News.com.au.* 5 December. Retrieved from: https://www.news.com.au/technology/gadgets/sex-robots-modelled-on-your-favourite-celebs-set-to-take-over-the-market-expert-warns/news-story/c6d3b0754933a20f22851e663b822f3b

MrDeepFake. (2021). *DeepFake Creation Guide*; *DeepFake Making Process*; *DeepFakeLab 2.0.* Retrieved from: https://mrdeepfakes.com/

Öhman, C. (2020). Introducing the pervert's dilemma: A contribution to the critique of Deepfake Pornography. *Ethics and Information Technology, 22,* 133–140.

PornHub. (2019). The 2019 Year in Review – Pornhub Insights. 11 December. Retrieved from: https://www.pornhub.com/insights/2019-year-in-review

Quinion, M. (2020). Happy slapping. *Worldwide Words.* Retrieved from: https:// www.worldwidewords.org/turnsofphrase/tp-hap1.htm

Refuge. (2020). 72% of Refuge service users identify experiencing tech abuse. Retrieved from: https://www.refuge.org.uk/72-of-refuge-service-users-identify-experiencing-tech-abuse/

Ringrose, J., & Lawrence, E. (2018). Remixing misandry, manspreading and dick pics: Networked feminist humour on tumblr. *Feminist Media Studies, 18*(4), 686–704.

Selbie, T., & Williams, C. (2021). Deepfake pornography could become an 'epidemic', expert warns. *BBC.* 27 May. Retrieved from: https://www.bbc.com/news/uk-scotland-57254636

Sensity, A. I. (2021). *The state of deepfakes 2020: Updates on statistics and trends.* Retrieved from: https://sensity.ai/reports/

Smith, M. (2017). *YouGov, UK.* Retrieved from: https://yougov.co.uk/topics/politics/articles-reports/2018/02/15/four-ten-female-millennials-been-sent-dick-pic

Smith, N. (2019). South Korean woman commits suicide after doctor filmed her using spycam, reports say. *Telegraph.* 2 October. Retrieved from: https://www.telegraph. co.uk/news/2019/10/02/south-korean-woman-commits-suicide-doctor-filmed-using-spycam/

Solsman, J.E. (2020). Deepfake bot on Telegram is violating women by forging nudes from regular pics. *CNET.* 22 October. Retrieved from: https://www.cnet.com/news/privacy/deepfake-bot-on-telegram-is-violating-women-by-forging-nudes-from-regular-pics/

Telford, T. (2019). 'The world is not yet ready for DeepNude': Creator kills app that uses AI to fake naked images of women. *Washington Post.* 28 June. Retrieved from: https://www.washingtonpost.com/business/2019/06/28/the-world-is-not-yet-ready-deepnude-creator-kills-app-that-uses-ai-fake-naked-images-women/

Thompson, C. (2018). A media archaeology of the creepshot. *Feminist Media Studies, 18*(4), 560–574.

Topping, A. (2012). 'Parasite' porn websites stealing images and videos posted by young people. *The Guardian.* 22 October. Retrieved from: https://www.theguardian.com/technology/2012/oct/22/parasite-porn-websites-images-videos

Van Der Meer, E. (2020). 'PERV' CAUGHT Sheriff's office worker, 28, 'spied on female roommate by hiding camera in vent in her bedroom'. *The Sun.* 25 May. Retrieved July 18 from: https://www.thesun.co.uk/news/11706984/ sheriffs-office-worker-spied-on-female-roommate-hiding-camera-bedroom/

Vesna, B. (2019). Video-recording attacks (happy slapping) – A complex form of peer violence in digital era. In R. Celec (Ed.), *Challenges of modern society from different perspectives* (pp. 19–34). Hamburg: Verlag Dr. Kovač.

Wyllie, J. (2020). Voyeur jailed after fitting hidden camera in Aberdeen bar changing room to spy on 'unrequited crush'. *The Press and Journal.* 28 February. Retrieved July 18 from: https://www.pressandjournal.co.uk/fp/news/aberdeen/2039447/ voyeur-jailed-after-fitting-hidden-camera-in-aberdeen-bar-changing-room-to-spy-on-unrequited-crush/

Westerlund, M. (2019). The emergence of deepfake technology: A review. *Technology Innovation Management Review, 9*(11), 39–52.

Women's Aid. (2020). *Online and digital abuse.* Retrieved from: https://www. womensaid.org.uk/information-support/what-is-domestic-abuse/onlinesafety/

Part 3

Wider implications and responses

9 Wider implications for workplaces, organisations, and public spaces *with Charlotta Niemistö*

Introduction

Digital gender-sexual violations have many wider implications beyond the immediate harm and personal lives. They impact on home, family and households, and wider communities, as in intimate partner[1] violence (IPV) and digital intimate partner violence (DIPV), and more widely on education, social life, politics, leisure, and the worlds of work. In this chapter, we elaborate on some of these impacts, with a focus on work and workplaces, and also other institutional, organisational and 'non-work' times and places, such as associations, schools, colleges and universities, community facilities, political and social movement organising, religious organisations, and sport clubs – all of which clearly have their own online presence.

The huge technological changes of recent decades have made it possible for abuse to be easy, instantaneous, asynchronous, mobile, and ubiquitous, continue in perpetuity, and impact not only the intended target, but also others associated with them, for example, friends, colleagues, and employers (Arnold, 2014). This opens up possibilities and potentials for new sociotechnological forms of violation and abuse, at a distance, physically separated, that form part of and extend immediate interpersonal violence and abuse, with wider implications for all social, organisational, and public spheres.

---

1 The term, 'partner', within IPV has been problematised as meaning more than simply current sexual or romantic partner or spouse. For example, in the context of arranged marriages, a partner might not be considered a 'romantic' partner. 'Partner' can be extended to ex-partners, and in some cases situations where one person, a close friend, acquaintance or colleague, defines themselves as a partner while the other does not. Local, cultural dimensions can be important here, adding to the complexity of differential understandings of people in a 'romantic' relationship. Violence involving other family, intimate and friendship relations may sometimes raise related challenges and be relevant in analytical, policy and practice development. In some communities and contexts, women's sexuality and body are controlled further in the name of 'honour', such that the making of the private and the intimate in instances of IBSA and DGSV by family or community becomes a means to discredit and ostracise.

DOI: 10.4324/9781003138273-13

At the same time, despite many decades of concerted efforts to improve legal and policy responses to GBV, VAW and IPV by justice systems, enduring shortcomings have been shown, nationally and internationally, including detrimental treatment of racialised and other marginalised groups (e.g., LGBTIQA+ people, people living in poverty), as well as victim-survivors' ambivalence to formal justice systems (Gangoli, Bates & Hester, 2019; McGlynn & Westmarland, 2019). In response, a growing chorus of scholars and activists argues for an anti-carceral feminism (see Chapter 5), proposing alternatives to reliance on state justice systems (Méndez, 2020; Richie, 2015; Tolmie, 2018; also see Rackley et al., 2021) – with consequent implications for economy and civil society. In this move from relying primarily on established justice systems, other sites, such as education, leisure, community infrastructures, employment and workplaces can play a key role in survivor-centred healing and holding perpetrators accountable for DGSV.

Blurring boundaries

A key feature of DGSV is that it often transcends borders and boundaries, such as between private and public spheres, thus continuing feminist critiques of strict analytical separations of private and public domains (Elshtain, 1981; Hill Collins, 2000). Domestic and leisure spaces, work, workplaces and other organisations are all also becoming more complex, with contemporary social and technological changes. These include the routine use of digital technologies, the interplay of the online and the offline, blurring of the work/life distinction, transnational forms of working and organising, zero-hour contracts, and reduced trade unionisation, creating major challenges for all concerned.

Surveillance and violation by abusive partners, ex-partners, 'friends' and acquaintances can itself be enabled in part by changing relations and boundaries of both private (family/household)/public (work/employment) and offline/online worlds. For example, for many workers, there is little or no clear divide between work and personal life. Blurrings of private/public, home/work and work/life boundaries have been exacerbated by restrictions in relation to the COVID-19 pandemic which required many more workers to work remotely from home, along with the rising figures of IPV and DIPV across the globe with home-working during lockdowns (Evans, Lindauer & Farrell, 2020; Human Rights Watch, 2020; OECD, 2020; also see DeFrancesco Soto, 2020). Changes in working life wrought by COVID-19 restrictions are a starker manifestation of recent changes in working and organisational patterns for many people.

DGSV takes many forms, including cyberstalking, online surveillance by partners, Internet- and image-based abuse, 'revenge pornography', spycamming/creepshots, cyberflashing reputation abuse, abuse via banking technology (including abusive messages on bank statements via tiny transfers of money), as well as tracking, surveillance, hacking, (s)extortion, electronic sabotage, spycamming, spyware use of augmented reality technology, deepfakes and deepfake sex robots, doxing, and impersonation. Conventional, widely available technologies are certainly widely used, such as e-mail, the Internet, global positioning systems, spyware, video cameras, and online databases (Southworth et al., 2007). There are also increasing applications of even more sophisticated technologies, both those specifically for surveillance, and the Internet of Things (IoT) – with multiple devices, ranging from cars to kettles, with embedded sensors, software, and other technologies connected and exchanging data with other devices and systems over the Internet.

Organisational impacts of DIPV

In the light of these blurring boundaries, IPV, DIPV, and similar forms of violation are now often in part digital, with the digital and non-digital merging and reinforcing each other in some instances (Hall & Hearn, 2017; Jane, 2016; Phippen & Brennan, 2021; Powell & Henry, 2017). Among those experiencing IPV, many experience DIPV. Refuge (2020), the UK domestic violence charity, found in 2019 that 72% of their service users had experienced abuse through technology, and 85% of respondents surveyed by Women's Aid (2020) in 2015 reported that the abuse they received online from a (ex-) partner was part of a pattern of abuse experienced offline (Hadley, 2017). In extreme cases, DIPV may lead on to homicide or result in suicide.

Perpetrators of DIPV can use new tools to conduct their abuse but the types and impacts of behaviour are familiar. However, Fernet et al. (2019) assess that, as a distinct type of IPV, DIPV necessitates distinct research and policy responses. Similarly, Harris and Woodlock (2019) argue that, while "digital coercive control", as they name it, is a form of gendered violence that is "enacted alongside other forms of abuse (physical, sexual, psychological, emotional or financial abuse) and/or 'traditional' (in person) stalking [it] is unique because of its *spacelessness*" (p. 530, italics in original). Woodlock's (2017) survey with 152 IPV advocates and 46 victim-survivors found that new technologies were commonly used for stalking, and other digital abuses. IPV is no longer confined to the close proximity of perpetrator and victim-survivor. Indeed, it may be that, in many locations, DIPV is becoming a normalised part of IPV rather than the exception. Marganski and Melander (2018) note that young adults have the highest rates of technology use and can be at highest risk of IPV (see EU FRA, 2014a, 2014b), and thus DIPV.

While in recent years there has been a growing body of research literature on DIPV (Al-Alosi, 2017; Douglas, Harris & Dragiewicz, 2019; Dragiewicz et al., 2018; Duerksen & Woodin, 2019; Gámez-Guadix, Borrajo & Calvete, 2018; Henry, Flynn & Powell, 2020; Taylor and Xia, 2018), this has mainly been directed to personal and domestic life rather than to impacts on victim-survivors' capacity to carry out paid employment, education, sport, or similar activities outside the home (Langlois and Slane, 2017). DIPV has, until recently, seldom been taken up directly in research and policy studies on workplaces and other organisations.[2] For example, the Society for Human Resource Management (2013) estimates that, despite the clear risks to employers and their employees, around 65 percent of employers in the US do not have formal workplace policies for IPV (let alone DIPV), even whilst around a fifth of employers having experienced the impact of IPV in the past 12 months.

While employment and other public activities, such as education, voluntary work in the community, political organising or sport have the potential to provide some independent movement and networks for victim-survivors as well as potential pathways for leaving a violent partner (Patton, 2003; Rothman et al., 2007), blurring of boundaries between work and home, and online/offline IPV, further entraps women within the control of their abusive partners. Being employed or active in similar public activities can sometimes provide some degree of protection against IPV (Beecham, 2009, 2014; Walby & Towers, 2018), as well as providing community contexts that play a significant role in workers' lives, and at times act as a means of surviving and coping. Thus, extra-domestic organisations, most obviously but not only workplaces, can be important in efforts to prevent IPV, protect victim-survivors, and challenge perpetrators. On the other hand, as well as providing some refuge for some victim-survivors of DIPV, new patterns and dynamics of working and public life can actually extend the reach of perpetrators to exert power and control – with lack of physical distance from the perpetrator during work time and lack of possibilities for colleagues to observe a victim-survivor's decreasing level of well-being. Likewise, prevention or impeding of work and/or study is a form of economic abuse, resulting in the victim-survivor's deprivation of current or future economic or financial resources.

Personal mobile phones, email accounts, social media platforms and other ICTs are commonly used for work and social purposes, and can also easily be used by abusive partners to monitor and contact victim-survivors. For example, when perpetrators are present while their partners are working or studying from home, they can listen to their partners' telephone calls and video meetings, question their partners about their behaviour and relationships with work or study colleagues, and distract and intimidate them during such interactions in ways that undermine their performance. Victim-survivors of image-based sexual violations also report perpetrators forwarding explicit images of them, including deepfakes (see Ayyub, 2018, for an

2 Violence and the world of work may seem, to some, worlds apart or, to others, inextricably connected. Either way, Violence Studies, on the one hand, and Workplace, Organisation, Education and Leisure Studies, on the other, have often not developed in close association. Strong tendencies towards disciplinary silos mean that different researchers tend to focus on violence to those focusing on workplaces, employment, education, organisations, and leisure. Yet when one reflects on how organisations work, and how violence and violation are organised, it is easy to see many interconnections – from organisations created to enact systematic violence, to use of violence instrumentally by corporations, to violent organisational sub-cultures, onto local, immediate micro-aggressions, and everyday normalisation of ageism, homophobia, racism, misogyny, sexism, and xenophobia (Hearn and Parkin, 2001).

example), to their boss and colleagues, so they may experience workplace harassment and/or even resign due to stress and embarrassment when facing their co-workers (SHRM, 2014). Perpetrators may contact colleagues and managers, who may be key social contacts for victim-survivors outside the home and immediate personal relationships, to gather or share information about their victim, identify their whereabouts or activity, besmirch their reputation, disrupt victim-survivors' work and contact with others, as well as to instil confusion and fear. And, the increasing number of spy camera instances reported (see, for example, Fussell, 2019; May & Lee, 2018), where women were recorded in work toilets and changing rooms, and other public and private spaces means some women avoid/are now cautious about using these space for fear of ending up on pornographic websites.

A specific example reported by Crowe (2016) from an interview she conducted with the victim-survivor, Tara Dozier, concerns how Dozier's ex-partner posted explicit images of her to a dedicated revenge pornography website along with her personal contact information, home address and employer. Dozier's explicit images have been viewed and shared extensively online thousands of times by co-workers, managers, business partners and customers, and this is reported to have impacted both her and her employer: "She's received death threats. Pedophiles [sic.] have been invited to attack her children. She lost her job" (Crowe, 2016, p. 1).

The impacts of DIPV may include time away from public activities due to injuries, emotional stress at home and work, time spent seeking help from health and legal professionals, and needing to move locality to escape or avoid the perpetrator (Beecham, 2009, 2014; Harris & Woodlock, 2019; Walby, 2004; Woodlock, 2017). DIPV may disrupt work, education and training and hinder the victim-survivor's chances of securing future employment. DIPV brings multiple harms, to individual employees, work communities, and businesses. There are parallels here with, as well as differences from, the growing online abuse against journalists, politicians and others in the public eye (see Chapter 5), and safety procedures and codes for their support and protection (also see Chapter 8).

DGSV in organisations and public spaces

DIPV is not the only form of digital violation that can take place in and affect work, workplaces, education and similar organisational settings. There are few forms or instances of DGSV that could not, in some way, be relevant to organisations and colleagues, instructors, supervisors and managers there, and that require engagement from these people. Recordings of telephone calls, let alone SMSs, emails, images and videos, can always be re-circulated onto, say, colleagues, clients and supervisors at the time of posting or subsequently, even years later. Also, as noted, for many such contexts, the boundary between work and personal life is not clear cut, so that drawing neat boundaries around (the walls of) many organisations has become nigh on impossible.

Digital violation may be posted outside work or study hours, away from those premises, and sent to devices away from work, but that apparent physical distance can be irrelevant, in terms of effects on the recipient(s) and maybe many others. This can relate to work and similar situations in variable ways, for example, at the physical workplace or organisation, during organisational time, say, spreading unfavourable rumours through intranets; within physical organisations, but not during work or organisational time, when malicious messages, images, or information is sent initially to or forwarded onto colleagues or clients, say, in the evening or at the weekend; during work or organisational time, but not in the physical place, for example, sending abusive, threatening digital messages when someone is working elsewhere on the tasks for which they are employed. DGSV can also be enacted in neither physical workplaces and organisations nor during working or organisational time, for example, malicious messages, images, often through social media, or information with either organisationally relevant content or personal content with impacts on work or organisation concerned; and also outside organisational time, and/or the physical place and/or is not directly relevant, but then has implications and effects for the organisation, in terms of, for example, collegial morale, the victim-survivor's personal reputation, or the support the victim survivor receives from the workplace managers and colleagues.

Posts on dedicated revenge porn and other websites have been found to contain the victim-survivor's personal information such as their full name, hometown/city, profession, employer, social media pages, telephone numbers, and email address, presumably so that others could damage the victim-survivor's reputation at work or study or similar. Such postings are becoming increasingly common and the impact for victim-survivors is often discussed on public forums such as Reddit and Quora where devastating and life-altering effects are reported. These include humiliation, shame and embarrassment with colleagues, personal and organisational reputation ruination, along with lost time, reduced productivity at work, and difficulties securing other work as those images are there for anyone to see for perpetuity (Lichter, 2013). The Society for Human Resource Management (SHRM) (2014) reports the increasing disclosure of personal information specifically to damage the victim-survivor's professional reputation and career, which in turn can have lasting corporate reputational effects. DGSV impacts on victim-survivors' reputations in the context of organisations and stakeholders, in terms of, for example, whether it is a supportive or woman-friendly college, sports club, social venue or employer.

In some cases, the victim-survivor may be unaware of messages or pictures sent by the perpetrator to colleagues or organisational contacts, even for extended periods of time, thus raising the question of how this is to be handled ethically, confidentially, and with justice. A situation where the victim-survivor could be humiliated and stigmatised within the organisational community, without even knowing of it, calls for a highly empathetic approach from colleagues and managers, in informing the victim-survivor-employee in a sensitive way. Immediate measures need to be enacted to retain a safe environment, including specific methods depending on whether the perpetrator is a member, at the edges (as with a customer) or outside of the work organisation and community.

The experience of being a victim-survivor can thus be affected, asynchronously, by the immediate situation and ICT context, including what happens before, during and after receipt of or learning for the first time of the abuse. In some workplaces and other organisations, access to ICT devices themselves, for perpetrating, experiencing or learning of digital abuse, might be restricted to different times of the day, such as during breaks. More specifically, different kinds of work and workplaces themselves vary from situations where the employee lives in the workplace, as with, say, domestic workers or agricultural workers in tied accommodation, or where work and home blur as in some family businesses, remote working or homeworking, through to where there are strict(er) separations of working time and of workplace, and where employees work fixed hours, work alone or do piece-rate work, as in, say, delivery work.

Such differing situations clearly raise differential boundary conditions and impacts on privacy, autonomy and safety, as well as in some cases the likely prospects for justice and the balance of power between relevant actors. Interlinked with these different contexts are further variations in different relations of the people and groupings to the organisation(s) concerned at or across boundaries. Thus, DGSV can involve:

- One or more of the perpetrators and/or (in)direct victim-survivors who may or may not be members of the organisation concerned;
- An 'external' perpetrator, including those in another organisation, customers or clients, who may abuse an 'internal' victim-survivor;
- An 'internal' perpetrator who may abuse an 'external' victim-survivor, including those in another organisation, customers or clients;
- An 'internal' perpetrator who may abuse an 'internal' victim-survivor, who may themselves be partners, ex-partners or in some other close relationship.

All these possibilities above can be complicated by differing, and sometimes contradictory, power dynamics between the perpetrator(s) and the victim-survivor(s) in and around the organisation concerned. The power dynamics of perpetrator-victim-survivor relation often reproduce and reinforce existing power differentials in the organisation or wider society, as, for example, when a relatively more senior man abuses, through DGSV, a relatively more junior woman. Alternatively, the perpetrator-victim-survivor relation may sometimes, in a sense, challenge, or at least work along a different vector from existing organisational and/or societal power differentials, as when a relatively more junior person abuses, through DGSV, a relatively more senior person. It is thus possible for dominant *societal* power differentials to be complicated, or contradicted, by relative *organisational* power and position, which in turn may be complicated by the *perpetrator-victim-survivor* relation. These possible dynamics and complications of DGSV in organisations are comparable to those that may operate with workplace harassment and bullying more generally.

DGSV can impact on organisational, as well as personal, security. Perpetrators may threaten security by guessing or forcing the victim–survivor to disclose passwords to work-related, associational or other organisational accounts, mobile and other electronic devices, with both personal and organisational consequences. Perpetrators may harass or intimidate with electronic messages and online posts and (threaten to)publicly disclose sensitive and/or intimate information to their colleagues. Such actions pose threats to both individual and corporate security (MacQuarrie et al., 2019). The ongoing impact of DGSV can be further heightened in organisational cultures that embody patriarchal or *laissez-faire* norms, by inappropriate organisational responses, organisational avoidance or a total lack of response and support (Ågotnes et al., 2018).

Data security breaches are amongst the top threats for organisations, and can include severe financial costs (Ponemon Institute, 2020). Where such breaches include members', employees' and customers' personal data, there is an increased risk of identity theft. Identity theft can result in employees taking time away from work to restore their identity, losing customer loyalty, missed business or development opportunities, and reputational damage as a security risk organisation. The risk of reputational damage from security breaches may impact on colleagues and employees (e.g., job satisfaction, well-being), customers (e.g., quality of the product), partners and stakeholders (e.g., organisational commitment) (Crowe, 2016; Kerrbach & Mignonac, 2006).

Policy and practice

Preventing and dealing with DGSV is a strategic organisational issue, a matter of organisational cultures respecting individual integrity, and an operational question in terms of rules, regulations and processes for support and prevention. All this is important for victim-survivors, perpetrators, colleagues and the whole organisational community. This is clearly important in work organisations, but it is also relevant, perhaps in more contingent ways, in 'non-work' organisations. A key question here is the extent of the relevant organisation's responsibility and accountability. For example, does a sports club, a religious organisation, a political party, and so on have a responsibility to address the DGSV experienced by or perpetrated by a member? Even if almost all organisations might be advised to consider their policies and practices in relation to DGSV, there are often unclear responsibilities in some of these wider organisational environments and scenarios we are discussing. Thus, while much of our discussion focuses on the responsibilities of employers and work communities, in the current state of practice it relates more unevenly to the situation in many other kinds of organisations and the recognition and practice of responsible leadership there.

Well-formulated organisational policies and practices can assist the long process of resistance against violence and abuse (e.g., Lewis & Marine, 2019; Lewis, Marine & Kenney, 2018). Formalised polices may include those addressing security concerns, employment contracts and agreements, disciplinary proceedings, job-protected leave for medical and legal proceedings, awareness-raising, training members of staff to be contact points for victim-survivors, training to identify victim-survivors and avoid tragedies, as well as working with other organisations such as support organisations, emergency services, and legal professionals. With the varying challenging conditions, organisations need to develop, from the very top, strategic organisational policy guidelines and leadership on safe working environments (Austin, 2021), rather than relying on one-size-fits-all and over-simplified procedures. Addressing these issues can mean wholesale organisational cultural change to create violation-free organisations (Hearn & Parkin, 2001), with clear policy leadership and zero tolerance of violence, bullying, harassment and DGSV, and high levels of organisational trust that victim-survivors will be taken seriously. Policy action involves positive and proactive measures:

- Monitoring the *prevalence* of DGSV in its multiple forms;
- *Preventive* measures, for example, staff training and information-circulation on DGSV and its changing forms, in line with the pursuit of human dignity and safety from violence and potential violence;
- *Protection* of (potential) victim-survivors, for example, data protection for those concerned, and establishing contact points and dedicated roles, with relevant expertise, similarly in keeping with the pursuit of human dignity and safety from violence and potential violence;
- *Disciplining*, and, in the context of the workplace, applying disciplinary procedures, as well as rehabilitation of perpetrators, as part of justice in stopping and dealing with DGSV;
- *Provision* of services for (potential) victim-survivors, that respects privacy and autonomy for victim-survivors, as well as for bystanders, colleagues and perpetrators;
- Coherent *overall policy* and practice development for the whole organisation and its members, including ensuring, where relevant, human resource management, general management and supervision are well-informed, developing *partnerships* with stakeholders with relevant expertise, and attending to gender, racialised and other power dynamics in DGSV, in seeking to redress imbalances of power within and across organisations.[3]

For example, SHRM (2014) suggests that the work employer:

- Speaks with the employee about the incident as soon as possible to let the employee know that the company is aware of the situation and supports them;

---

3 These seven italicised Ps are drawn from UniSAFE, 2021.

- Provides the employee with material support and contact information about support organisations;
- Ensures the employee's safety and online security; and
- Limits the impact in and for the workplace, regarding maximum confidentiality, warnings and disciplinary measures against further disclosure.

Having said all this, formal policies alone can often have limited effects on well-being, or be only partially implemented, as informal cultures, attitudes, and support from colleagues and leadership can be more significant for well-being in day-to-day organisational life. Employers and similar leaderships have a responsibility for setting the overall tone of the culture, and for making clear that DGSV is a misuse of ICTs and employees' and members' time, that damages well-being, security and morale, and that will be dealt with and not tolerated. Moreover, consideration needs to be given to possible unintended consequences of placing DGSV into occupational, employee, health or well-being framings, and how these relate to social justice, human rights, anti-violence, or feminist framings.

Implication for specific groupings in organisations

Policy and practice also need to be developed in relation to specific groupings within and beyond the organisation, specifically: direct victim-survivors; perpetrators; colleagues of victim-survivors and/or perpetrators, as relevant; instructors, supervisors, managers and board members; as well as other stakeholders. We briefly consider these groups in turn.

Direct victim-survivors: in providing support, it is advisable to connect with established and expert 'victim-survivor support' services, including some that are themselves online. In terms of internal organisational process, informed consent for victim-survivors regarding pursuit of a legal case against a perpetrator needs to be taken very seriously, as does the minimising of further harm and further invasion of privacy.

Perpetrators: while there is undoubted value in taking a victimological approach, a shortcoming is that it can play down or even render invisible the perpetrators. This can lead to policies and practices which focus on supporting members who are victim-survivors without acknowledging that, amongst colleagues, there may also be perpetrators. Members may use their organisational time and resources to perpetrate DGSV against those who may work in the same or a different organisation. In dealing with perpetrators, and potential perpetrators, most workplaces will already have general disciplinary procedures, including a system of formal warnings, that can be built upon. Such disciplinary procedures need to be reviewed to include restricting/preventing a perpetrator's access to ICT, and, if warranted, dismissal. Very importantly, some business sectors, most obviously ICT, technology, engineering, design and social media sectors, have further responsibilities to counter DGSV, as, for example, through 'Coercive control resistant design'

(Nuttall et al., 2019), whereby technological design takes on means to block coercive uses.

Colleagues and co-members: DGSV can also (directly) involve multiple colleagues, for example, as group experience of or collusion in humiliation, as in misogynist forms of so-called canteen or locker room cultures (Curry, 1991; Gregory, 2009), and individual victim-survivors can suffer multiple forms of violation, thus adding to power imbalances. Colleagues can be involved in a variety of ways, as indirect victim-survivors, as supporters of direct victim-survivors, reporters of others' abuse, as bystanders, even as colluding with perpetrators. They may be approached by the perpetrator to gather or spread information about the victim-survivor. Being a colleague in these situations can have major effects, including 'triggering' and reactivating earlier experiences of abuse, which can lead to decreased work capacity for the colleague(s) and, thus, affect entire teams and units. This may raise what may seem novel demands for teamwork, organisational collaboration, communality and collegial relationality. Such more collective and even communal situations can interact in complex ways, in and with, say, teamwork relations.

Supervisors, managers, leaders, board members, entrepreneurs and owners: these groups have a special responsibility to deal with DGSV and its impacts, in developing strategy, policy and culture, and in terms of organisations and businesses as legal entities. This includes being fully trained on the topic, being cognisant of gender and other power dynamics, observing data protection for those concerned, and avoidance of conflicts of interest. Many organisations and legal regimes are increasingly specifying policies on data protection and storage, and on the uses and possible misuses of work-based or similar ICTs for non-work purposes. There are also sometimes complex inter-organisational relations to deal with, when, for example, a member of another organisation (A) with which there is collaboration perpetrates DGSV against a member of the collaborating organisation (B), and so the situation involves more formal organisational connections and processes, even across international borders. Managers and supervisors themselves can be victim-survivors. This can be invisible in the organisation yet have serious consequences for the unit or organisation they lead in the form of decreased leadership capacity. Managers can also be perpetrators, so appropriate accountable policy and practice needs to be in place when DGSV is alleged or demonstrated (see Roofeh, 2021).

Furthermore, if the digital abuse is perpetrated from an employee's place of work or from employer-issued devices, the organisation may be liable, depending on the jurisdiction, for the action of their employees (Ryan, 2016). Depending on the judicial context, plaintiffs could argue for the ethical and legal responsibility of organisations under doctrine of *respondeat superior* whereby the organisation is responsible for their employees' actions (Brazzano, 2020). Joshua Dale, a specialist Australian lawyer in the field (Ryan, 2016, p. 1), suggests that:

> if an incident of revenge porn occurred in a workplace setting and injury is suffered, the employer would potentially be exposed to a claim

under workers' compensation provisions … if successful, could result in damages paid for any psychological injury suffered. Compensation can include economic loss, medical expenses and lump sum compensation … In at least one case of revenge porn, more than $30,000 in damages was paid as a result of the significant embarrassment, anxiety and distress suffered by the complainant as a result of the defendant sharing the images.

A transnational coda

All the discussion in this chapter needs to be understood in terms of the changing nature of public space and public domains which in many contexts is now both inherently virtual and characteristically transnational. DGSV is no longer local, or even national, in its spread, but can operate across borders, cultures, legal regimes, religions, nationalities, racialisations, languages, perhaps especially so with the increasing visualisation of media, culture and communication (Hearn and Hall, 2021).

Thus, for example, in terms of working life, a particular challenge is the impact of transnational forms of working and for employing organisations, global corporations, transnational social movements and international NGOs, operating within different (inter)national jurisdictions, whereby policy and practice may become a cross-border, inter-organisational concern, including in some cases engagement with international service providers. This is especially important for employers operating transnationally in multiple jurisdictions, given civil laws and penalties are likely to differ across territories. Even if liability is not pursued, accusations against an employee may expose the employer to reputational damage or other unwelcome consequences (Brazzano, 2020). Likewise, IT, Human Resource Management and legal departments need to ensure their organisation is adequately protected from such transnational digital violence and abuse.

All of this is partly a question of DGSVs in and across different societal, and indeed legal, contexts, but it also concerns the development of new forms of transnational cultural, mediatised, and hybridised spaces – which themselves may be used for violation in new and more complex ways, across language and culture.

Conclusion

We have examined the manifestations and implications of DGSV in a range of organisational and public contexts, with a particular focus on DIPV. Focusing on the specific context of the workplace, it has revealed the complex matrix of experiences and responsibilities involved when DGSV occurs in work or similar environments. In most cases of DGSV, the perpetrator(s) and victim-survivor(s) are likely to be involved in some form of work or working environment, and so the impacts and implications of DGSV are likely to manifest at least in part within work and organisational life. Likewise, the majority of working environments are themselves likely to be impacted by DGSV, even when this is not explicitly acknowledged in the work community. As a result, leaders of work and other organisations have an important role to play in responding to and preventing DGSV amongst their employees, clients and indeed in their collaborations with other organisations.

References

Ågotnes, K. W., Einarsen, S. V., Hetland, J., & Skogstad, A. (2018). The moderating effect of laissez-faire leadership on the relationship between co-worker conflicts and new cases of workplace bullying: a true prospective design. *Human Resource Management Journal, 28*(4), 555–568.

Al-Alosi, H. (2017). Cyber-violence: Digital abuse in the context of domestic violence. *University of New South Wales Law Journal, 40*(4), 1573–1603.

Arnold, M. S. (2014). United States: Revenge porn: A disturbing picture. *Mondaq.* 7 August. Retrieved from: https://www.mondaq.com/unitedstates/discrimination-disability-sexual-harassment/333158/revenge-porn-a-disturbing-picture

Austin, K. (2021). Firms told to look out for domestic abuse signs. *BBC News.* Retrieved from: https://www.bbc.com/news/business-55644222

Ayyub, R. (2018). I was the victim of a deepfake porn plot intended to silence me. *Huffington Post.* 21 November. Retrieved from: https://www.huffingtonpost.co.uk/entry/deepfake-porn_uk_5bf2c126e4b0f32bd58ba316

Beecham, D. (2009). *The impact of intimate partner abuse on women's experiences of the workplace: A qualitative study,* Doctoral thesis. Warwick University, Coventry.

Beecham, D. (2014). An exploration of the role of employment as a coping resource for women experiencing intimate partner abuse. *Violence and Victims, 29*(4), 594–606.

Brazzano, R. (2020). Zoombombing, sexting and revenge porn, oh my! *New York Law Journal* 10 June. Retrieved from: https://www.law.com/newyorklawjournal/2020/06/10/zoombombing-sexting-and-revenge-porn-oh-my/?slreturn=20200702090539

Crowe, M. (2016). '55,000 people have seen me naked': A story of 'revenge porn' and the lawyers who are trying to stop it. *Puget Sound Business Journal.* 5 August. Retrieved from: https://www.bizjournals.com/seattle/blog/techflash/2016/08/55-000-people-have-seen-me-naked-a-story-of.html

Curry, T. J. (1991). Fraternal bonding in the locker room: A profeminist analysis of talk about competition and women. *Sociology of Sport Journal, 8*(3), 119–135.

DeFrancesco Soto, V. M. (2020). America's recovery from the 2020 "Shecession": Building a female future of childcare and work. Texas: LBJ School of Public Affairs. Retrieved from: https://repositories.lib.utexas.edu/handle/2152/83388

Douglas, H., Harris, B. A., & Dragiewicz, M. (2019). Technology-facilitated domestic and family violence: Women's experiences. *British Journal of Criminology, 59*(3), 551–570.

Dragiewicz, M., Burgess, J., Matamoros-Fernández, A., Salter, M., Suzor, N. P., Woodlock, D., & Harris, B. (2018). Technology facilitated coercive control: Domestic violence and the competing roles of digital media platforms. *Feminist Media Studies, 18*(4), 609–625.

Duerksen, K. N., & Woodin, E. M. (2019). Technological intimate partner violence: Exploring technology-related perpetration factors and overlap with in-person intimate partner violence. *Computers in Human Behavior, 98*, 223–231.

Elshtain, J. B. (1981). *Public man, private woman: Women in social and political thought.* Princeton, NJ: Princeton University Press.

EU Agency for Fundamental Rights (FRA). (2014a). *Violence against women: An EU wide survey - main results report.*

EU Agency for Fundamental Rights (FRA). (2014b). *Violence against women: An EU wide survey - survey methodology, sample and fieldwork.*

Evans, M. L., Lindauer, M., & Farrell, M. E. (2020). A pandemic within a pandemic — Intimate partner violence during Covid-19. *The New England Journal of Medicine.* 16 September. Retrieved from: https://www.nejm.org/doi/full/10.1056/NEJMp2024046

Fernet, M., Lapierre, A., Hebert, M., & Cousineau, M. M. (2019). A systematic review of literature on cyber intimate partner victimization in adolescent girls and women. *Computers in Human Behavior, 100*, 11–25. doi:10.1016/j.chb.2019.06.005

Fussell, S. (2019). Airbnb has a hidden-camera problem. *The Atlantic.* 26 March. Retrieved from: https://www.theatlantic.com/technology/archive/2019/03/what-happens-when-you-find-cameras-your-airbnb/585007/

Gámez-Guadix, M., Borrajo, E., & Calvete, E. (2018). Partner abuse, control and violence through internet and smartphones: Characteristics, evaluation and prevention. *Papeles del Psicólogo, 39*(3), 218–227.

Gangoli, G., Bates, L., & Hester, M. (2019). What does justice mean to black and minority ethnic (BME) victims/survivors of gender-based violence? *Journal of Ethnic and Migration Studies, 46*(15), 3119–3135.

Gregory, M. (2009). Inside the locker room: Male homosociability in the advertising industry. *Gender Work and Organization, 16*(3), 323–347.

Hadley, L. (2017). *Tackling domestic abuse in a digital age. A Recommendations Report on Online Abuse by the All-Party Parliamentary Group on Domestic Violence.* Bristol: Women's Aid Federation of England.

Hall, M., & Hearn, J. (2017). *Revenge pornography: Gender, sexualities and motivations.* Abingdon: Routledge.

Harris, B. A., & Woodlock, D. (2019). Digital coercive control: Insights from two landmark domestic violence studies. *British Journal of Criminology, 59*(3), 530–550.

Hearn, J., & Hall, M. (2021). The transnationalization of sexual violation: The case of "revenge pornography" as a theoretical and political problematic. In R. Y. Zhou, C. Sinding & D. Goellnicht (Eds.), *Sexualities, transnationalism, and globalization: New perspectives* (pp. 92–106). New York: Routledge.

Hearn, J., & Parkin, W. (2001). *Gender, sexuality and violence in organizations.* London: Sage.

Henry, N., Flynn, A., & Powell, A. (2020). Technology-facilitated domestic and sexual violence: A review. *Violence Against Women, 26*(15-16), 1828–1854.

Hill Collins, P. (2000). *Black feminist thought* (2nd ed.). New York: Routledge.

Human Rights Watch. (2020). Women face rising risk of violence during Covid-19. 3 July. Retrieved from: https://www.hrw.org/news/2020/07/03/women-face-rising-risk-violence-during-covid-19

Jane, E. (2016). *Misogyny online: A short (and brutish) history.* London: Sage.

Kerrbach, O., & Mignonac, K. (2006). How organisational image affects employee attitudes. *Human Resources Management Journal, 14*(4), 76–88.

Langlois, G., & Slane, A. (2017). Economies of reputation: The case of revenge porn. *Communication and Critical/Cultural Studies*, *14*(2), 120–138.

Lewis, R., & Marine, S. (Eds.). (2019). Special issue, Transforming campus cultures: Activism to end gender-based violence. *Violence Against Women*, 25(11), 1283–1289. https://doi.org/10.1177/1077801219844598

Lewis, R., Marine, S., & Kenney, K. (2018). 'I get together with my friends and try to change it': Young feminist students resist 'laddism', 'rape culture' and 'everyday sexism'. *Journal of Gender Studies*, 27(1), 56–72.

Lichter, S. (2013). Unwanted exposure: Civil and criminal liability for revenge porn hosts and posters. *JOLT Digest: Harvard Journal of Law and Technology*. 27 May. Retrieved from http://jolt.law.harvard.edu/digest/privacy/unwanted-exposure-civil-and-criminal-liability-for-revenge-porn-hosts-and-posters

May, T., & Lee, S. (2018). Is there a spy camera in that bathroom? In Seoul, 8,000 workers will check. *The New York Times*. 3 September. Retrieved from: https://www.nytimes.com/2018/09/03/world/asia/korea-toilet-camera.html

McGlynn, C., & Westmarland, N. (2019). Kaleidoscopic justice: Sexual violence and victim-survivors' perceptions of justice. *Social & Legal Studies*, *28*(2), 179–201.

MacQuarrie, B., Scott, K., Lim, D., Olszowy, L., Saxton, M. D., & MacGregor, J. (2019). Understanding domestic violence as a workplace problem. In R. J. Burke & A. M. Richardsen (Eds.), *Increasing occupational health and safety in workplaces: Individual, work and organizational factors* (pp. 93–114). Cheltenham: Edward Elgar.

Marganski, A., & Melander, L., (2018). Intimate partner violence victimization in the cyber and real world: Examining the extent of cyber aggression experiences and its association with in-person dating violence. *Journal of Interpersonal Violence*, *33*(7), 1071–1095.

Méndez, X. (2020). Beyond Nassar: A transformative justice and decolonial feminist approach to campus sexual assault. *Frontiers: A Journal of Women Studies*, *41*(2), 82–104.

Nuttall, L., Evans, J., Franklin, M., & James, S. B. (2019). *Coercive control resistant design: The key to safer technology*. IBM Corporation. Retrieved from: https://www.ibm.com/blogs/policy/wp-content/uploads/2020/05/CoerciveControl-ResistantDesign.pdf

OECD. (2020). Women at the core of the fight against COVID-19 crisis. 1 April. Retrieved from: https://www.oecd.org/coronavirus/policy-responses/women-at-the-core-of-the-fight-against-covid-19-crisis-553a8269/

Patton S. (2003). *Pathways: How women leave violent men*. Hobart, Tasmania: Government of Tasmania.

Phippen, A., & Brennan, M. (2021). *Sexting and revenge pornography: Legislative and social dimensions of a modern digital phenomenon*. London: Routledge.

Ponemon Institute. (2020). *Cybersecurity in the remote work era: A global risk report*. October. Retrieved from: https://www.keepersecurity.com/en_GB/ponemon2020.html?campaignid=386642075&adgroupid=1207264219120960&adid=&hsa_acc=2895762531&hsa_cam=11384568876&hsa_grp=1207264219120960&hsa_ad=&hsa_src=s&hsa_tgt=kwd-75454345750388:loc-188&hsa_kw=%2-Bponemon&hsa_mt=e&hsa_net=adwords&hsa_ver=3&msclkid=fb2a4ac563151b3c40552a4b1df0c550&utm_source=bing&utm_medium=cpc&utm_campaign=B2B%3A%20Search%20-%20Ponemon%20-%20EN%20-%20EMEA&utm_term=%2Bponemon&utm_content=Ponemon%20-%20Broad

Powell, A., & Henry, N. (2017). *Sexual violence in a digital age*. Houndmills: Palgrave Macmillan.

Refuge. (2020). 72% of Refuge service users identify experiencing tech abuse. Retrieved from: http://www.refuge.org.uk/72-of-refuge-service-users-identify-experiencing-tech-abuse/

Rackley, E., McGlynn, C., Johnson, K., Henry, N., Flynn, A., Powell, A., & Gavey, N. (2021). Seeking justice and redress for victim-survivors of image-based sexual abuse. *Feminist Legal Studies.* doi: 10.1007/s10691-021-09460-8.

Richie, B. E. (2015). Reimagining the movement to end gender violence: Anti-racism, prison abolition, women of color feminisms, and other radical visions of justice. *University of Miami Race & Social Justice Law Review, 5*(2), 257–273.

Roofeh, A. (2021). Many new solutions to workplace sexual harassment in a post #MeToo era, but will they do the trick? In G. Chandra & I. Erlingsdóttir (Eds.), *The Routledge handbook of the politics of the #MeToo movement* (pp. 199–220). London: Routledge.

Rothman, E. F., Hathaway, J., Stidsen, A., & de Vries, H. F. (2007). How employment helps female victims of intimate partner violence: A qualitative study. *Journal of Occupational Health Psychology, 12*(2), 136–143.

Ryan, E. (2016). Revenge porn and workplace implications. *Lawyers Weekly.* 7 November. Retrieved from: https://www.lawyersweekly.com.au/sme-law/19899-revenge-porn-and-workplace-implications

Society for Human Resource Management. (2013). The workplace impact of domestic and sexual violence and stalking. 1 February. Retrieved from: https://www.shrm.org/hr-today/trends-and-forecasting/research-and-surveys/Pages/shrm-workplace-impact-domestic-sexual-violence-stalking.aspx

Society for Human Resource Management. (2014). *A disturbing picture: Revenge porn is a vicious new way to smear someone's professional reputation.* 21 July. Retrieved from: https://www.shrm.org/hr-today/news/hr-magazine/Pages/0814-revenge-porn.aspx

Southworth, C., Finn, J., Dawson, S., Fraser, C., & Tucker, S. (2007). Intimate partner violence, technology, and stalking. *Violence Against Women, 13*(8), 842–856. Retrieved from: https://doi.org/10.1177/1077801207302045

Taylor, S., & Xia, Y. (2018). Cyber partner abuse: A systematic review. *Violence and Victims, 33*(6), 983–1011.

Tolmie, J. (2018). Coercive control: To criminalize or not to criminalize? *Criminology & Criminal Justice, 18*(1), 50–66.

UniSAFE. (2021). Gender-based violence and institutional responses: Building a knowledge base and operational tools to make universities and research organisations safe. Retrieved from: https://cordis.europa.eu/project/id/101006261

Walby, S. (2004). *The cost of domestic violence.* Women & Equality Unit. Retrieved from: https://eprints.lancs.ac.uk/id/eprint/55255/1/cost_of_dv_report_sept04.pdf

Walby, S. & Towers, J. (2018). Untangling the concept of coercive control: Theorizing domestic violent crime. *Criminology & Criminal Justice, 18*(1), 7–28.

Woodlock, D. (2017). The abuse of technology in domestic violence and stalking. *Violence Against Women, 23*(5), 584–602.

Women's Aid. (2020). *Online and digital abuse.* Retrieved from: https://www.womensaid.org.uk/information-support/what-is-domestic-abuse/onlinesafety/

10 Socio-legal-technical considerations

Introduction

We have explored some of the forms of DGSV and highlighted some of the perpetrator motivations in this book. Some countries have implemented laws as deterrents to DGSV and to prosecute those who perpetrate. But despite these moves we highlight a number of challenges that remain, such as the absence of universal DGSV laws, and international laws when DGSV is transnational in some respect.

Legislation is not the only consideration. Social and cultural dimensions need to be considered too in order, for example, to change unhealthy attitudes and oppressive practices in gendered-sexual relations, and gender relations more generally, where abuses are either normalised or the victim-survivor is blamed for being complicit in some way. We highlight the need for both educational and technological interventions to change attitudes and behaviours, and further discuss issues around consent.

There has also been an increasing number of charities, support groups, feminist networks, activists, academics, and others who have been working to raise awareness of the different emerging forms of DGSV and their harmful impacts on victim-survivors and those close to them. These actions, both individual and collective, campaign for and work towards legislative, social attitude and behavioural changes, additional interventions from state and non-state actors, and more support for victim-survivors. We discuss some of these socio-legal-technical considerations in this chapter.

DOI: 10.4324/9781003138273-14

National contexts[1]

Universal laws able to convict DGSV perpetrators do not exist. In 2016, Mary Anne Franks (2016, p. 3) reported:

> In 2009, the Philippines became the first country to criminalize nonconsensual pornography, with a penalty of up to 7 years' imprisonment.[2] The Australian state of Victoria outlawed non-consensual pornography in 2013. In 2014, Israel became the first country to classify non-consensual pornography as sexual assault, punishable by up to 5 years' imprisonment; Canada criminalized this conduct the same year.[3] Germany and Japan have now made revenge porn a criminal offence. England and Wales joined these countries in February 2015. New Zealand outlawed the practice in July 2015. Northern Ireland and Scotland followed suit in February and March 2016, respectively.

In many countries, the legal frameworks for prosecuting DGSV perpetrators are either non-existent or political conditions or cultural aspects make it difficult to secure convictions. For example, Lyons et al. (2016, p. 1) found that in China there is no specific law for any form of DGSV.[4] As such, the 'human flesh search engine'[5] has grown in notoriety. In the Russia Federation, the government is reported to either be behind, or at least complicit in, some forms of online sexual abuse, for example, homophobia is indirectly encouraged by the 2013 laws on homosexual propaganda, and sexual abuses are rarely investigated as securing a conviction is unlikely due in part to the difficulty of securing necessary evidence. Although Russia has no specific laws against DGSV, these violations could be covered by recent amendments to the Russian general data protection law (Federal Law No. 152–FZ on Personal Data, 2020), which requires organisations or individuals to seek consent to publish or disseminate personal data (Zanfir-Fortuna & Iminova, 2021).

A somewhat different context has been reported in other countries such as Colombia, India, and the Democratic Republic of Congo. DGSV in countries is often linked to party political motives. For example, in Columbia paramilitary groups are presumed to be behind some DGSV as a means to silence or intimidate women's rights campaigners who speak out against violence

---

1 It should be noted that the following legal and governmental, and technological and political responses, were correct at the time of writing. However, we would like to point out to readers that the landscape is constantly changing.

2 World Intellectual Property Organization, *Anti-Photo and Video Voyeurism Act of 2009* (Republic Act No. 9995). Retrieved from: www.wipo.int/edocs/lexdocs/laws/en/ph/ph137en.pdf

3 House of Commons of Canada, Bill C-13.

4 However, there is now legislation in Hong Kong (Feng, 2021).

5 A crowd sourcing phenomenon in China whereby a person's identity can be sources and shared often in order to shame and expose them (Baasanjav, Fernback & Pan, 2019).

against women (Lyons et al., 2016). In India, DGSV has been reported to be used against political opposition to the nationalist Bharatiya Janata Party (BJP) (Ayyub, 2018). The situation in the Democratic Republic of Congo is reported (Lyons et al., 2016) to be much worse since sexual violence and online abuse against women are generally either not taken seriously or completely dismissed by the authorities. However, it should be noted that the recording of sexualised materials for political motives is nothing new and was a legitimate method of intelligence and security agencies, especially during the Cold War, and known as 'sex-espionage' (Mijalković, 2014). But, today, with access to relatively easy to use modern technologies, the non-specialist can engage in such abuse for political and other motives, and this is frequently gendered as we highlight in Chapter 5 where feminists are textually abused online.

Not only is legislation for the prosecution of DGSV not universal, but securing convictions can be difficult, even where there is more developed legislation. Moreover, even in countries where there are laws criminalising DGSV, these do not necessarily cover all forms, and, indeed, reform of DGSV laws is often slow to include newer and changing forms of DGSV. As the Law Commission for England and Wales (2021, p. 1) highlights, "the law has not kept up with this behaviour, resulting in significant gaps that have left victims unprotected".

Transnational legal and technological challenges

Information and Communication Technologies (ICTs) contribute to fundamental change in forms of control, privacy, autonomy, and democracy, with the technology for both decentralised TAZs (temporary autonomous zones) and strong centralised surveillance – with consequent implications beyond and across national boundaries. Global capitalism, ICTs, and virtuality more broadly challenge historical constructions of the autonomous, sovereign nation-state and hegemonic politics of social space. In political, policy and legal terms, interventions to counter DGSV need to be both local/national and transnational, and include legislative, policy and technological responses and frameworks to curb it, awareness-raising, victim-survivor support, perpetrator re-education, and social movement, especially feminist, activism that contests the phenomenon (Hall & Hearn, 2019; Hall, Hearn & Lewis, 2022 Hearn & Hall, 2019).

The situation is further complicated where DGSVs occur across national boundaries and involve multiple jurisdictions. Tackling DGSV poses several challenges transnationally. Despite the existence of domestic regulations in some countries (e.g., the UK, Germany, Japan; see Lyons et al., 2016 for country-specific details), international laws do not yet exist. But given the transnational dimension of these forms of abuse and violations, there is clear need for viable laws and regulations at transnational and global levels. Indeed, differences in legal frameworks for online sexual abuses and violations between countries means it is difficult for victim-survivors to bring prosecutions where a crime is committed in another country. Indeed, tackling perpetrators is a transnational issue, but largely dependent on national legal jurisdictions. For example, the ex-boyfriend of the YouTube musician Chrissy Chambers recorded secret non-consensual sexual videos of her. The videos were recorded in the US where she lives but posted online in the UK. Even though the offence took place in the US, she had to pursue the case under UK law, because that was where the videos were posted. A four-year legal battle eventually secured a conviction (Kleeman, 2018).

Criminal justice prosecutors may also be hindered by the ease of how such abuses and violations cross national borders. Before the former dedicated revenge porn Internet site MyEx.com was closed down by the US Federal Trade Commission (2018) and the state of Nevada, it was reported to be operated by anonymous individuals in the US in coordination with colleagues in the Philippines, and hosted by Web Solutions B.V. in the Netherlands, where there was no specific revenge porn law, even while the site had global reach (Steinbaugh, 2014). This meant that almost anyone, in most countries around the world, apart from where the Internet is partially blocked, could anonymously upload non-consensual explicit images and videos without fear of prosecution, not least because of differences in national legal frameworks. Combined with the anonymity and deceptions employed by cyber criminals, attribution is impeded as is interrogation of suspects and apprehension of offenders.

Internet service providers and social media platforms need to take more responsibility for material posted across national borders. Currently, there is no requirement for social media platforms, such as Facebook, to be proactive in stopping the posting of sexually explicit non-consensual images, only a requirement for the removal of such images within a reasonable period of time. The onus is on others reporting these images to social media platforms. However, the time difference between posting, reporting, and removal can mean that images are distributed further afield. In 2016, a 14-year-old girl aimed to sue Facebook in the Belfast High Court after naked photos of her were posted on the platform as an act of revenge. Although Facebook removed the images when notified, the images had already been republished multiple times by individuals on other platforms and porn sites (England, 2016). However, Facebook (2019) has recently become more proactive, launching the support hub 'Not Without My Consent' covering its platforms (Facebook, Instagram, Messenger, WhatsApp) so that images can be identified and removed, and victim-survivors provided with access to organisations and resources where support can be provided.

Those Internet organisations providing platforms for posting DGSV might face future civil actions in which victim-survivors' claim for damages to reputation, health impacts, and so on. Arguably, stronger civil laws should be in place so that victim-survivors can sue perpetrators for damages. Without laws on cross-border DGSV, pursuing perpetrators and those who facilitate these crimes has been, and is likely to be in the future, very difficult. Criminalisation of DGSV may act as a deterrent for some, but not all (Hall & Hearn, 2019; Hall, Hearn, & Lewis, 2022; Hearn & Hall, 2019).

The complications of copyright

In some forms of DGSVs such as pornographic deepfakes, there are copyright and data protection issues that can hinder legal processes and prosecution. For example, the World Intellectual Property Organization (2020), published a *Conversation on intellectual property (IP) and artificial intelligence (AI)*. The revised paper highlights the following issues with deepfake pornography which can impinge on issues around consent, ownership, the right of use and distribution, and thus prosecution:

(i)   Is copyright an appropriate vehicle for the regulation of deep fakes?
(ii) Since deep fakes are created based on data that may be the subject of copyright, should the deep fake benefit from copyright?
(iii) If deep fakes should benefit from copyright, to whom should the copyright in the deep fake belong?
(iv) If deep fakes benefit from copyright, should there be a system of equitable remuneration for persons whose likenesses and "performances" are used in a deep fake?

(WIPO, 2020, p. 9)

Because of issues related to human rights, protection from harm, privacy, data protection, and so on, the concern for WIPO is whether copyright should be given which may protect the perpetrator, rather than who it should be given to. This highlights that it would be wrong to give copyright to person A, where consent was not originally provided by person B and person B was harmed as a result of person A's actions. However, as the Internet Justice Society (Çolak, 2021) point out, the victim-survivor is unlikely to have obtained copyright on their images even if taken by themselves. Thus, instead, the Internet Justice Society (Çolak, 2021), suggests prosecutions could be based on infringements of the EU General Data Protection Regulation (GDPR) under the maintenance of accurate data, which deepfake pornography clearly contravenes. In this way, consent questions are not raised.

The centrality of consent

Cultural norms and political motives are, of course, not the only dimensions relevant to DGSV and organised responses to it, as we have highlighted throughout the book; other dimensions include vengeance, men profiting from homosocial peer status and/or notoriety, entertainment, opportunity, empowerment, commercial and personal profit, for no particular reason at all, and other (un)known reasons (Franks, 2016). Yet what underlies all forms of DGSV is the question of consent. As we discussed in the Conclusion to Chapter 8, the question of consent may vary between different forms of DGSV and between the moment of taking the image, to making it, dissemination, receiving, and forwarding on, and even elaborating on it.

However, some commentators (Tyler, 2016) argue that consent is questionable even in the production of sexual materials such as home porn movies and sexting where initial consent is presumed. This is for three reasons. First, women's continued economic, political, social, and sexual inequality contributes to a form of cultural coercion into various forms of porn production. Second, sexual violence and abuse against women is common in all forms of porn. And, finally, the porn industry rests on the worldwide sexual objectification of women. Thus, at a more general level of gender and economic class structures, all porn can be potentially understood as coercive or non-consensual because its existence contributes to gendered inequality, and men, as a class, benefit, collectively, at the expense of women.

Questions of consent may have significant impacts for the psychological, emotional, and social well-being of the victim-survivor, and in terms of prosecution of perpetrators. For example, even in countries such as England and Wales, where DGSVs such as so-called 'revenge pornography' can be prosecuted under Section 33 of the Criminal Justice and Courts Act 2015 (Crown Prosecution Service, 2017), victim-survivors are often unwilling to come forward over concerns of victim-survivor-blaming. This can be especially so where consent to take the image was presumed to have been given, for example, via sexting, or in a previous romantic relationship (Marcum, Zaitzow & Higgins, 2021; Starr & Lavis, 2018).

Huber (2018) also highlights several other legal issues in the prosecution of DGSV. For example, legal definitions of different DGSV mean some forms of DGSV may not be deemed DGSV. Examples include a woman photographed in her underwear, or topless on a public beach, or in a state of religious undress. Laws often also require proof that the perpetrator intended to cause distress, partly so that excessive criminalisation is prevented, but as Huber's (2018) interviews with activists point out, non-consensual image taking, making, and distribution are always likely to cause distress. Even when victim-survivors do come forward, they are often not protected by anonymity, and so risk public shame, embarrassment, and further abuse.

Victim-survivor support and empowerment services

Many programmes to support victim-survivors of gender and sexually based crimes tend to focus on how to reduce the risk of revictimisation (Eckhardt et al., 2013). But once images are posted it is difficult to retract them because of the speed of dissemination in e-space by others (Lichter, 2013). However, there have been some efforts to remove images. For example, in 2015 the UK-based charity South West Grid for Learning (SWGfL) in partnership with the UK-based Revenge Porn Helpline (RPH) launched a free tool 'Stop-Non-Consensual Intimate Image Abuse' (StopNCII.org) for victim-survivors of DGSV by generating a hashtag for their intimate images. StopNCII.org is then able to share those hashtags with partner organisations in order for them to detect and remove them so they cannot be shared. The project has more than 50 organisational members from Africa, Europe, the Middle-East, and North America, reporting a 90% removal rate, and successfully removing more than 200,000 individual images (StopNCII.org, 2021: https://stopncii.org/about-us/).

There are also country specific support programmes, feminist networks, and charities that help victim-survivors deal with the legal process of bringing offenders to court by providing advice and guidance on legislation, processes and procedures, image removal, directing victim-survivors to support groups and to legal scholars who specialise in DGSV, and other such services (Levendowski, 2014). For example, a US feminist network of legal scholars named *Legal Voice* (2018) offers advice and guidance on the following:

> What Is "Nonconsensual Pornography"?; Is It Illegal?; What If I Am Under 18?; What If the Perpetrator Is Under 18?; What Is the Punishment?; What If I Was the One Who Took the Picture or Video?; How Do I Report This to the Police? Will They Do Anything?; What If the Person Posted the Images from Another State or Country?; What If I Am an Undocumented Immigrant?; How Do I Get the Images off the Internet?; Who Else Can I Sue?; Where Can I Go for Help?

But despite the growing number of specialist support services, these need to be strengthened to include supporting victim-survivors with the myriad of impacts of DGSV. As Chrissy Chambers who was a victim-survivor of DGSV commented in a BBC (2018, p. 1) interview: "It has affected my life in every way imaginable and I'm sure it will continue to for the rest of my life". Work at the University of Primorska, Science and Research Centre, Slovenia, in conjunction with project partners at University of Trieste (Italy), Isonomia (Spain), University of Aalborg (Denmark), University of Vienna (Austria), and local actors (University of Primorska, Science and Research Centre, 2016) suggests that specialist support services and protocols of cooperation between relevant authorities facing non-consensual online sharing of sexually explicit images should be strengthened both locally and transnationally. This would include: mapping specialist support services, sharing best practices, and promoting cooperation and multi-disciplinary networking among national authorities, and non-governmental organisations for safe(r) Internet use. Clearly, some work and successes have been achieved (e.g., StopNCII.org), but with the ever-changing terrain of DGSV, as we have highlighted, much more certainly needs to be done.

Education, awareness-raising, and campaigns

Digital gender-sexual violations has been reported to be widespread among young people (Lundgren & Amin, 2015), which makes them vulnerable to a lifelong trajectory of violence, as victim-survivors or perpetrators; thus, robust responses are required. Given the transnational dimensions to gender and sexual violences, such as 'upskirting' and 'sexual happy slapping', there is clear need to raise global awareness, including how risks can be both nearby/immediate and geographically/transnationally distant. One method of doing so is to include this on the sex and relationship curriculum (Martellozzo et al., 2016). Even in countries where sex and relationship education are compulsory, the primary focus is generally on sexuality, health, and what constitutes a healthy relationship; this should include how to deal with, and act appropriately and ethically, when relationships end. Indeed, charities, educational groups and institutions, and campaigns more generally report that many teenagers are not being taught about issues like sexting, online pornography, sexual consent, and equal relationships (BBC, 2014; Taylor, 2014; NSPCC, 2022). School-, education- and campaign-based interventions should address such issues as non-violent conflict resolution, communication skills, help-seeking, unequal gender norms, power and control in relationships, and normalisation of sexual violences (Wolfe et al., 2009).

A number of feminist campaigns such as Crash Override network, Gadgette, Women, Action and the Media (WAM), TrollBusters (see Alexander 2016), #HerNetHerRights, and CONSENT (Williams 2017), have become major drivers of opposition to cyberabuse, drawing on lessons from other transnational feminist campaigns (Carr, 2013; Jane, 2017). And feminist networks such as Women Against Violence Europe (2021) have organised conferences to discuss tackling cyberviolence against women and girls. In addition, individual feminist non-governmental organisations such as the Women of Uganda Network (WOUGNET) (2020) have hosted sessions on DGSV, for example, at the RightsCon online 2020 conference. There is also an increasing number of conferences, seminars, workshops, and study groups by activists, academics, researchers, policy-makers, and politicians engaging in ways to tackle the myriad of DGSV (e.g., Public Exchange Policy, 2021). A number of victim-survivor activists have been successful in assisting the process of changing legislation. For example, 'revenge porn' victim-survivor Megan Renee testified to the Irish Parliament (Labour, 2020), contributing to the implementation of the 'Harassment, Harmful Communications and Related Offences Bill' (Pogatchnik, 2020).

There have also been various forms of more direct and sometimes bodily resistance, online or offline. These include, perhaps most famously, the 'Free the nipple' campaign. Beginning in the US, in part through the 2014 film of that name, directed by Lina Esco and written by Hunter Richards, that aimed to bring attention to the wider issue of societal taboos on public exposure of female breasts, it was reinvigorated in Iceland in 2015 as a feminist response to the online abuse directed at a young woman after she posted herself topless to promote gender equality. This led to various women supporting her and a 'Free nipples day' with various events in schools, colleges, the University of Iceland, swimming pools and outside the Houses of Parliament on 26 March 2015.

Such actions can be related to other feminist bodily attempts to oppose sexism, and other oppressions, through women's own use of their bodies, naked or not. In some ways, they can be related to other recent feminist protests such as Femen and Slut Walks. Together, these various bodily initiatives have led to significant debates, often online, including between feminists on the political pros and cons of baring the breast for political ends. These arguments include the feminist case for inverting the gaze of sexism, pornography and other DGSV; critiques thereof as reproducing the reduction of women to bodies and body parts; their effectiveness or lack of effectiveness for change; the focus on what are said by some to be less important issues to the neglect of larger issues. For example, Gyða Margrét Pétursdóttir, Associate Professor in Gender Studies at the University of Iceland, was reported to comment on the Icelandic campaign thus:

> And there's a question whether this will increase the power [women] have over their own bodies or whether it will strengthen the notion that the power is held by others and affirm the traditional ideas of women instead of revolutionizing them.
>
> (Arnarsdóttir, 2015, p. 1)

Annadís G. Rúdólfsdóttir and Ásta Jóhannsdóttir (2018) have provided a much fuller description and analysis of the 2015 events in Iceland, and various, mainly feminist, interpretations of them across four phases of activity: 'The Revolution: Claiming the body back from Patriarchy'; 'Feminist reactions to #FreetheNipple: Is this a Revolution?'; 'Patriarchy strikes back'; and 'Defiance through Solidarity against Patriarchy'. They locate their analysis within a broader discussion of young femininity and feminism in a post-feminist, digital age, including 'the intricate relationship between social media and mainstream media' in which 'many of the news items consisted entirely of selected texts from the social media network'.

Bringing this kind of angry protest into the realm of DGSV may be hard, for some, to imagine. However, it is in such ways that the ongoing and complex politics of and against DGSV are likely to develop, as women, and perhaps some men and further genders, challenge virtual power with and through their own bodies, and the exposure of their bodies. This is one part and one example of the wider politics of gender, sexuality, feminism, bodies and embodiments, not least in the recognition, and thereafter disruption, of the association, and even equation, of women with bodies. These politics are being rethought and re-practiced, especially in the light of the socio-affordances made available by advanced technologies. They entail the recognition of the power of bodies and embodiment, even as virtual(ised) bodies, yet without conflating these with women or other gendered, sexual(ised) persons.

Conclusion

The growing number of forms of (un)known DGSV makes tackling them challenging for any state(s) or non-state actor(s). Feminist and legal scholars, activists, charities, and others have been at the forefront of various ways to tackle DGSV. There have clearly been some successes as we have highlighted, such as changes in legislation, technology, activist campaigns, and social perceptions. However, more clearly needs to be done, at the local, national, and international levels. This needs to be a concerted effort, with more cooperation and sharing of resources between states to develop international laws for the detection of DGSV and prosecution of perpetrators, regulation of technologies, and between all actors working to change social and cultural perceptions of DGSV and gender-sexual relations as a whole. Changes to education curricula are likely to help, but wider social changes are needed, and these require protocols of cooperation and resource-sharing between relevant authorities, policy-makers, activists, support groups, legislators, academics, and others, locally, nationally, and transnationally as we have highlighted in this chapter. Without them, more women, and girls (and some men and boys) with become victim-survivors of DGSV. It is within our collective means to tackle DGSV, gender-sexual violations, and gender violations and inequalities more generally.

References

Alexander, L. (2016). Online abuse: How women are fighting back. *The Guardian*. 13 April. Retrieved from: www.theguardian.com/technology/2016/apr/13/online-abuse-how-women-are-fighting-back

Arnarsdóttir, E. S. (2015). 'Free the Nipple' Day's success disputed in Iceland. *Iceland Review Online*. Retrieved from: http://icelandreview.com/news/2015/03/27/free-nipple-days-success-disputed-iceland.

Ayyub, R. (2018). I was the victim of a deepfake porn plot intended to silence me. *Huffington Post*. 21 November. Retrieved from: https://www.huffingtonpost.co.uk/entry/deepfake-porn_uk_5bf2c126e4b0f32bd58ba316

Baasanjav, U. B., Fernback, J., & Pan, X. (2019). A critical discourse analysis of the human flesh search engine. *Media Asia*, 46(1–2), 18–34.

BBC. (2014). *Is revenge porn already illegal in England?* 28 December. Retrieved from: www.bbc.co.uk/news/uk-england-30308942

BBC. (2018). *Chrissy Chambers: Revenge porn almost killed me.* 18 January. Retrieved from: https://www.bbc.com/news/technology-42733034

Carr, J.L. (2013). The SlutWalk movement: A study in transnational feminist activism. *Journal of Feminist Scholarship*, 4(1), 24–38.

Çolak, B. (2021). Legal Issues of Deepfakes. *Internet Justice Society*. 19 January. Retrieved from: https://www.internetjustsociety.org/legal-issues-of-deepfakes

Crown Prosecution Service. (2017). Revenge Pornography - Guidelines on prosecuting the offence of disclosing private sexual photographs and films. 24 January. Retrieved from: https://www.cps.gov.uk/legal-guidance/revenge-pornography-guidelines-prosecuting-offence-disclosing-private-sexual

Eckhardt, C. I., Murphy, C. M., Whitaker, D. J., Sprunger, J., Dykstra, R., & Woodard, K. (2013). The effectiveness of intervention programs for perpetrators and victims of intimate partner violence. *Partner Abuse*, 4(2), 196–231.

Facebook. (2019). *Not without my consent.* Retrieved from: https://www.facebook.com/safety/notwithoutmyconsent

Feng, J. (2021). Hong Kong outlaws upskirt photos and deepfake pornography. *SupChina*. 12 October. Retrieved from: https://supchina.com/2021/10/12/hong-kong-outlaws-upskirt-photos-and-deepfake-pornography/

Franks, M. A. (2016). Drafting an effective "revenge porn" law: A guide for legislators. *Cyber Civil Rights Initiative*. Retrieved from: www.cybercivilrights.org/guide-to-legislation/.

Hall, M., & Hearn, J. (2019). Revenge pornography and manhood acts: A discourse analysis of perpetrators' accounts. *Journal of Gender Studies, 28*(2), 158–170.

Hall, M., Hearn, J., & Lewis, R. (2022). 'Upskirting', homosociality, and craftmanship: A thematic analysis of perpetrator and viewer interactions. *Violence Against Women, 28*(2), 532–550.

Hearn, J., & Hall, M. (2019). "This is my cheating ex": Gender and sexuality in revenge porn. *Sexualities, 22*(5–6), 860–882.

Huber, A. R. (2018). Revenge porn law is failing victims – Here's why. *The Conversation*. 25 January. Retrieved from: https://theconversation.com/revenge-porn-law-is-failing-victims-heres-why-90497

Jane, E.A. (2017). 'Dude … stop the spread': Antagonism, agonism, and# manspreading on social media. *International Journal of Cultural Studies, 20*(5), 459–475.

Kleeman, J. (2018). YouTube star wins damages in landmark UK 'revenge porn' case. *The Guardian*. 17 January. Retrieved from: https://www.theguardian.com/technology/2018/jan/17/youtube-star-chrissy-chambers-wins-damages-in-landmark-uk-revenge-porn-case

Labour. (2020). Bill to tackle revenge porn must become law. 25 July. Retrieved from: https://labour.ie/news/2020/07/25/bill-to-tackle-revenge-porn-must-become-law/

Law Commission for England and Wales. (2021). Reforms to laws around intimate image abuse proposed to better protect victims. 26 February. Retrieved from: https://www.lawcom.gov.uk/reforms-to-laws-around-intimate-image-abuse-proposed-to-better-protect-victims/

Legal Voice. (2018). *Know your rights: Nonconsensual pornography ("Revenge porn")*. April. Retrieved from: https://www.legalvoice.org/nonconsensual-pornography

Levendowski, A. (2014). Our best weapon against revenge porn: Copyright law? *The Atlantic*. 4 February. Retrieved from: www.theatlantic.com/technology/archive/2014/02/our-best-weapon-against-revenge-porn-copyright-law/283564/.

Lichter, S. (2013). Unwanted exposure: Civil and criminal liability for revenge porn hosts and posters. *JOLT Digest: Harvard Journal of Law and Technology*. 27 May. Retrieved from https://jolt.law.harvard.edu/digest/unwanted-exposure-civil-and-criminal-liability-for-revenge-porn-hosts-and-posters.

Lundgren, R., & Amin, A. (2015). Addressing intimate partner violence and sexual violence among adolescents: Emerging evidence of effectiveness. *Journal of Adolescent Health, 56*(1), S42–S50.

Lyons, K., Phillips, T., Walker, S., Henley, J., Farrell, P., & Carpentier, M. (2016). Online abuse: How different countries deal with it. *The Guardian*. 12 April. Retrieved from: www.theguardian.com/technology/2016/apr/12/online-abuse-how-harrassment-revenge-pornography-different-countries-deal-with-it?CMP=share_btn_link.

Marcum, C. D., Zaitzow, B. H., & Higgins, G. E. (2021). The role of sexting and related behaviors to victimization via nonconsensual pornography: An exploratory analysis of university students. *Journal of Aggression, Conflict and Peace Research*. 11 September. doi: 10.1108/JACPR-02-2021-0578.

Martellozzo, E., Monaghan, A., Adler, J. R., Davidson, J., Leyva, R., & Horvath, M. A. (2016). *"I wasn't sure it was normal to watch it…" A quantitative and qualitative examination of the impact of online pornography on the values, attitudes, beliefs and behaviours of children and young people*. Project Report. Middlesex University, NSPCC, OCC. doi:10.6084/m9.figshare.3382393

Mijalković, S. (2014). 'Sex-espionage' as a method of intelligence and security agencies. *Bezbednost, Beograd, 56*(1), 5–22. Retrieved from: https://cyber.haifa.ac.il/images/Publications/Dark%20and%20Deep%20Webs%20Liberty%20or%20A%20buse.pdf

NSPCC. (2022). *Sexting: advice for professionals*. 16 March. Retrieved from: https://learning.nspcc.org.uk/research-resources/briefings/sexting-advice-professionals

Pogatchnik, S. (2020). Ireland brings in tough laws on revenge porn and online bullying. *Politico*. 17 December. Retrieved from: https://www.politico.eu/article/ireland-brings-in-tough-laws-on-revenge-porn-and-online-bullying/

Public Exchange Policy. (2021). Supporting Victims of Image Based Sexual Abuse: Improving Criminal Justice Responses to Digital Forms of Domestic Abuse. 13 May. Retrieved from: https://www.publicpolicyexchange.co.uk/event.php?eventUID=LE13-PPE

Rúdólfsdóttir, A. G., & Jóhannsdóttir, Á. (2018). Fuck patriarchy! An analysis of digital mainstream media discussion of the #FreetheNipple activities in Iceland in March 2015. *Feminism & Psychology, 28*(1), 133–151

Starr, T. & Lavis, T. (2018). Perceptions of revenge pornography and victim blame. *International Journal of Cyber Criminology, 12*(2), 427–438.

Steinbaugh, A. (2014). Revenge porn site MyEx.com Sued for copyright infringement. 7 March. Retrieved from: http://adamsteinbaugh.com/2014/03/07/revenge-porn-site-myex-com-sued-for-copyright-infringement

StopNCII.org. (2021). *About Us*. Retrieved from: https://stopncii.org/about-us/

Taylor, J. (2014). New calls to change sex and relationship education. *BBC*. 28 January. Retrieved from: www.bbc.co.uk/newsbeat/article/25921487/new-calls-to-change-sex-and-relationship-education

Tyler, M., 2016. All porn is revenge porn [online]. *Feminist Current*. 24 February. Retrieved from: www.feministcurrent.com/2016/02/24/all-porn-is-revenge-porn

University of Primorska, Science and Research Centre, Slovenia. (2016). *Revenge porn: Tackling non-consensual sharing of sexually explicit images in cyber space*. Unpublished proposal to The European Parliament and the Council Daphne as part of the General Programme "Fundamental Rights and Justice".

US Federal Trade Commission. (2018). Emp Media Inc. (MyEx.com). 22 June. Retrieved from: https://www.ftc.gov/enforcement/cases-proceedings/162-3052/emp-media-inc-myexcom

Williams, C. (2017). Young women mobilise against 'revenge porn' and online abuse [online]. *Open Democracy* 30 October. Retrieved from: https://www.opendemocracy.net/en/5050/young-women-mobilise-against-revenge-porn-online-abuse/

Wolfe, D. A., Crooks, C., Jaffe, P., Chiodo, D., Hughes, R., Ellis, W., … & Donner, A. (2009). A school-based program to prevent adolescent dating violence: A cluster randomized trial. *Archives of Pediatrics & Adolescent Medicine, 163*(8), 692–699.

Women Against Violence Europe. (2021). CYBERSAFE: Conference on changing attitudes among teenagers on cyber violence against women and girls. 14 October. Retrieved from: https://wave-network.org/cybersafe-conference-on-changing-attitudes-among-teenagers-on-cyber-violence-against-women-and-girls/

Women of Uganda Network. (2020). Not 'revenge porn': Non-consensual intimate imagery i-Uganda. *RightsCon Online 2020.* Retrieved from: https://wougnet.org/website/news/newsingle/49

World Intellectual Property Organization. (2020). Revised Issues Paper on Intellectual Property Policy and Artificial Intelligence. 29 May. Retrieved from: https://www.wipo.int/meetings/en/doc_details.jsp?doc_id=499504

Zanfir-Fortuna, G. & Iminova, R. (2021). Russia: New law requires express consent for making personal data available to the public and for any subsequent dissemination. *Future of Privacy Forum.* 1 March. Retrieved from: https://fpf.org/blog/russia-new-law-requires-express-consent-for-making-personal-data-available-to-the-public-and-for-any-subsequent-dissemination/

11 Afterword

Key issues now and for the future

Introduction

The digital world is now very much a part of everyday life for more than half of the world's populations (Internet World Stats, 2021). But whilst this provides many benefits, such as maintaining distant relationships, increasing the speed of communications, and accessing a wider range of goods and services, there has been a price to pay for some. Becoming victim-survivors of cybercrime and cyberbullying, facing psychological stresses and pressures to conform to 'ideal' ways to look, and losing balance between work and non-work time, are some of the consequences of the increasingly digital world. Our focus has been on digital gender-sexual violations. Our aim has not been to provide a comprehensive review of all forms of DGSV, as we wonder if that is even possible as technologies and their social affordances develop and change; rather, our aim has been to explore some of these urgent issues, such as discussing terminology considerations, how these might be contextualised, what motivates people to commit such acts, the impacts on victim-survivors, and the various online and offline responses.

In this Afterword, we briefly discuss further important considerations for understanding DGSV now and for the future: sex, gender, and sexuality; men talking and writing about violence and violation; binary gender and sexuality positions in doing violence; ambiguities and transgressions; the power practices of micro-techno-masculinities; online/offline spaces; and what the future of DGSVs might look like. We finish on a more positive note by highlighting that, whilst the digital world has opened up a space for new (and old) form of gender-sexual violations, it has also become a space in which individuals and groups across the world tackle these very violations through different forms of collaboration and activism.

Sex, gender, and sexuality

Throughout this book, we have examined digital violations in relation to gender, sex, sexuality, and the sexual, with its own ambiguities. As noted in Chapter 1, all these terms can have different meanings and connotations,

DOI: 10.4324/9781003138273-15

depending partly on context, not to mention their different equivalents, or not so equivalents, in different languages. When working in and writing on this field of activity, finding the best and most accurate language is, at times, not easy. We have opted to use the portmanteau word, gender-sexual, to express some of the range of intentions, meanings, and forms of viola-tion, as well some of the ambiguities, that can sometimes occur with digital violations.

There is a continuing set of societal debates, that are especially variable when viewed internationally, on the possible usages of 'sex' and 'gender', and their connections or not. Although these debates are loudest in relation to transgender in some parts of the world, the politics and practice of terminology – around gender, sex, sexual, sexuality – are complicated in the virtual world, with diverse (re)presentations, visualisations and violations not always easily categorisable or recognisable as specifically only sexed, sexual or gendered. Rather some combination of 'sex', 'sexuality', and 'gendering' may well be recognisable or experienced. Here, even these three very words can become less than accurate, hence terms like 'gender-sex', 'gex', and our own rendering, the 'gender-sexual'.

These questions are reminiscent of earlier, and ongoing, discussions of the differences between, say, gender violence, gendered violence, gender-based violence, sexual violence, and 'sexual sexual violence' (sic.) (cf. Boyle, 2019; Graaff, 2021; Wise and Stanley, 1984). After all, is there any violence to women that is not in some way gendered and not sexual? Is there any violence more broadly that is not gendered – in some way? It is quite hard to think of examples of violence that are non-gendered. The very notion of gender-based violence includes more than violence to women; anti-trans violence, anti-gay violence, and violence between men, amongst other exam-ples, are gender-based, or at least gender-related.

All these debates and discussions are not just innocent and 'technical mat-ters'. They are all political with bodily effects. They are also deepened and furthered by interrogation in relation to both intersectional power dynamics, and digitalisation and the virtual world. Moreover, the intersectional land-scape is not fixed, but itself develops and changes, with newly recognised marginalisations and oppressions. And somewhat similarly, digitalisation and the virtual world are also subject to major changes, and unknowns in the future, with, for example, AI/AGI, deepfakes, holograms, heightened interactivity, and immersive/virtual reality, all of which can be exploited for DGSVs. Such developing technologies do not just and only exist as discursive representations, but are usable material-discursive, IRL-virtual violations and harms.

Men talking and writing about violence and violation

When men do, talk about, and more specifically write about their own dig-ital violence, as with 'revenge porn', image-based sexual abuse, and online abuse towards feminists, they do several things. They are not only doing violence and violation, but, in writing violence, are often seeking to establish credibility, using one or more strategies, that invoke: simple, unapologetic, oppressive misogyny; potential, taken-for-granted homosocial 'reasonableness' appealing to an unknown (male) audience; or a diminished, more vulnerable 'victim-survivor' position. The table is turned, the narrative inverted, away from framing their actions as doing violence. Men's posts on MeEx.com often positioned themselves as wronged victim-survivors and the ex-partner as a perpetrator of a form of gender violence/abuse. Most posters claimed the women deserved being posted, constructing this, in their terms, as legitimate interpersonal revenge. Such online posts are often both precise in their explicitly misogynistic characterisations of the allegedly misdemeaning woman, and invested in masculinised, hierarchical, heterosexual, intimate relationships, and contexts. Similarly, men's abuse of feminists online invokes misogynistic world views in which women accept their subordination by men in all spheres of life. Image-based violation is double-layered – in the non-consensual sharing and distribution of sexual images, photographs, and videos, and in the misogynist texts accompanying the images, often directed to an unspecified, unknown male audience, who sometimes adds supportive dialogical responses. Moreover, men's writing about upskirting can be considered as a triple violation. The violation is created initially, by photographing or videoing without consent; then, by posting, sharing and distribution of those images, with accompanying written text; and, finally, by the celebratory, collective, homosocial written commentaries by other posters on those postings adding a further layer of violation. Importantly, sometimes the victim-survivor may not learn of the digital violation at all or until much later, which both brings the complications of delayed impact, and legitimates further violence and violation.

Binary gender and sexuality positions in doing violence

What is clear from our analysis and discussions is that the display of gender and sexual positions is through antagonism, violation, power and control, towards those who are, or have been, the object of desire. DGSV is thus part of a whole range of gender and sexual phenomena, for example: gendered violence and abuse; sexual assault; cyberbullying and cyberstalking; normalisation of sexually abusive and misogynist online public space. Thus, DGSVs are understandable through the lens of gender and sexual dynamics and constructions, binary gender and sexual positionings and the use of sexual meanings. The structure and directionality of DGSV, and its non-consensual, violating, and abusive forms in the written texts of perpetrators parallel the dynamics of power and control in unhealthy (intimate) gender-sexual relationships, becoming overridden by the 'logic' of desire and counter-desire, made possible in extended form by the affordances of ICTs. The virtual world becomes orientated monologically, not dialogically or interactively. DGSV is justified by blaming the victim-survivor. The precise textual devices by which DGSV is differentially practiced, and justified, is then less about the affordances of

ICTs and more about gender-sexual positions and possibilities within dominant gender-sexual orders. It is through these devices, such as the appeal to similar (to the poster) others, that the gender-sexual differences in online postings are explicitly enacted. Men's practices of DGSV and the discourses employed within and around them, can be seen as part of the dominant repertoires of men and masculinities. In this sense, they are perhaps less novel than they may appear at first sight; rather, they are extensions and elaborations of well-charted ways of dominating and abusing others, especially in the cultural context of the extensive sexist and misogynist texts online. Thus, given the mass of DGSV seems to be strongly based in binary positionings, it reproduces, and performs, broader gender hegemony.

Ambiguities and transgressions

Gender-sexual dynamics, with their generally binary 'logic' are complicated further by the technological affordances available. In this way, it is a cliché but true to say that DGSV is a product of its time. Much of the power of DGSV and the damage it causes comes from both its ambiguities and its transgressions, across several boundaries. The ambiguous and transgressive nature of DGSV is part and parcel of the work of the normalisation of sexually abusive online environments, and of violence and abuse online more generally. Crucially, such violence and abuse is simply and unambiguously legitimate to its doers, adherents, and sponsors. The routine domination by men's voices and posts in online fora (Herring, Johnson & DiBenedetto, 1995) has in practice, and in a rather short time period, easily escalated to the greater propensity and power of men to insult and abuse, especially when there is less facial or eye contact (Lapidot-Lefler & Barak, 2012). This spread and diffusion can to some extent be attributed to the so-called 'online disinhibition effect' (Suler, 2004), coupled with processes of peer pressure, imitation, contagion, and multimodal media crossovers, in front of real or imagined audiences: to put it simply, a virtual homosocial mob. Social psychological processes around both disinhibition and audience-serving have to be placed into a structural context of gender domination beyond the immediate psychological processes concerned. They also have to be placed in the transnational, deterritorialised, translocal and hybrid context, extending the diverse forms and processes of such transnational violences in gender-sexual relations. Transnational virtual violences are enacted in dispersion, as dispersed and distanced delocalised violences (cf. Brage, Gordaliza & Orte, 2014). Specifically, DGSVs occur in a wide variety of transnational contexts, for example, transnational dispersed families, migration, employment, holidays, and others, and often linked to vulnerabilities.

The power practices of micro-techno-masculinities

Within these broad contexts of ambiguity and transgressions DGSV can be seen largely, though not exclusively, as an example of (some) men's gendered power practices in their engagement with technological patriarchies.

The co-production of masculinity and technology has been studied in many locales and forms, for example, men's gendered engagement with tinkering, technical skill and simple fascination with technologies (Faulkner, 2000; Lohan & Faulkner, 2004). Indeed, we discussed craftsmanship in Chapter 7. The analysis of techno-masculinity, or techno-masculinities, often focuses on the intersection of technology and masculinised gender power relations as a relatively new basis of power at the societal level. Thus, many issues that relate to men, masculinities, ICTs, and technologies are also present in DGSV. These include the presence and problematising of stereotypes around men, women, and technology; and the paradoxically remote technological possibilities for online homosociality and abuse, as we have shown. DGSV can be seen as raising some new issues and creating some new phenomena around the practices of techno-masculinity, such as the globalisation of violence and abuse. These may in turn challenge and reshape the homogeneity of both hegemonic masculinity and dominant forms of patriarchal techno-masculinity. Taking this argument one step further, we might think of these developments as part of micro-techno-masculinities and micro-technologies of the masculine self, socially and technologically mediated (see Pooley, 2013), and with a somewhat different form and process to those macro-techno-masculinities that figure so strongly in debates on globalisation and the place of ICTs.

Online/offline spaces

DGSV throws up many questions about experiences of both time and space. ICTs provide the possibility to extend patriarchal power across space and time, and DGSV puts that potentiality for patriarchal power into practice, spatially and temporally. Early hopes that the virtual world would provide a space to re-imagine gender relations and provide a haven for free speech and democracy have long since been dashed. Patriarchy is too pernicious and too adaptive to allow this new space to develop free of its influence. Indeed, some aspects of the virtual world have *emerged from* misogynistic roots (see Oliver, 2015, for an account of the misogynistic actions by the creators of Facebook, Snapchat, and Tinder). The offline world offers a virtually limitless space for perpetrators of DGSV (mostly men and boys) to abuse, humiliate, sexualise, shame, threaten, intimidate, sexually objectify, belittle, exclude, and terrify their victim-survivors (mostly women and girls). One impact is to make the online world unwelcoming to women, including women who do not conform to heterosexual imaginings and sexual fantasies. Online abuse, for example, (attempts to) exclude from online spaces women, especially feminist women but also women in politics, journalism and other occupations which require them to use their voice (as we discussed in Chapter 5). For some women, minimising one's voice and presence in these spaces is the pragmatic solution. However, for others, this abuse galvanises them in their politics and political activity.

DGSV is experienced not only in the online spaces in which it occurs. As we have presented in the preceding chapters, the spaces of DGSV include the intersections of the offline and online worlds, as well as the offline world. For example, some types of DGSV involve actions in the offline world (e.g., taking consensual or non-consensual photographs and videos) which are used non-consensually online, on, for example, 'revenge porn' or 'upskirting' websites (as discussed in Chapters 6 and 7, respectively). Most forms of DGSV manifest online but their impacts are experienced offline. Psychological impacts of having one's (altered) image disseminated are embodied reactions to such experiences, as is fear of (sexual) assault and of destruction of one's reputation if one's identity is circulated online.

Moreover, many of these forms of DGSV are likely to have wider impacts offline beyond the individual victim-survivor to women as a group. Fear of having one's image taken non-consensually, as in upskirting, or having consensual images used in sexualised and abusive ways (as in 'revenge pornography' and 'deepfakes') are likely to be currently impacting women and girls across societies. To add to the male gaze, and its internalisation by most women, women now contend with the possibility of constant surveillance through these forms of DGSV. The ubiquity of panoptic patriarchy conveys to women that no aspects, even the most private, intimate parts, of their lives, are off limits to perpetrators who wish to abuse them. In these ways, DGSV erodes easy distinctions between online and offline space and private and public space. Our discussion in this book adds to previous scholarship which has challenged these distinctions, and adds to scholarship on the re-gendering of social space (e.g., Delphy & Leonard Barker, 1992; Hearn, 1992; Landes, 1998; Lewis et al., 2017).

The impacts of DGSV on time are, in some ways, more complex and even contradictory. Patriarchal power is not only extended across physical and social space, it is also made temporally ubiquitous. With DGSV, time is not linear or chronological. DGSV can be present and experienced instantaneously, or many days, months, or even years afterwards, or for perpetuity. DGSVs can be received online when long separated from the perpetrator, and in the middle of any other task or experience, for example, by text while about to go for a job interview, in the middle of a meeting, on holiday, or at whatever intimate moment is imaginable. ICTs and DGSV extend the reach and impact of perpetrators and patriarchal power both quantitatively and qualitatively.

Future considerations

We highlighted in our Introduction how various forms of DGSV have been a long time in the making with historical roots in the historical symbiotic relationship between, for example, gender-sexual violence and abuse, pornography and technology (Rosen, 2010). With increasing Internet speed, technology-related education, technological developments that make using different types of software more accessible to non-specialists, the growth in people using the Internet, and the increase in the number of Internet platforms and websites for DGSV in both the surface and dark net means that the different forms of DGSV have increased and evolved. And we suspect the forms are likely to evolve further in the future. For example, when we began researching DGSV, sexual Zoombombing was relatively unheard of, and deepfake pornography was just coming into public awareness in the media and is policy discussions. Sexual Zoombombing is partly a product of its time – the COVID-19 pandemic lockdowns facilitated increased homeworking and virtual meetings between colleagues provided additional opportunities for some people to hack into those meetings and display pornographic materials to attendees.

We are not aiming to make predictions or speculate, but there are some significant markers that warrant consideration for researchers, activists, technology developers, and policy-maker. For example, we pointed out in Chapter 8 that the actors such as Angelina Jolie and Scarlett Johansson had their faces placed on sex robots in 2016, which were set to retail for between $2,000–3,000 (Glaser, 2016; Michael, 2016). More recently, it was reported (Winer, 2022) that Israeli Instagram model Yael Cohen Aris is suing a Chinese company for making a sex doll that looks exactly like her. Producing pornography-related online and offline materials that look like others (mostly women and girls) could become more prevalent with developments in artificial intelligence (e.g., deepfake technologies used for pornographic intent).

Similarly, we also highlight the risks in merging artificial intelligence and augmented reality pornography. Currently augmented reality pornography allows the user/viewer to watch animated pornography of 'ideal' women, giving them some control with visuals to decide what the animation does. It may not be a large step for AI to produce 'real' faces and bodies of women and girls in augmented reality pornography. But whilst the risks of some modern technologies, such as Google Glasses for spying were highlighted (Leonard, 2013), others that can be misused for DGSV are likely to follow. Although policy-makers and technology developers have responded to some of these concerns – for example, banning the silent smartphone camera apps without a shutter click sound in South Korea and Japan, reduce misuse of smartphones for upskirting (United Press International, 2013) – further considerations and actions on current and new technologies (e.g., the use of spy cameras such as on drones, shoes, and pens for DGSV) will be needed by in the future researchers, policy-makers, activists, technology developers, and people more generally.

Activisms

As much as the virtual world has produced myriad forms of DGSV that were unimaginable a few years ago, so too it has enabled a level of international, intersectional, real-time activism that was previously beyond the capacity of many campaigners. Social media is now home to endless permutations of feminism, activism against DGSV, campaigning, support groups, and victim-survivor narratives (Sotirin, Bergvall & Shoos, 2020). This explosion in online feminist activism is not without its problems; is it contributing to the re-shaping of feminism as an individualistic enterprise in keeping with neo-liberal ideology? Does it create cultural discourse without material action? Does it enable men's surveillance of feminism (Megarry, 2018)? These important questions notwithstanding, the development of extensive and varied feminist activism online around the globe provides space to resist and challenge DGSV, as well as to support those impacted by it. It is this work together with scholarship that has the potential to shift discourses, cultures and practices, as well as policies and legislation that may help make the virtual world a safer, more egalitarian space.

References

Boyle, K. (2019). What's in a name? Theorising the Inter-relationships of gender and violence. *Feminist Theory*, *20*(1), 19–36.

Brage, L. B., Gordaliza, R. P., & Orte, C. (2014). Delocalized prostitution: Occultation of the new modalities of violence. *Procedia – Social and Behavioural Sciences*, *161*(19), 90–95.

Delphy, C., & Leonard Barker, D. (1992). *Familiar exploitation*. Cambridge: Polity in association with Blackwell.

Faulkner, W. (2000). Dualisms, hierarchies, and gender in engineering. *Social Studies of Science*, *30*(5), 759–792.

Glaser, A. (2016). The Scarlett Johansson bot is the robotic future of objectifying women. *Wired*. 4 April. Retrieved from: https://www.wired.com/2016/04/the-scarlett-johansson-bot-signals-some-icky-things-about-our-future/

Graaff, K. (2021). The implications of a narrow understanding of gender-based violence. *Feminist Encounters: A Journal of Critical Studies in Culture and Politics*, *5*(1), 12. doi: 10.20897/femenc/9749.

Hearn, J. (1992). *Men in the public eye*. London: Routledge.

Herring, S., Johnson, D. A., & DiBenedetto, T. (1995). 'This discussion is going too far!' Male resistance to female participation on the internet. In K. Hall & M. Bucholtz (Eds.), *Gender articulated: Language and the socially constructed self* (pp. 67–98). New York: Routledge.

Internet World Stats. (2021). *Usage and populations*. 31 March. Retrieved form: https://www.internetworldstats.com/stats.htm

Landes, J. B. (Ed.). (1998). *Feminism, the public and the private*. Oxford: Oxford University Press.

Lapidot-Lefler, N., & Barak, A. (2012). Effects of anonymity, invisibility, and lack of eye-contact on toxic online disinhibition. *Computers in Human Behavior*, *28*(2), 434–443.

Leonard, T. (2013). Google's sinister glasses will turn the whole world into search giant's spies. *Mail Online*. 18 March. Retrieved from: https://www.dailymail.co.uk/news/article-2295004/Google-Glass-Googles-sinister-glasses-turn-world-search-giants-spies.html

Lewis, R., Rowe, M., & Wiper, C. (2017). Online abuse of feminists as an emerging form of violence against women and girls'. *British Journal of Criminology*, *57*(6), 1462–1481.

Lohan, M., & Faulkner, W. (2004). Masculinities and technology: Some introductory remarks. *Men and Masculinities*, *6*(4), 319–329.

Megarry, J. (2018). Under the watchful eyes of men: Theorising the implications of male surveillance practices for feminist activism on social media. *Feminist Media Studies, 18*(6), 1070–1085.

Michael, T. (2016). Sex robots modelled on your favourite celebs set to take over the market, expert warns. *News.com.au.* 5 December. Retrieved from: https://www.news.com.au/technology/gadgets/sex/robots-modelled-on-your-favourite-celebs-set-to-take-over-the-market-expert-warns/news/story/c6d3b0754933a20f22851e663b822f3b

Oliver, K. (2015). Rape as spectator sport and creepshot entertainment: Social media and the valorization of lack of consent. *American Studies Journal, 16*(2), 1–15.

Pooley, J. (2013). Sociology and the socially mediated self. In S. Waisbord (Ed.), *Media sociology: A reappraisal* (pp. 224–247). Cambridge: Polity.

Rosen, R. (2010). *Beaver street: A history of modern pornography: From the birth of phone sex to the skin mag in cyberspace: An investigative memoir.* London: Headpress.

Sotirin, P., Bergvall, V. L., & Shoos, D. L. (Eds.). (2020). *Feminist vigilance.* Cham: Palgrave Macmillan.

Suler, J. (2004). The online disinhibition effect. *CyberPsychology & Behavior, 7*(3), 321–326.

United Press International. (2013). *S. Korea say no more silent camera apps.* 29 March. Retrieved from: https://www.upi.com/Science_News/Technology/2013/03/29/S-Korea-say-no-more-silent-camera-apps/46721364588057/

Winer, S. (2022). Israeli woman sues after unwittingly inspiring a sex doll. *The Times of Israel.* 11 January. Retrieved from: https://www.timesofisrael.com/israeli-woman-sues-after-unwittingly-inspiring-a-sex-doll/

Wise, S, & Stanley, L. (1984). Sexual sexual politics—An editorial introduction. *Women's Studies International Forum, 7*(1), 1–6.

Index

Note: Page numbers followed by "n" denote endnotes.

activism 37, 180–181
Adams, C. 76
addiction (to the Internet) 6
adjective order (in naming) 22
AdultDeepFakes.com 131–132
Airdropping 135–137
ambiguities 177
anonymity 5, 49
antimeria 100–101n5
artificial intelligence (AI) 2n6, 129–130, 180
augmented reality (AR) 2n7
augmented reality pornography 133–134, 180
awareness-raising 167–169

banter/chat (misogynistic) 99
binary gender 176–177
boundary blurring 5, 31, 146–147

campaigns 167–169
Candid Zone: craftmanship 100–106; data collection 61–62; discourse analysis 62–63; overview 60–61; underage girls 61; victim-blaming 101
catfishing 50n1
celebrity deepfakes 131–132
chat/banter (misogynistic) 99
commitments from online platforms 37, 164
Committee on Standards in Public Life 37
communities online 51
compensation/damages 156
concepts see naming
confidentiality (notions of) 5
consent: centrality of 165–166; lack of 16, 138; 'non-consensual distribution' (term) 16; responsibility around 16

copyright 165
couplets (in naming) 15–16
Covid 113, 146, 180
craftmanship (upskirting and The Candid Zone) 99–106
Criado-Perez, C. 77, 87
'cyber' (term) 19
'cyber addiction' 6
Cyber Civil Rights Initiative 16
cyberflashing 135–137
cyberstalking 4–5

damages/compensation 156
Daneback, K. 5
death threats 79–82
deception (online) 49–50
DeepFaceLab 2.0 131n3
deepfake pornography 129–134
'deep learning' 130
Deeptrace report 133
Deep Web 48–49, 50
DGSV: within continuum of GBV 28–29; as gender-sexual practices 29–30; researching 66–68
'digi' (term) 18–19
digital hate 35–37
digital intimate partner violence (DIPV) 147–149
discourse analysis 62–63
downblousing 107

education 167–169
elements of DGSV: interconnections between 20–23; overview 18–19
'emotional labour' 76
emotive responses to data 66–68
envy (and homosociality) 103–104
ethical considerations (for research) 64–66

European Union's Fundamental Rights
   Agency 4–5, 74
excluding (function of online abuse)
   84–86
exoticisation 39

FaceApp 131n2
Facebook 33, 37, 48, 164, 178
'facilitated' (use of term) 19
fantasies (as normative) 131–132
Faulkner, W. 32
feminism *see* online abuse of feminists
flashing 135–137
Frappening, The 1, 35
'Free the nipple' campaign 168–169
Fundamental Rights Agency (FRA) 4–5,
   74
future of DGSV 179–180

Gamergate 36, 81
Gardiner, B. 76
gender: sex and 19–20, 174–175; use of
   term 19
gender-based violence: conceptualisation
   of 27–29; DGSV within continuum of
   28–29; statistics 28
gender differences: pornography use 4;
   revenge pornography 5
gender-sexual practices (DSGV as) 29–30
gender-technologisation 31–33
globalisation of sexuality 6
Google 37; Glasses 148
gratitude (and homosociality) 102

Hall, M. 2, 8, 67, 112, 113
happy slapping 137–138
hate (digital) 35–37
hate crime 37
Hearn, J. 2, 8, 34, 67, 112, 113
'hidden labour' 76
Hochschild, A. 76
homosociality 98–108; advice-seeking
   104–105; on The Candid Zone
   100–106; envy 103–104; gratitude 102;
   humour/banter 99; respect 102–103;
   'risk-taking' and status 101–102, 104
humour (misogynistic) 99

identity: co-construction of 52; online
   deception 49–50; revealing oneself
   50–52; self-presentation 48–49
ideology (misogynistic) 89
image-based sexual abuse (IBSA) 16
impacts of online abuse of feminists
   82–84

incels 36, 88–90, 88n7
information and computer technologies
   (ICTs): affordances of 30–31;
   co-production of masculinity and 177–
   178; DGSV as part of technologisation
   30; effect on how sex is done 2–3;
   gender-technologisation 31–33; given
   agency in terms used 19; intersection
   with gender and sexuality 22–23;
   relationship with pornography 2
intentions of perpetrator 36
interaction online (forms of) 47
Internet: forms of online interaction
   47; new possibilities from 2–3; social
   benefits 50–51; usage 46–47
Internet addiction 6
Internet service providers 164
intersecting identities 88
'intimate image abuse' 16
intimate partner violence (IPV) 145n1,
   147–149

Johnson, P. 2
Jyrkinen, M. 34

Kelly, L. 76, 78

Law 9, 16, 37, 96, 132, 136–137, 155–
   156, 161–166, 170
Law Commission (UK) 16, 37, 136
Lewis, R. 15, 36, 73–92
LGBTIQA+ 5, 146

male sexual fantasies (as normative)
   131–132
manosphere 36–37
masculinities 30, 98–99, 177–178
Massey, K. 4
mass murders 89
materiality (self-evident) 22
mediatisation 39–40
men writing violence 175–176
methods of analysis 57–69
MGTOW (Men Going Their Own Way)
   36
microaggressions (accumulations of) 29n2
misogyny: DGSV through the lens of
   35–37; 'hybrid masculinity' within
   98–99; as an ideology 89; impacts
   of 36–37; materialist perspective of
   90–91; in origins of Facebook 33;
   policing 37; polite 107–108; upskirting
   as 97–99
motives of perpetrator 36
MyEx.com *see* revenge pornography

naming 15–26; couplets 15–16; 'digital sexual' *vs.* 'sexual digital' violation 21–22; order of adjectives 22; process of 15–16; for specific forms of abuse 17–18; terms used (most common) 16, *see also* elements of DGSV
national contexts (legal) 162–163
National Survey of Porn Use, Relationships, and Sexual Socialization (NSPRSS) 3
normalisation (as a coping strategy) 82–83
'Not Without My Consent' hub 164

Onion Router (TOR) 48–49
online abuse of feminists 73–92; data analysis 60; data collection 58–60; explaining/understanding 86–92; function of 84–86; galvanising effect of 86; impacts 82–84; statistics 74–77; women's experiences 77–82
online communities 51
online dating 49–50
online/offline boundary blurring 5, 31, 146–147, 178–179
organisations 145–157; colleagues 155; DGSV policy/practice 152–156; direct victim-survivors support 154; forms of DGSV in 149–152; impacts of DIPV 147–149; liability of 155–156; managers 155; perpetrators 154–155; power dynamics 151–152; transnational factors 156
orientalism 39

patriarchal power 178–179
penis disparagement 118–120
Penney, J. 1
performances (self-image and) 48
perpetrators: of DGSV 5
'pervert's dilemma' 131
PEW Research Centre 75
photographic skills 105–106
'pick-up artists' 36
Plan International 75
polite misogyny 107–108
politicians (intimidation of) 37, 76–77
PornHub 3
pornographisation 33–35
pornography: addiction 6; changing forms/meanings 33; industry 2; link to sexual risk-taking 4; normalisation 4, 34; statistics 3–4
power: dynamics at work 151–152; practices 177–178

privacy: notions of 5; online 52–53
publicisation processes 39–40
public spaces: DGSV in 149–152

racism 39
rape threats 79–82
relationship (framed in terminology used) 17
removing images 166–167
researching: DGSV 66–68; *see also* Candid Zone; online abuse of feminists; revenge pornography
respect (and homosociality) 102–103
responsibilisation 37
revenge pornography 112–128; data collection 64–66; female-to-female 120–123; female-to-male 118–120; gender hegemony in 125–126; lockdowns and 113; male-to-female 114–116; male-to-male 116–118; MyEx.com 164; objectives of 116–117, 123–126; overview 63–64, 112–114, 123–126; penis disparagement 118–120; personal information on 150; self-legitimation of 124–125; statistics 5
risk-taking: sexual 4, 117; and status 101–102, 104
Ross, W. M. 5
Rowe, M. 15, 36, 73–92; *see also* Lewis

Safety Net Project 22
self-presentation 48–49
sex: and gender 19–20, 174–175; use of term 19
sexting (statistics) 3
'sexualed' 22n3
sexual happy slapping 137–138
sexuality (use of term) 19
sexual spycamming 134–135
silencing function of online abuse 84–86
Snapchat 33, 178
social construction 23
social media platforms 37, 164
social support 51–52
socio-legal-technical considerations: awareness-raising 167–169; consent questions 165–166; copyright 165; cyberflashing 136, 137; deepfakes 132; national contexts 162–163; organisational liability 155–156; transnational challenges 163–165; upskirting 96; victim-survivor support/empowerment services 166–167
sockpuppetting 130n1

spycamming 134–135
StopNCII.org 16, 166–167
support: in organisations 154;
    programmes 166–167; social 51–52
'survivor' (term) 5n9

technofeminism 31–33
technologies of violence 21
technologisation 30–33
technology *see* information and computer
    technologies (ICTs)
technology-focused terms 16, 17
terms used *see* naming
terrorism (incel ideology as) 89–90
thematic analysis 57–58
Tiktok 37
Tinder 33, 178
transnationalisation 38–39, 163–165
triggering effect 84
trust manipulation 22
Turkle, S. 49
Twitter 37

UK Law Commission 16, 37, 136
under-reporting of DGSV 3–4
upskirting 98–108; as craftmanship
    99–108; as double abuse 97; history
    of 96–97; as homosociality/misogyny
    97–99; legal position 96; talking about
    as polite misogyny 107–108, *see also*
    Candid Zone

US National Network to End Domestic
    Violence 22

Vera-Gray, F. 76
'victim' (term) 5n9
victim-blaming 101, 117
violence: conceptualisation of 28;
    technologies of 21; use of
    term 18, 20
'virtual addiction' 6
voyeurism 134–135

Wiper, C. 15, 36, 73–92; *see also* Lewis
women: online abuse towards 74–75;
    politicians (as targets) 37, 76–77
words *see* naming
workplaces: 145–157; colleagues 155;
    DGSV policy/practice 152–156;
    direct victim-survivors support 154;
    forms of DGSV in 149–152; impacts
    of DIPV 147–149; liability of 155–
    156; managers 155; orientalism 39;
    perpetrators 154–155; power dynamics
    151–152; transnational factors 156
World Intellectual Property
    Organization 165

young people: and pornography 3–4; and
    sexting 3; and victimisation 5

Zoombombing 135–136

Made in the USA
Coppell, TX
09 January 2023